EDUCATIONAL LEADERSHIP FOR ORGANISATIONAL LEARNING AND IMPROVED STUDENT OUTCOMES

STUDIES IN EDUCATIONAL LEADERSHIP

VOLUME 3

SCOPE OF THE SERIES

Leadership we know makes all the difference in success or failures of organizations. This series will bring together in a highly readable way the most recent insights in successful leadership. Emphasis will be placed on research focused on pre-collegiate educational organizations. Volumes should address issues related to leadership at all levels of the educational system and be written in a style accessible to scholars, educational practitioners and policy makers throughout the world.

The volumes – monographs and edited volumes – should represent work from different parts in the world.

The titles published in this series are listed at the end of this volume.

EDUCATIONAL LEADERSHIP FOR ORGANISATIONAL LEARNING AND IMPROVED STUDENT OUTCOMES

by

WILLIAM MULFORD

*University of Tasmania,
Hobart, Australia*

HALIA SILINS

*Flinders University of South Australia,
Adelaide, Australia*

and

KENNETH LEITHWOOD

*OISE/University of Toronto,
Toronto, Canada*

KLUWER ACADEMIC PUBLISHERS

DORDRECHT / BOSTON / LONDON

A C.I.P. Catalogue record for this book is available from the Library of Congress.

ISBN 1-4020-3761-9 (PB)

ISBN 1-4020-1987-4 (HB)
ISBN 1-4020-2199-2 (e-book)

Published by Kluwer Academic Publishers,
P.O. Box 17, 3300 AA Dordrecht, The Netherlands.

Sold and distributed in North, Central and South America
by Kluwer Academic Publishers,
101 Philip Drive, Norwell, MA 02061, U.S.A.

In all other countries, sold and distributed
by Kluwer Academic Publishers,
P.O. Box 322, 3300 AH Dordrecht, The Netherlands.

Printed on acid-free paper

Printed in the Netherlands.

TABLE OF CONTENTS

SECTION 1: THE CRITICAL ROLE OF LEADERSHIP FOR ORGANIZATIONAL LEARNING AND IMPROVED STUDENT OUTCOMES

SECTION 2: USING THE BOOK

ACKNOWLEDGEMENTS

Pamela Bishop for her total integrity and support for the disadvantaged. The finest of educators. A member of the Leadership for Organizational Learning and Student Outcomes research team, she had a major responsibility for the writing of the case studies used in this book.

Silja Zarins educator par excellence. As a member of the Leadership for Organizational Learning and Student Outcomes research team, her contribution progressed our work in many ways. Her early assistance in the development of the survey instruments is particularly recognized here.

LIST OF TABLES

LIST OF FIGURES

SECTION 1:

THE CRITICAL ROLE OF LEADERSHIP FOR ORGANIZATIONAL LEARNING AND IMPROVED STUDENT OUTCOMES

CHAPTER 1

THE CRITICAL ROLE OF LEADERSHIP FOR ORGANIZATIONAL LEARNING AND IMPROVED STUDENT OUTCOMES

INTRODUCTION

The current context for educational leadership increasingly involves large-scale, if not global, cultural, technological, economic, and political forces for change. Given such outside pressures, loss of control of some of the educational agenda by those in schools is inevitable. For example, the information age has caused those in schools to lose their privileged access to knowledge and its dissemination. At the same time, and seemingly as a reaction against too much decentralisation, education systems in many countries have tightened centralised control mechanisms through accountability devices such as high states testing, performance management and competency frameworks. In brief, the external world of the educational leader is one of increasing loss of control, change, complexity, diversity, and intensity (Leithwood & Hallinger, 2002)

Paradoxically, and at the same time, the role of the educational leader within his or her school is one of greater responsibility. The growing importance of the educational leader is evidenced not only by reference to results of his or her pivotal role in effective schools (see, for example, Marks, Louis, & Printy, 2000; Silins & Mulford, 2002), but also the increasing preparedness on the part of governments to invest in the leaders of their schools and their training (see, for example, Gronn, 2002; National College for School Leadership [NCSL], n.d.).

There is a greater understanding that too often educational reforms have been thwarted by the robust nature of established school practices. It is clear that reforms, no matter how well conceptualised or powerfully sponsored, are likely to fail in the face of cultural resistance from those in schools (Bishop & Mulford, 1999; Louden & Wallace, 1994; McLaughlin, 1998; Sarason, 1998). But some forms of school leadership and restructuring are proving to be more beneficial than others. For example, schools moving from competitive, top-down forms of power to more collective and facilitative forms (Mulford, 1994) are finding greater success, as are those attempting to make not only first-order changes (i.e., in curriculum and

1

instruction) but also those second-order changes which support efforts to implement first-order changes (i.e., culture and structure).

Given that certain forms of restructuring challenge some existing teacher paradigms, resistance to change is predictable. Smylie, Lazarus, and Brownlee-Conyers (1996) have shown, for example, that the greater the participative nature of decision-making, the greater the increase in perceived accountability, the more organizational learning opportunities for teachers. The greater the increases in accountability, the more learning opportunities available, the greater the reports of instructional improvement. The greater the reports of instructional improvement, the more positive the teacher-reported student outcomes, and the more likely improvements in reading and mathematics achievement test scores. However, at each stage of this sequence, teachers also reported a decline in perceived individual autonomy. The change in paradigm is away from the teacher in his or her own classroom to the development of learning communities which value differences and support critical reflection and encourage members to question, challenge and debate teaching and learning issues (Peters, Dobbins, & Johnson, 1996).

How to do this is far from clear, but we believe the area of organizational learning (OL) offers valuable clues. The indications are that the successful restructuring agenda depends on teams of leaders, whole staffs and school personnel, working together in genuine collaboration. The challenges these groups face require significant development of their collective, as well as their individual, capacities.

The evidence on which this book is based, publications such as *Organisational Learning in Schools* (edited by Leithwood & Louis, 1998), *Understanding Schools As Intelligent Systems* (edited by Leithwood, 2000), *The Ethical Dimensions of School Leadership* (Begley & Johansson, 2003), and the research project, *Leadership for Organisational Learning and Student Outcomes* (LOLSO; Mulford, 1998; Mulford & Silins, 2001, 2003; Silins & Mulford, 2002a, b, c; Silins, Mulford, Zarins, & Bishop, 2000; Silins, Zarins, & Mulford, 2002), addresses the need to extend present understandings of school reform initiatives that aim to change collective school practices with the intention of supporting enhanced student learning. After a brief comment regarding the importance of using only quality evidence in school reform efforts, this chapter details quality evidence from the LOLSO research project. The results from LOLSO's teacher surveys ("teacher voice") and student surveys ("pupil voice") are organised around six of the project's major research questions:

- how is the concept of OL defined in schools ("teacher voice")?
- what leadership practices promote OL in schools ("teacher voice")?
- what are some outcomes of schooling other than academic achievement ("pupil voice")?
- what are the relationships between the non-academic and academic outcomes of schooling?
- does school leadership and/or organizational learning contribute to student outcomes? and,

- what other factors contribute to student outcomes?

The chapter then discusses four implications of this evidence as well as linking them to the evidence from recent introductory books in the area. Other contemporary research is also introduced. We conclude with a plea that given the accumulation and consistent quality of the evidence from across systems and countries, we no longer need to involve ourselves with just *impressions* of effective leadership. We have a way forward that links to organizational learning and improved student outcomes.

SORTING THE WHEAT FROM THE CHAFF

As we have already said, reforms for schools, no matter how well conceptualised, powerfully sponsored, brilliantly structured, or closely audited are likely to fail in the face of cultural resistance from those in schools. By their actions, or inaction, students (Rudduck & Flutter, 2000), teachers (Berends, 2000), middle managers (Busher & Harris, 2000), and principals (Leithwood & Duke, 1999) help determine the fate of what happens in schools, including attempts at reform.

Sometimes this is not a bad thing, for many a school has been badly disillusioned by the galloping hoofbeats of the itinerant peddlers behind the new movements who ride in and out again extorting their latest elixirs (Slavin, 1996). On the other hand, there are reforms that may have great potential for school reform. To have these advances fall to the same fate as the latest gimmickry or short-term political opportunism benefits no one, especially those in schools for they are the people most responsible for the long-term improvement of schools and the children in them (Prestine, 1998).

Where do those in schools start sorting the wheat from the chaff, genuine growth potents offering long-term improvement from the elixirs and short-term opportunism? The current and growing emphasis on evidence informed policy and practice is as good a place as any (The Evidence for Policy and Practice Information and Co-ordinating Centre [EPPI-Centre], 2001). However, if one is seeking to establish a useful evidence base for school improvement then one also needs to establish the value of the evidence that is presented. The old computer adage "garbage in, garbage out" remains as relevant today as it has always been.

In this section we present some quality evidence for those considering school reform. We believe it is quality evidence because it has integrity, predictive validity, and clearly defined variables. The evidence has integrity in the sense that it is complex enough to come closer to the reality faced by schools than much of previous research in the area, has been gathered from other than principals (who tend to overestimate the effectiveness of reforms when compared with their teachers – see McCall et al., 2001; Mulford, Kendall, Kendall, Bishop, & Hogan, 2000; Mulford, Kendall, Kendall, Lamb, & Hogan, 2001) and has been collected by other than those involved in the design or implementation of the reform. It has predictive validity because it attempts to link leadership with organizational learning and student outcomes. The link to student outcomes is a rare event indeed in the research literature on educational leadership and school improvement.

THE EVIDENCE

The LOLSO Research Project addressed the need to extend present understandings of school reform initiatives that aim to change school practices with the intention of supporting enhanced student learning. LOLSO was unique in a number of ways including its:

- large sample;
- longitudinal nature;
- attempt to clearly define its variables;
- inclusion of the concept of OL;
- use of student and teacher "voice";
- examination of the relationships among a large number of variables, specifically leadership processes, organizational learning and student outcomes taking into account a number of contextual variables such as socio-economic status (SES), home educational environment and school size;
- use of a measure of student outcomes that is wider than academic achievement;
- being carried out by those not involved in the design or implementation of the school restructuring initiatives; and,
- use of findings to develop a set of problem based learning professional development materials for educational leaders (that is, this book).

Research Design

LOLSO's research design required four phases of data collection and analysis conducted over 4 years:

- In Phase 1, surveys of 3,500 Year 10 students and 2,500 of their teachers and principals were conducted in half the secondary schools in South Australia and all the secondary schools in Tasmania, Australia (a total of 96 schools).
- In the second phase of the study, cross-sectional and longitudinal case studies of best practice were collected from four schools selected from the sample to triangulate and enrich the information generated by the survey data.
- In the third phase, South Australian Year 12 students, teachers and principals were resurveyed.
- The fourth phase saw the results from the quantitative and qualitative data used to develop and trial professional development interventions for school leaders.

In brief, the project's research design allowed for iterative cycles of theory development and testing, using multiple forms of evidence.

Results

Results from LOLSO's teacher surveys ("teacher voice") and student surveys ("pupil voice") can be organised around six of the project's major research questions. In what follows, a figure summarizing the answer to the question precedes the written explanation.

1. **How is the concept of OL defined in schools ("teacher voice")?** (see Figure 1)

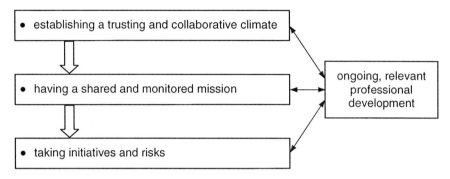

Figure 1. The four factors defining OL.

OL was found to involve *sequentially* establishing a trusting and collaborative climate, having a shared and monitored mission, and taking initiatives and risks within the context of supportive, ongoing, relevant professional development.

2. **What leadership practices promote OL in schools (teacher voice)?** (see Figure 2)

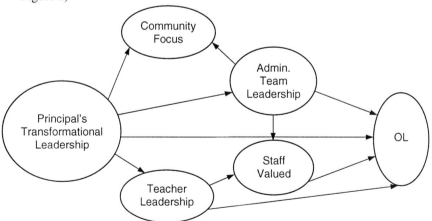

Figure 2. Factors influencing OL.

The LOLSO research demonstrated clearly that the predominant conditions accounting for variations in OL between secondary schools were a principal skilled in transformational leadership and administrators and teachers who are actively involved in the core work of the school. In brief, leadership that makes a difference to a high school having a community focus, staff feeling valued and OL is transformational and distributed. Having a community focus means that the teachers perceive the school as having productive working relations with the community and that school's administrators are sensitive to the community, work with community representatives and incorporate community values in the school. The principal who is transformational focuses on:

- **Individual Support** – providing moral support, shows appreciation for the work of individual staff and takes their opinion into account when making decisions.
- **Culture** – promoting an atmosphere of caring and trust among staff, sets a respectful tone for interaction with students and demonstrates a willingness to change his or her practices in the light of new understandings.
- **Structure** – establishing a school structure that promotes participative decision making, supports delegation and distributed leadership and encourages teacher autonomy for making decisions.
- **Vision and Goals** – working toward whole staff consensus in establishing school priorities and communicates these priorities and goals to students and staff giving a sense of overall purpose.
- **Performance Expectation** – having high expectations for teachers and for students and expects staff to be effective and innovative.
- **Intellectual Stimulation** – encouraging staff to reflect on what they are trying to achieve with students and how they are doing it; facilitates opportunities for staff to learn from each other and models continual learning in his or her own practice.

What is important is that staff are actively and collectively participating in the school and feel that their contributions are valued.

We also found that the principal's gender or the teacher's years in education or their school, age, or gender were not factors promoting OL, but school size was. The larger metropolitan schools of over 900 students, staffed by experienced and ageing teachers, did not provide the environment most conducive to transformational leadership or teacher distributed leadership. Perhaps surprisingly, having a community focus was not found to be related to promoting OL.

3. What are some outcomes of schooling other than academic achievement (pupil voice)? (see Figure 3)

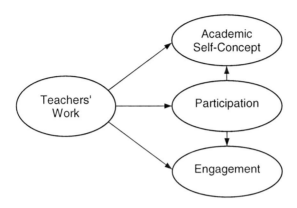

Figure 3. Influence of Teachers' Work on Academic Self-Concept, Participation, and Engagement.

There have been consistent and growing calls for broader measures of school success beyond academic achievement. (Department for Education and Science [DfES], 2001; Elliot & Voss, 1974; McGaw, Piper, Banks, & Evans, 1992) For example, alienation of pupils from school can be a critical step leading to failure to complete schooling and is especially important for middle and senior high school students. Pupils who experience acceptance, or belongingness, are more highly motivated and engaged in learning and more committed to school. Engagement and commitment are closely linked to student performance, and more importantly, to the quality of student learning (Osterman, 2000).

The LOLSO Research Project took such calls on board and included surveys of Year 10 and Year 12 pupil views of their schooling. The following factors emerged from the statistical analysis of their responses:

- Teachers' Work – pupils
  - like the way the teachers teach,
  - see a variety of activities, constant challenge and good organisation in class, and
  - believe teachers discuss their work with them and expect them to do their best work.

- **Academic Self-Concept** – pupils are
  - confident of success and graduating,
  - satisfied with marks now and at the end of the year, and

  ○ satisfied with the extent of their learning and ability to understand
    material.

- **Participation** – pupils
  ○ respond to questions and enjoy giving their opinion,
  ○ set goals,
  ○ participate in extracurricular activities, and
  ○ have low number of days where they were late and/or skipped classes.

- **Engagement** – pupils
  ○ are satisfied with student-teacher and student-student relationships,
  ○ identify with their school, and
  ○ see the usefulness of schoolwork for future life.

The findings on the relationships among these four non-academic achievement
student outcomes reinforce the importance of the teachers' work for academic self-
concept, participation and engagement. They also highlight the central role
participation, that is the active, behavioural dimension, has for the attitudinal
dimensions of academic self-concept and engagement.

4. **What are the relationships between the non-academic and academic
   outcomes of schooling?** (see Figure 4)

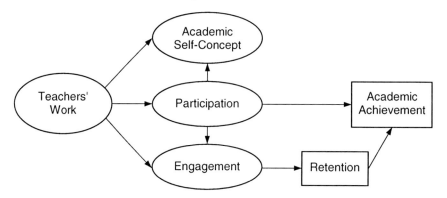

*Figure 4. Teachers' Work and the relationships between non-academic and academic student
outcomes.*

The LOLSO Research Project gathered data from over half of its student sample
on whether or not they continued on from Year 10 to Year 12 (Retention) and their
five subject aggregate Tertiary Entrance score from the Secondary Assessment
Board of South Australia's formal assessment procedure (Academic Assessment).

We found that students who stay in school and completed Year 12 and who
participate in school are most likely to achieve academically. Retention is more
likely when students are engaged with school. In other words, engagement is a direct
predictor of retention but only indirectly influences achievement (through retention).

The contra-intuitive result that academic self-concept is not a predictor of engagement, retention or achievement should be noted.

Other (see Figure 6) results indicated that the size and socio-economic status (SES) of the school and the pupil's perception of their home educational environment also influenced non-academic and academic student outcomes. Home educational environment involves having a space and aids for study as well as having discussions about and help with-school work and conversations about world events.

Larger schools were more likely to have students with higher academic self-concept but to have lower student participation. Schools of higher SES were more likely to have students with higher academic self-concept, retention and academic achievement but lower perceptions of teachers' work. There was a very strong positive relationship between home educational environment and teachers' work and participation and a less strong but still positive relationship between home educational environment and academic self-concept.

5. Does school leadership and/or organizational learning contribute to student outcomes? (see Figure 5 on the next page)

Both positional (principal) and distributed (administrative team and teacher) leadership is only indirectly related to student outcomes. OL, or a "collective teacher efficacy," is the important intervening variable between leadership and teacher work and then student outcomes. Said another way; leadership contributes to organizational learning which in turn influences what happens in the core business of the school; the teaching and learning. It influences the way teachers organise and conduct their instruction, their educational interactions with students, and the challenges and expectations teachers' place on their pupils. The higher the teachers' ratings of the school on the four sequential dimensions defining organizational learning, the more positively teachers' work is perceived in classrooms by their pupils. Pupils' positive perception of teachers' work directly promotes participation in school, academic self-concept and engagement with school. Pupil participation is directly and pupil engagement indirectly, through retention, related to academic achievement.

6. What other factors contribute to student outcomes? (see Figure 6 on page 11)

To repeat earlier findings, larger schools were not only less likely to promote transformational or teacher distributed leadership but were also more likely to have students with higher academic self-concept and lower student participation. In addition, schools of higher SES were more likely to have students with higher academic self-concept, retention and academic achievement but lower perceptions of teachers' work. Higher SES was related to having a positive home educational

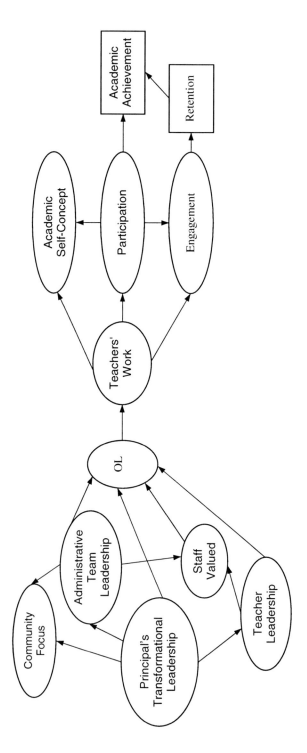

Figure 5. Effects of Leadership, OL, and Teachers' Work on student outcomes.

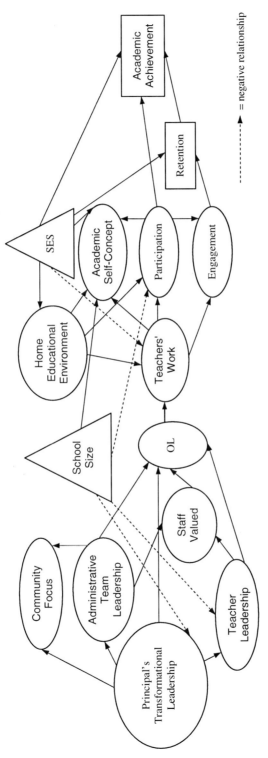

Figure 6. Influence of School Size and SES on student outcomes.

environment. Also, there were very strong positive relationships between home educational environment (pupil provided with study space and aides) and teachers' work and participation and a less strong but still positive relationship between home educational environment and academic self-concept.

Student participation and engagement in school were either directly or indirectly related to retention and academic achievement. What was important was that pupils, just like teachers, are actively participating in the school and feel that their contributions are valued. However, neither pupil academic self-concept nor the school having a community focus was directly or indirectly related to any of the other student outcomes.

FOUR IMPLICATIONS

There are at least four clear implications for educational leadership, for organizational learning, and improved student outcomes arising from the quality evidence provided in the LOLSO research conducted by Mulford and Silins (see Mulford, 1998; Mulford & Silins, 2001, 2003; Silins & Mulford, 2002a, 2002b, 2002c; Silins et al., 2000; Silins et al., 2002) – transformational and distributed leadership, a focus on development/learning, broad measures of student outcomes, and the importance of context.

Transformational and Distributed Leadership

The first of four implications is that leadership that makes a difference in schools is both position based (principal) and distributed (administrative team and teacher) and that the effects of both these forms of leadership on student outcomes is indirect (through OL and teacher work).

The positional/principal leadership we are talking about is what is termed *transformational*. Leithwood, Jantzi, and Steinbach (1998) found that along with district initiatives and school culture, transformational leadership had the strongest direct and indirect effects on OL. Transformational leadership here involved eight dimensions: identifies and articulates a vision, fosters the acceptance of group goals, conveys high performance expectations, provides appropriate models, provides individualised support, provides intellectual stimulation, builds a productive school climate, and helps structure the school to enhance participation in decisions. Silins and Mulford (2002) found both direct and indirect (through distributed leadership and staff feeling valued) relationships between a similar measure of transformational leadership and OL. Louis and Kruse (1998) found that one element of transformational leadership, the intellectual vision of the principal, was a powerful stimulus for collective learning in their school.

Silins and Mulford (2002) identified two types of distributed leadership, administrative team and the teacher. Both were found to contribute directly to OL and indirectly (through OL and teachers' work) to student outcomes. What was found important was the collective efficacy of the staff, their ability to engage in organizational learning. Ben-Peretz and Schonmann's (1998) study of teachers' lounges illustrates "just how interdependent are teachers' senses of professional community and the collective learning that occurs in that community" (p. 64). What these authors found most important was a teaching culture "characterised by strong norms of collegiality" (p. 64). How the teachers are treated is reflected in how the students perceive the teacher's work which, in turn, is related to the outcomes of their schooling.

This first implication is consistent with the findings of a recent review of the research literature that identified three major and aligned elements in successful school reform (Silins & Mulford, 2002). The first element relates to how people are treated. Success is more likely where people act rather than are always reacting, are empowered, involved in decision-making through a transparent, facilitative and supportive structure, and are trusted, respected and encouraged. The second element concerns a professional community. A professional community involves shared norms and values including valuing differences and diversity, a focus on continuous enhancement of learning for all students, de-privatisation of practice, collaboration, and critical reflective dialogue, especially that based on performance data. The final element relates to the presence of a capacity for learning. This capacity is most readily identified in an ongoing, optimistic, caring, nurturing professional development program.

Our emphasis on distributed leadership is consistent with the UK government's White Paper (DfES, 2001) on education and some of the directions espoused by its National College for School Leadership (NCSL, n.d.). The White Paper, for example, states that "Only if we can build on the commitment and enthusiasm of all those who work in schools will we succeed in implementing a truly diverse secondary system" (p. 15). It talks about "Education with character" and the importance of the school's ethos for successfully achieving such character. The NCSL's documentation points out that their work is founded on four beliefs including that "Our most successful schools are self-improving" and that "Leadership in such schools tends to be shared." Elsewhere, NCSL gives priority to concepts such as *capacity, dispersed leadership,* and *learning communities.*

Our emphasis on transformational and distributed leadership is also consistent with the early findings from the Programme for International Student Assessment (PISA; Organization for Economic Cooperation and Development [OECD], 2001a). PISA represents a new commitment by the governments of OECD countries to monitor the outcomes of education systems every 3 years in terms of student achievement and within a common framework and set of assessment instruments that are internationally agreed upon. PISA 2000 assessed young people's ability to apply their knowledge and skills in reading, mathematic and science to real life problems and situations, rather than how well they had learned a specific curriculum. A sample of 265,000 15-year-old students from 32 countries also answered questions about themselves including their home backgrounds, their attitudes to school and learning, and strategies they used when studying. The students' school principals were asked about their schools including the atmosphere and resources for learning and the kinds of programs the students were studying. Confirming Lee and Smith's (2001, p. 156) conclusion that, "schools influence their student learning by how they organise themselves," PISA found that overall school level factors accounted for 31% of variation in reading among schools within countries and 21% among countries. Together with home background factors these percentages increased to 72 and 43, respectively.

While there was no single factor in the PISA results that explained why some schools or countries had better results, school policies and practices that tend to be associated with success in reading (taking account of other observed school and home background factors) included a number closely related to transformational and distributed leadership, as well as OL. These policies and practices were: student use of school resources (library, computers, laboratories); university qualified teachers; student:staff ratio from 10:1 to 25:1; school policy and practice (as reported by principals) regarding teacher expectations of student performance, teacher morale and commitment and school (not teacher) autonomy; classroom practice (as perceived by students) involving positive teacher-student relations, good disciplinary climate and, to a lesser extent, emphasis on academic performance and high demands on students (including homework).

The rejection in our findings of "the great man or woman" theory of leadership should be noted. Faith in one person, "the leader," as the instrument for successful implementation of the government's educational policy, let alone broader and longer term educational outcomes, might bring initial albeit temporary success but the dependency relationship that it establishes will eventually ensure mediocrity if not failure. There is a clear difference here between our research and the influential British Hay-McBer (n.d.) model of excellence for school leaders. In contrast to the Hay-McBer "model", we do not give emphasis to the leader showing initiative by acting decisively, having impact by persuasion, calculation and influencing, or creating the vision through, for example, strategic thinking. Nowhere is the difference clearer than in our different interpretations of the concept *transformational leadership.* The Hay McBer emphasis on the "drive and the ability to take the role of leader, provide clear direction, and enthuse and motivate others" (p. 12) is a mile away from our stress on support, care, trust, participation, facilitation, and whole staff consensus.

Development/Learning

The second implication is that successful school reform is all about development and, therefore, learning. As Stoll, MacBeath, Smith, and Robertson (2001, p. 171) conclude, "the learning opportunities for generations of pupils are determined by the extent to which their schools are themselves able to learn and grow." Hersey and Blanchard (1988) made this point some time ago in respect of a leader's use of a task and/or relationship emphasis depending on the maturity of the group he or she was leading (see Figure 7).

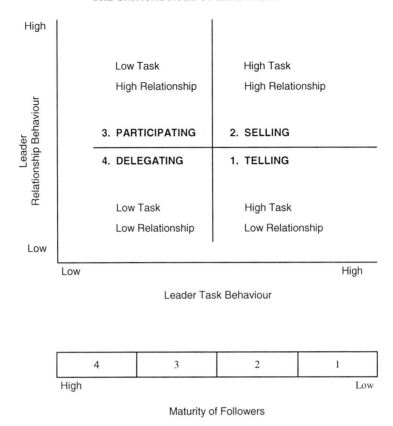

Figure 7. Linking leader relationship and leader task behaviour to maturity of followers.

A group low in maturity would need a *telling* style of leadership (high task, low relationship). At the next level of group maturity the leader would need a *selling* style (high task, high relationship), then *participating* style (low task, high relationship), and finally, with a group high in maturity a *delegating* style (low task, low relationship). The weakness of this model, however, is that it is not really about development. For example, if a leader keeps using only telling or selling style when working with an immature group, then the group is never going to become more mature. Of course, this assumes one wants a mature group, that is, a group (a school staff) that has the ability (skill, knowledge, experience) and willingness (motivated, committed, self- confident) to take responsibility for directing its own behaviour!

In other words, one needs to first get the personal/interpersonal, distributed leadership, collective teacher efficacy or trusting and collaborative climate "right." Once the personal/interpersonal is "right" then it can be used to focus on the educational/instructional, including having a shared and monitored mission. As Cousins (1998, p. 146) found, collaborative evaluation in itself holds "potential for fostering individual and collective learning." Once the educational/instructional is "right" and there is confidence in what the school is doing and why it is doing it, then the leaders and school can move to taking risks/development/learning/change. Such stages are confirmed in research by Mitchell and Sackney (1998) that examines the development of OL in a Canadian elementary school.

Mitchell and Sackney (1998, p. 188) found not only the importance of two cognitive and two affective antecedents to OL, but they also identified three distinct phases of development. The cognitive antecedents were the *processes of reflection* and *professional conversation*; the affective antecedents were *invitation to participate* and *affirmation of contributions*. The three interrelated phases were: (a) *naming and framing* (discussions characterized by description, storytelling, and suggestion), (b) *analysing and integrating* (analysis and evaluation of current practice), and (c) *applying and experimenting* (discussions about implementation plans). Mitchell and Sackney's phases as well as ours (establishing a trusting and collaborative climate, having a shared and monitored mission and taking initiatives and risks in a context of supportive, ongoing, relevant professional development) have elements that are remarkably consistent with Stringfields's (1998) research on conditions for high reliability schools. These conditions include commitment to and clarity regarding goals, systematic staff training, mutual monitoring and taking performance evaluations seriously, having powerful data bases, and being hierarchically structured but also with collegial decision-making regardless of rank.

Development implies another important principle—one needs stability for change, one needs to constantly move ahead but without losing one's roots. Put another way, one needs a base or agreed position from which to develop; one needs to stand for something, to first be "grounded." As Leithwood et al. (1998, p. 88) found, a "coherent sense of direction for the school is crucial in fostering organisational learning." Admittedly, unlearning the past can be a significant challenge to schools engaged in significant restructuring (Louis & Kruse, 1998). Leithwood and Louis (1998, p. 8) advise: "Learning seems to occur most productively when staffs use both internal and external sources of information, when important assumptions underlying the work of the school are given ongoing attention, when teachers' learning occurs in systematic ways, and when teachers think about their roles in new ways."

Broad Measures of Student Outcomes

The fourth implication is the need to broaden what counts for effective education beyond academic achievement. Self-concept is a case in point. Even though we, along with others, (Silins & Murray-Harvey, 2000) found that academic self-concept did not link to other student outcomes, including academic achievement, it does not follow that academic self-concept is not an important student outcome. For example, pupil self-concept has been shown to be related to later life successes such as employment and earnings (Feinstein, 2000). Data from this British cohort study followed all children born in UK in the first week of April 1970 and surveyed them again in 1975, 1980, 1986, 1991, and 1996. In 1980, at the age of 10, over 12,000 children were tested for mathematics and reading ability; their self-esteem and locus of control were also assessed. The children's teachers were questioned about their behavioural attributes of conduct disorder, peer relations, attentiveness, and extraversion. In 1996, at the age of 26, the young people were asked about their highest qualification attained, earnings, and employment history. The economist Feinstein (2000) summarizes his findings as follows:

> Attentiveness in school has been shown to be a key aspect of human capital production, also influencing female wages even conditioning on qualifications. Boys with high levels of conduct disorder are much more likely to experience unemployment but higher self-esteem will both reduce the likelihood of that unemployment lasting more than a year and, for all males, increase wages. The locus of control measure . . . is an important predictor of female wages . . . . Good peer relations are important in the labour market, particularly for girls, reducing the probability of unemployment and increasing female wages. (p. 22)

> [These results] suggest strongly that more attention might be paid to the non-academic behaviour and development of children as a means of identifying future difficulties and labour market opportunities. It also suggests that schooling ought not be assessed solely on the basis of the production of reading and maths ability. (p. 20)

Findings such as this, as well as those from the LOLSO Research Project, add weight to views expressing concerns about the sole reliance on academic achievement as the measure of a school's success (DfEE, 1999; DfES, 2001). Perhaps the most significant of these studies is OECD's (2001a) PISA. On average PISA found that those who like school perform better than those who do not. PISA makes the point strongly that students need to leave school not just with sound subject-matter knowledge and skills but also have to be ready to continue learning throughout life. In order to do so, they must be able to manage their own learning, being motivated and engaged as well as having learning strategies. Yet, in 20 out of 28 countries, PISA found more than one in four students considered school a place where they did not want to go (up to 42% in Belgium, 38% in Italy, and 35% in the United States). In almost half the OECD countries, the majority of students also agreed or strongly agreed that school was a place in which they felt bored.

While a positive disposition to academic subjects remains an important educational goal in its own right, PISA 2000 results show that this interest not only varies widely but also is closely associated with performance. The aspect of student engagement found to be most closely associated with reading performance was students' ability to control the learning process, that is, figuring out what they need to learn, work out as they go what concepts they have not understood, look for additional information when they do not understand, check whether they remember what they have learned, and make sure they have remembered the most important things.

The use of "pupil voice" may be timely for research (Fielding, 1999) is now "beginning to encounter students expressing doubts about the genuineness of their school's interest in their progress and well-being as persons, as distinct from their contributions to their school's league table position. [The result is that] contract replaces community as the bond of human association" (p. 286). Another study by Cullingford (2001) based on interviews with 195 Year 10 and 11 pupils found their attitudes towards school to be uniformly negative. Most worrying, however, was that teachers were beginning to be seen by their students as only representing other people's wills as they seek out the best means to adapt to the requirements of academic achievement results and inspection – "every effort that a teacher makes to cajole the pupils into more work is interpreted as a sign of the teacher's selfish insecurity . . . all appears to be done for the sake of the external powers" (p. 7).

Context

The third implication of the LOSO research is that the context for leadership and school reform must be taken more into account. Variables such as SES, home educational environment and school size have a clear interactive effect on leadership, the school and student outcomes. Reynolds (n.d.), for example, is wary of any belief in "one right way" leadership pointing out that socially difficult schools may involve leadership that is more initiating and more effective schools more managing. Recent research by Harris and Chapman (2001) examining leadership in schools facing challenging contexts has shown that effective leadership in these schools is tight on values, purposes and direction but loose on involving others in leadership activity. The result of such leadership is clear direction and widespread involvement. But given our first implication on the importance of distributed leadership for significant and long-term school reform, we need to be careful here. As Barnett, McCormick, and Conners (2001) have found, a visionary principal can actually distract teachers from concentrating on teaching and learning, let alone have ownership of the vision!

Our results help to resurface the school size debate and add weight to the research drawing attention to the advantages of smaller schools (Cotton, 1997; Lee & Loeb, 2000; Sammons, Thomas, Mortimore, Owen, & Pennell, 1994). For example, Heck (2000) found that larger elementary schools produced smaller gains in reading, language and mathematics between third and sixth grades. This issue has been recognized in some parts of the United States with large schools now dividing themselves into sub-schools in order to provide the web of support necessary for student and teacher identification and involvement with the school and improved learning outcomes (Hodges, 2000).

The lack of a link found in the LOLSO research between the school having a community focus and organizational learning or student outcomes is potentially problematic. On the basis of our results, and if a choice needs to be made between working with and being sensitive to the community and improving home educational environments, then the latter will have more direct and immediate "payoff" for student outcomes. The success of the Excellence in Cities education mentors program in UK is a case in point. (Coughlan, 2001; Radice, 2001) Of course, having a strong community focus may be important for other reasons such as for the development of social capital in the community, especially in poor inner city and rural communities (Kilpatrick, Johns, Mulford, Falk, & Prescott, 2002).

OECD's (2001a) PISA study found differences in the performance between schools accounted for much of the variation in student performance in some countries. Varying amounts of within-school and between-school differences in performance were associated with the individual's socio-economic background, however the socio-economic composition of a school's population was found to be an even stronger predictor. The association between family background and student reading performance also differed greatly from one country to another. Students from privileged social backgrounds tended to perform better, but differences were less pronounced in some countries than in others. Within school differences were more likely to be influenced by SES where there were differentiated school systems. A stronger predictor of performance was whether students had a "classical culture" in their homes, such as literature and works of art. Higher parent/mother's education, having both parents living at home and, consistent with our results, more social and cultural communication between parents and their children (discussing books to eating meals together) were also associated with better student performance.

CONCLUSION: NO NEED TO CONTINUE TO BUILD IN CANVAS?

We have clearly moved on from the introductory position in Leithwood and Louis's (1998) book: "A review of empirical research on organisational learning in schools alone would make a very quick read indeed" (p. 7). In fact, the evidence from the LOLSO research project and the implications for positive school reform that arise from these results are consistent with Leithwood and Louis' (1998) conclusions that:

> Schools as organisations contain both a need for change and disorderliness, and also a demand for stability and a cohesive story about "where we have been and where we are going." Schools need to engage in fundamental and risky learning, and they need to organise themselves into communities of caring and trust. These two processes must coexist, for the chapters presented in this volume suggest they are interdependent as well as oppositional. (p. 283)

Our results and implications are also consistent with other contemporary research in the area. For example, in the United States, both Goddard, Hoy, and Hoy (2000) and Heck (2000) have found close links between school environments and improved student learning. Goddard et al. found that "collective teacher efficacy is a significant predictor of student achievement . . . [and] is greater in magnitude than any one of the demographic controls [including SES]" (p. 500). They conclude: "A one unit increase in collective teacher efficacy is associated with an increase of more than 40% of a standard deviation in student achievement" (p. 501). Heck (2000) found that higher SES was directly related to greater student improvement and that larger schools produced smaller student gains. He also showed that schools where the principal's leadership was rated as more supportive and directed towards instructional excellence and school improvement, and where the school climate was seen in positive terms "produced greater-than-expected improvements in student learning over time" (pp. 538-539).

In UK detailed case study research (Maden, 2001) following up on 11 effective schools in disadvantaged areas some 5 years after the initial investigation has found that the levers of change and improvement included:

distributed leadership ["It is tempting to dwell solely on the head teacher as a kind of miracle worker, but these heads know that, above all else, securing improvement comes through the hearts and minds of teachers" (p. 319), and "Extra mental and emotional energy seems to be triggered off by a shared sense of achievement, particularly when this is the result of the real efforts of staff and pupils" (p. 330)];

organizational learning ["It is probable that 'school capacity' is the single most important matter in trying to identify how and why some schools maintain and sustain improvement" (p. 320)]; and,

pupil participation and engagement ["Effective headship seems always to include the nurturing of leadership opportunities for teachers, but also . . . for pupils" (p. 327).]

In their chapter bringing together the lessons from a book of international research on leadership for change and school reform, Riley and Louis (2000) focused on leadership that is more than role-based, that is leadership as an organic activity involving the formation of a network of values-driven relationships. Integral to the success of such dispersed leadership are both pupil and teacher voice.

Finally, an OECD (2001b) nine-country study on innovative initiatives in school management also concluded that, "Changes designed with little involvement of those destined to use them are rarely effective . . . In that sense every teacher is a school leader . . . . It is striking . . . how frequently team-working is cited as a key ingredient to the success of new approaches to school management" (p. 55). The study pointed out that, "In such learning organisations, individuals and teams become reflective practitioners and are able to review their own situations and deal with problems or challenges as they arise" (p. 55).

It will be noted that our research, as well as this other contemporary research, places much less emphasis on the organizational, managerial or strategic than has previously been the case. This should not be surprising when it is realized that there is very little evidence to link such an emphasis to either OL or student outcomes. Elsewhere, Mulford (2002a, 2002b) has discussed such "transactional" leadership as too readily having the potential for "façades of orderly purposefulness," "doing things right rather than doing the right thing," "building in canvas," or "procedural illusions of effectiveness."

Sizer (1984) has talked about *Horace's Compromise*, that is working toward a façade of orderly purposefulness, exchanging minima in pursuit of the least hassle for everyone. Sometimes this compromise can be likened to "doing things right" rather than "doing the right thing." As Sergiovanni (2000) noted, it has the same purpose as the latest military technology of "building in canvas," that is, folding canvas tanks and canvas missile launchers designed to serve as decoys and to create an illusion of strength. Thus the purpose for education is to provide the right public face thus gaining the freedom for the government to interpret, decide, and function in ways that make short-term political but not necessarily long-term educational sense.

Meyer and Rowan (1977, as cited in Hannaway, 1978) pointed out that procedural illusions can be employed to maintain the myth of education and function to legitimize it to the outside world. In the absence of clear-cut output measures we turn to processes as outputs. For example, there are precise rules to classify (and credential) types of principals, types of teachers, types of students, and sets of topics. All these rules and regulations, competency lists, strategic plans, examinations, and so on give confidence to the outside (and to many of those inside) that the education system and its schools know what they are doing.

The structure of the system or school is the functioning myth of the organisation that operates not necessarily to regulate intra-organizational activity, but to explain it, account for it, and to legitimate it to the members outside the organization and to the wider society. The transactions in educational organizations are concerned with legitimacy. Structures are offered that are congruent with the social expectations and understandings about what education should be doing, e.g., process goals explicitly stated by an education department to help maintain or develop this legitimacy may influence the use of certain "approved" consultants, the creation of organizational sub-units such as an audit section or office of review, the setting up of national examination boards and training institutions, and so on. While such actions may have little proven positive effect on what goes on in schools, classroom or with pupils, they do, at the time of their creation, demonstrate congruence with the goals and expectations of the wider society as perceived by the department or authority.

Here we are talking about high visibility and the *impression* of decisiveness of action. Such goal displacement does, of course, raise important moral questions, especially if you believe, as we do, that deception has no place in education and its leadership or administration.

Where does our evidence sit in the educational leader's world of increased centrally mandated change? Galton (2000) replies to this question well in terms of teachers:

> By making certain techniques mandatory you run the danger of turning teachers into *technicians* who concentrate on the method and cease to concern themselves with ways that methods must be modified to take account of the needs of individual pupils. As we face the demands of a new century, creating a teaching profession which while technically competent was imaginatively sterile would be a recipe for disaster. (p. 203, emphasis in original)

As it is for teachers, so we believe it is for leadership for organizational learning and improved student outcomes.

ORGANIZATION OF THE BOOK

There are four sections to this book:

1. **An introductory rationale.** The chapter that makes up this section has made the case for evidence informed decision making and then provided quality evidence outlining the critical role of leadership for organizational learning for improved student outcomes in schools;

2. **Advice for using the book.** This section consists of two chapters. Chapter 2 details the reasons for the choice of problem-based learning as the vehicle for the professional development materials that form the major part of this book. These are professional development materials that aim to improve leadership for organizational learning and improved student outcomes. Chapter 3 provides suggestions for use of the book, including a one-day and two-day workshop, and advice on group development and warm-up activities for use for such group development before moving to the problem-based learning package in Section 3;

3. **A problem-based learning, evidence informed, professional development package for aspiring and actual school leaders.** This section is made up of five chapters. Chapter 4 details the problem, performance specifications, learning objectives, resources, and guiding questions. Chapter 5 consists of the Altona High School case study and Chapter 6 the Heronwood High School case study. Appendix 3 contains a short version of the Altona case study and Appendix 4 contains a short version of the Heronwood case study. Chapter 7 introduces the survey and other data from Altona and Heronwood.

4. **A challenge**. The final Chapter 8 provides refined versions of the diagnostic instruments used in the research that forms the basis of this book and challenges readers to use them in their own schools. The book concludes with two other appendixes containing two additional readings, a list of the references used, and a list of other readings.

SECTION 2:

USING THE BOOK

CHAPTER 2

PROBLEM-BASED LEARNING: A VEHICLE FOR PROFESSIONAL DEVELOPMENT OF SCHOOL LEADERS

INTRODUCTION

The use of the material contained in this book for the professional development of school leaders will depend on the time available and the number of participants involved. At least a one-day workshop is recommended with a minimum of 10 participants. Two or three days would be better and would allow for an increase in the number of participants.

Trialing of the material in several educational systems in different countries suggests that they work best with aspiring and early career principals or experienced principals who have not employed a data or evidence-based approach to problem solving.

You are encouraged to experiment with the workshop design. However, our trialing has found the best sequence before, during and after a one or two-day workshop would be as prescribed here. Alternatively, a two and three-day workshop, especially where it was residential and the participants worked in the evening, would see much more time spent at each stage. Other structured experiences could be added to the sequence of warm-up activities (see later in this Section). Much more time could be spent on analysing and applying the case study material, survey data and readings. Participants could be given both case studies to compare and contrast. Greater time could be provided for feedback on the group presentations and a session could be held where participants complete and analyse the LOLSO questionnaires for their own schools. Finally, an exciting development would be to experiment with translating the materials into distance materials and/or ICT for the whole or part of the workshop.

Before making suggestions for a one- and two-day workshop and warm-up activities, we outline our reasons for choosing problem-based leaning as our vehicle for best understanding and developing skills in educational leadership for organizational learning and improved student outcomes.

WHY PROBLEM-BASED LEARNING?

Introduction

Almost two decades ago one of the authors (Mulford, 1984) set down some thoughts on three interrelated aspects concerning the teaching of educational leadership. These areas were: first, the learners and their stages of development, their tendency toward dependence, and their needs regarding competence and belonging; second, the learning context, including assessment requirements, mode of delivery (for example, block or weekly meeting modes), and inclusion of students from different organizational backgrounds; and, third, how learning objectives might be met through different teaching approaches. It was concluded at the time that it would only be when we as teachers expect of ourselves what we expect of our students, that is that performance depends not only on intuitive skill or "art", but also on explainable techniques and procedures, that the craft of educational leadership would be transformed into a profession.

  This conclusion remains as relevant today as at the time it was made. Dramatic shifts have occurred in who is learning as well as in when and where they are learning. In addition, the knowledge explosion is calling into question long-held beliefs about what participants need to learn, while newly emerging tools for accessing, creating, displaying and assessing information are transforming the nature of the learning process itself. The who, when, where, what, and how of learning continue to change.

  Unfortunately, there is a widely acknowledged failure of common curricular approaches in many professional fields to take such changes in learning into account and therefore to meet client needs (in the field of educational leadership see, for example, Murphy, 1990). Educational leadership programs have traditionally sought to teach prospective and practicing leaders through curriculum content that focuses on theories and concepts derived from the social sciences (Cooper & Boyd, 1987 and other chapters in the same book). What is more, the predominant modes of instruction have been lecture and group discussion with alternative approaches such as case studies, simulations and experiential learning finding occasional favour (Hallinger & Wimpleberg, 1992).

  These traditional methods of organising the curriculum and its delivery appear to result in knowledge that can usually be recalled when the learner is asked specifically to do so but to not be used spontaneously in problem-solving contexts (Bransford, Franks, Vye, & Sherwood, 1989). While course developers may see relevance of such knowledge to the tasks they confront on the job in such contexts, graduates of the programs may not, or at least not significantly so (Bridges & Hallinger, 1992).

  It is our view that the *teachers'* interests continue to dominate the teaching infrastructure in leadership programs while participants remain as little more than passive recipients of the teachers' decision-making regarding content, process and evaluation. This situation is unfortunate.

Towards a Better Way of Teaching and Learning

Given that it is impossible to keep up with the "knowledge explosion" and, further, that much of the knowledge required for successful practice is constructed through social action, we believe that it is outmoded and unrealistic to regard courses in educational leadership as being a body of received knowledge or a complete preparation for a life-long career acquired through "teacher-centred" activities. Rather, we are concerned to ensure programs reflect the "real world" of the practitioner and that learning is transferred through embedding knowledge and skill acquisition in learning contexts that are similar in significant ways to those encountered in the real world. For the educational leader this world is one of ambiguity, where problems not facts or information are the starting point, where one works with and through others, where value is given to shared practitioner craft knowledge, where task and personal assessment tends to be formative rather than summative, and where self-directed learning will be essential as professionals pursue their careers.

One promising approach to help reflect this real world is Problem-Based Learning (PBL).

Problem-Based Learning

What is PBL, what are its major goals and basic principles? Why use PBL? What difference does PBL make?

What Is PBL, What Are Its Major Goals and Basic Principles?

- **What is it?**

PBL is a way of constructing and teaching courses using problems as the stimulus and focus for participant activity. It is an instructional strategy that organizes knowledge around problems rather than the disciplines and aims to achieve not only the solution of the difficulty, but also the discovery of the method of accomplishing this result. The approach derives from an epistemological teaching model of constructivism—knowledge is something the learner must construct for and by himself or herself. As individuals pursue their goals by selectively interacting with others, they adapt, or create for themselves, representational models of reality which guide their actions. Knowledge is tentative and socially constructed. PBL gives importance to learners observing, reflecting on their observations, collaborating with peers, negotiating meaning, and arriving at consensus.

- **Major goals**

The major goals of PBL include:

  ○ **acquisition of the knowledge base** underlying practice—learning within the context of practice and integrating basic knowledge with professional practice;
  ○ **development of interpersonal skills**, for example, group work;
  ○ **development of problem-solving skills**, for example, to analyse problems, identify what knowledge and skills are required to deal with a problem, acquire relevant knowledge and skills, apply what has been learned to seek a solution to the problem;
  ○ **development of life-long learning skills** and **motivations**, for example, self-directed learning ability and continuing professional education; and,
  ○ **acquisition of the motivation for learning**.

- **Basic principles**

The success of PBL depends on a product (the problem solution) and learning (knowledge-skills-values acquired) while maintaining and/or enhancing morale (including working through/with others). Several basic principles run through such an approach, including:

  ○ holistic approach to discipline and education;
  ○ orientation towards the professional practice;
  ○ integration of knowledge from different domains and of knowledge, skills and attitudes
  ○ students responsible for their own learning;
  ○ knowledge and skills actively acquired; and,
  ○ cooperation rather than competition.

More specifically, for educational leadership programs, Hallinger and Bridges (1995) have proposed seven key PBL principles:

  ○ **Challenge Focus** – PBL stimulates new learning for action with a problem in the foreground, supported by disciplinary knowledge in the background;
  ○ **Collaborative Teaching** – human resources include clinicians, multi-disciplinary experts, students as expert practitioners, all acting as models;
  ○ **Self-Directed Learning** – limited resources in practice means that adult learners must learn how to organize their learning, including their use of time;
  ○ **Cooperative Group Learning** – while case methods simulate reality, PBL develops team problem-solving capacities, culture and leadership;
  ○ **Implementation Focus** – where case methods invite projections, PBL asks for analysis, critical reflection, plans, action, outcomes and evaluation;

- ○ **Formative Evaluation** – summative data compare outcomes with plans—PBL supplements summative evaluation with formative evaluation of different types; and,
- ○ **Project Focus** – teams are provided with a challenge, guiding questions, learning resources, product specifications and formative assessment.

Why Use PBL?

We use PBL because it is a strategy for achieving excellence, quality assurance and accountability. It helps achieve abilities we want to see in our graduates, abilities such as knowledge of discipline, an ability to think like an educational leader, ability to integrate learning from different disciplines, ability to learn for themselves, ability to problem solve, ability to work collaboratively as a member of a team, ability to self and peer assess (self judgement), and being interesting, interested, motivated.

Active initiation and participation by those affected by change is one of the essential factors in successful implementation of change. Participants learn best through interacting with their environment in order to make personal meaning of their world. PBL uses teaching methods which emphasize the unique nature of each individual's system or structure of meanings, while recognising the shared nature of much human understanding. It takes account of the manner in which participants learn. Learners engage in a dialectic process in which every person's knowledge is respected and counted on. Learners experience control over their own learning.

The group work in PBL can help simulate group situations from practice. The negotiation function of the tutorial is at least as important as the integration process. Negotiated orientation, and ongoing reorientation of the problem, context and solution towards each other, and ongoing maintenance of the terms of mutual understanding are essential to quality outcomes.

But we need to be aware that PBL changes teacher-learner relationships. A teacher who sees learning as essentially a matter of mastering a body of "facts" is likely to adopt a substantially different approach to teaching from the one who sees learning as a dynamic interaction between the learner and a constantly changing world. A belief in a participant-centred approach to learning is central to the implementation of PBL, with the role of teacher becoming one of facilitator who aims to empower participants. Positive regard for participants forms the basis of genuine communication between facilitator and participant.

What Difference Does PBL Make?

The effectiveness of PBL in preparing professionals for their roles has been studied most extensively in the context of training in medicine. Research with public health nurses in a one year post registration in Australia and Sweden (Brown & Appel, 1993) indicates that there was no significant difference between the groups with regard to their perceptions of the knowledge gained. However the PBL graduates claim to have learned important skills such as responding to novel situations, solving of conflicts, self directed learning, self awareness and the possibility to be creative to a larger extent than their colleagues from comparison groups. Compared with conventional medical instruction for physicians, PBL has been found to be nurturing and enjoyable, to promote good achievement in clinical examinations and faculty evaluations but not necessarily in basic science examinations, and to be associated with graduates entering family medicine (Albanese & Mitchell, 1993).

The translation of PBL from medical education to educational leadership is only at a relatively early stage and thus few results of systematic empirical research are readily available. However, those results that are available show much promise. Student and staff feedback in North America (Hallinger & Bridges, 1994) and our own programs (Grady, Mulford, & Macpherson, 1995) has found that educational leaders rate PBL very positively in regard to their:

- acquisition of knowledge relevant to the educational administrator's role;
- ability to think like, for example, someone responsible for effective implementation, for making and interpreting policy and for leading at school or system level;
- ability to integrate learning from a number of disciplines and so develop personal theories concerning education;
- development of skills in solving complex problems in educational settings;
- capacity to make sound judgements about matters; and,
- perceptions of the degree of alignment of their *education* and *professional work*.

Given its goals, principles, reasons for use, and evidence of its success, we believe our choice of PBL as the vehicle for best understanding and developing skills in educational leadership for organizational learning and improved student outcomes to be a wise one. In what follows, we outline our advice regarding the before, during and after of both a one-day and a two-day workshop using the PBL materials that form the crux of this book.

BEFORE, DURING, AND AFTER A ONE-DAY WORKSHOP

Before

1. Pre-reading: a copy of this book for each participant with instructions to have read either the Altona or Heronwood case study (in long - Chapter 5 or 6 - or short - Appendix 3 or 4 - form) and case study outline, the first chapter of this book and one of the two readings.
   [To ensure a spread in the total group, you might want to specify the same case study but a different reading for each member of groups of approximately 6 participants.]

2. Consideration should be given to having participants use the survey instruments in Section 4 in their school and bringing the collated results to the workshop.

During

3. Lose time to gain time: Warm-up activity **Interdependence** (45 minutes) – see materials at the end of this Section of the book.
[If the case studies were sent out as pre-reading, then group participants for this activity by the case study they received, as this will be the group they will work in for the remainder of the workshop.]

4. Problem-Based Learning Package (15 minutes):

   4.1. Read through Section 3: Problem-Based Learning Package with participants and answer any questions. Use can be made of the *Action Plan Summary* overhead projector master (Figure 9 in Chapter 4) to reinforce the task at hand.

   4.2. Locate and refer to the survey data guide and data as well as the readings.

5. Form teams (of approximately 6) and set them to work.
[If the case studies were sent out as pre-reading, teams should be formed based on the case they received. Otherwise, use the same groups formed for the warm-up activity "Interdependence." Ensure each team has a space in which to work that is relatively independent of the other groups and any other activities at the venue. Provide each team with materials to facilitate their work, including large sheets of white paper, marker pens, tape, and overhead transparencies. Some teams may request access to PowerPoint, Data Show and other presentation technologies to assist with their task. Facilitators make themselves available for teams on request and/or circulate around teams having input on request.]

6. Review: after lunch bring all groups together for approximately 15 minutes so that they can be reminded of the task, provided with an opportunity for feedback and questions, and given an overview of the first Section of this book (with the aim of having the research findings used to justify their plan of action).

7. Conclusion: one hour before the scheduled completion of the workshop, team presentations are made and feedback provide on the value of the workshop.

   7.1 Team presentations
   [As these must not exceed 10 minutes each, it may be helpful to remind presenters when they have 5 and 2 minutes left.]

   7.2. Feedback from the Superintendent's school review committee and discussion. (At least 20 minutes)
   [The more realistic you can make this committee the better. Outsiders are preferable to those involved in the workshop. If you can enlist the services of a Superintendent and/or other senior Departmental officers, so much the better.
   In a situation where there are multiple groups working on the same case study, it has been found useful to let the Superintendent's school review committee hear all the presentations on the particular case study before feedback and discussion.]

7.3. Feedback on the workshop itself.

[Consideration should be given to having participants challenged to use the survey instruments in Section 4 in their school.]

After

8. Participants are encouraged to use the survey instruments in Section 4 in their school, collate the results and relate them with data and learnings from this workshop.

BEFORE, DURING, AND AFTER A TWO-DAY WORKSHOP

Before

1. Pre-reading: a copy this book for each participant with instructions to have read either the Altona or Heronwood case study (in long - Chapter 5 or 6 - or short - Appendix 3 or 4 - form) and case study outline, the first chapter of this book and one of the two readings.

   [To ensure a spread in the total group, you might want to specify the same case study but a different reading for each member of groups of approximately 6 participants.]

2. Have participants use the survey instruments in Section 4 in their school and bring the collated results to the workshop.

During

3. Lose time to gain time: Warm-up activity (60 minutes)

   3.1. Ice-Breaker (15 minutes)

   3.2. Interdependence (45 minutes)

   3.3. Trading (45 minutes)

   [If the case studies were sent out as pre-reading, then group participants for this activity by the case study they received, as this will be the group they will work in for the remainder of the workshop.]

4. Problem-Based Learning Package (45 minutes)

   4.1. Read through Section 3: Problem-Based Learning Package with participants and answer any questions. Use can be made of the Action Plan Summary overhead projector master included as part of Section 3 (Figure 9) to reinforce the task at hand.

4.2. Locate and refer to the case studies and case study outlines

4.3. Locate and refer to the survey data guide and data as well as readings.

5. Form teams (of approximately 6) and set them to work
   [If the case studies were sent out as pre-reading, teams should be formed based on the case they received. Otherwise, use the same groups formed for the warm-up activity "Interdependence."
   Ensure each team has a space in which to work that is relatively independent of the other groups and any other activities at the venue. Provide each team with materials to facilitate their work, including large sheets of white paper, marker pens, tape, and overhead transparencies. Some teams may request access to PowerPoint, Data Show and other presentation technologies to assist with their task.
   Facilitators make themselves available for teams on request and/or circulate around teams having input on request.]

6. Review: at the start of Day 2, it has been found useful to bring all groups together for approximately one hour so that they can be reminded of the task, discussion held on the stages of development experienced by their PBL group (see the next chapter), provided with an opportunity for feedback and questions, and given an overview of the first Section of this book (with the aim of having them used to justify their plan of action).

7. Conclusion: two hours before the completion of the workshop at the end of day two, team presentations, feedback, application to back home work situation, and program evaluation.

   7.1. Team presentations
        [As these must not exceed 15 minutes each, it may be helpful to remind presenters when they have 5 and 2 minutes left.]

   7.2. Feedback from the Superintendent's school review committee and discussion. (At least 30 minutes)
        [The more realistic you can make this committee the better. Outsiders are preferable to those involved in the workshop. If you can enlist the services of a Superintendent and/or other senior Departmental officers, so much the better. In a situation where there are multiple groups working on the same case study, it has been found useful to let the Superintendent's school review committee hear all the presentations on the particular case study before feedback and discussion.]

   7.3. In case study groups, sharing data gathered before the workshop from their school using the collated survey instruments in Section 4, comparing and contrasting results with those from the case study schools, and providing suggestions and advice to the whole group on the learnings including areas in need of change to make the instrumentation more helpful.

   7.4. Feedback on the workshop itself.

After

8. If survey instruments were not used, then participants are encouraged use the survey instruments in Section 4 in their school, collate the results and relate the them with data and learnings from this workshop.

These plans for a one-day and two-day workshop are only suggestions arising from the piloting of our materials. As we said at the start of this chapter, we encourage readers to experiment with the workshop design to best suit your particular needs. However, given that PBL involves groups and the effectiveness of those groups will in large measure determine the success of the program, we strongly urge that attention be given to the groups and their development. This is the subject of the next chapter.

CHAPTER 3

GROUP DEVELOPMENT AND WARM-UP ACTIVITIES

INTRODUCTION: LOSE TIME TO GAIN TIME

A strong message that has emerged from the educational leadership literature is that those in schools must learn how to lose time in order to gain time (Mulford, 1994, 1998). Awareness of, and skill development in, group and organizational processes is a first step in any effective change. Instead of others trying to insert something into the school's culture, the school, and especially its leadership, should first be trying to help that culture develop an awareness of and responsiveness to itself.

One way to approach these processes is to base professional development, increased cooperative effort, increased sharing of power and responsibility, on predictable stages of group development. Use can be made of the Stages of Group Development overhead projector master (Figure 8) included in this Section as part of presenting the reasons for the use of the warm-up activities. At some point, perhaps during the review at the commencement of the second day, participants could reflect on the development of their own workshop group.

At the first or **forming** stage, group members are polite, they avoid conflict, and they are concerned about being accepted or rejected. At the second stage, **storming**, group members become involved in conflict because of concern about status, power and organisation. The "pecking order," of "who is good at what," needs to be sorted out. The third stage, **norming**, sees more cohesion between members as there is more affection, open-mindedness and a willingness to share. However, pressures to conform to the group may detract from the task at hand. Next comes the **performing** stage, or work stage. It is characterized by an increase in task orientation and an open exchange of feedback. The next stage is **transforming**. This stage represents a refinement of the performing stage. It indicates that the group does not just continue performing the same tasks well, that it learns from feedback about those tasks and how they are undertaking them and, if necessary, changes the tasks and/or the methods of achieving them. There can also be a **dorming** stage that interacts with the performing and transforming stages. It is the time for "pulling back on the oars," for resting and recuperating, for letting the momentum of success allow the group to "coast" for while. Dorming helps to prevent group and/or individual burnout. Finally, there is a **mourning** stage, which can occur after whichever of the stages the

35

group has reached and is triggered by the impending dissolution of the group. At this stage members reassert their independence from the group and start to disengage.

Not only are there a number of clearly identifiable and sequential stages of development, but also much can be done to assist the group make the transitions through to the more effective later stages of performing or transforming. If left to their own devices, groups may not progress beyond the earlier less productive stages of forming, storming, and norming.

Many leaders and group facilitators are aware of the need to provide an "ice-breaker" when a new group first comes together, whether that be in the form of a specific set of exercises and/or discussion over refreshments. However, this is usually as far as the intervention goes and group members are then expected to get on with the task at hand.

Of all the transitions between stages of group development, the transition from storming to norming and norming to performing are perhaps the most crucial. Leaders need to be able to support group members, especially through a key stage where together they change from being managers of conflict to leaders who surface conflicts that must be addressed for the group to move forward. This surfacing and productive use of conflict requires hard listening that is alert to conflict, active encouragement to voice frustrations, and respect and honesty, including permitting others to criticize the leaders decisions. Making these transitions also requires the leader to ensure that the growing social cohesion is used for the good of the tasks at hand.

Activities

Structured Experiences have been found to be an excellent way to assist with group development (Mulford, Watson, & Vallee, 1981). Three examples follow that we have found to be useful warm-up activities for LOLSO Problem-Based Learning project. The first, **Ice-Breaker**, provides an opportunity for sharing information and mixing. The second, **Interdependence**, explores the effects of collaboration and competition in group problem-solving as well as how task-relevant information is shared. The third, **Trading**, helps participants become aware that individuals can react differently to exactly the same stimuli and that a person's view can be affected by the position taken by the group. All of these objectives link closely to progressing groups beyond the early stages of group development.

For each of the three structured experiences that follows, we outline its goals, use, process, and variations before providing any accompanying handouts.

In longer workshops we encourage greater use of structured experiences appropriately selected and used to advance groups through the sequential stages of group development (from the large resource base available elsewhere, for example, Johnston & Johnston; 1975, Mulford et al., 1981; Pfeiffer, 1991; Schmuck & Runkel, 1994; Schmuck & Schmuck; 1988, Senge et al., 1999; and Silbermann, 1999). Some examples of well known structured experience found useful for advancing groups through some of the stages would be:

- **Forming to Storming**
  - Who's Here
  - Autobiographies

- **Storming to Norming**
  - One-Way, Two-Way Communication
  - Broken Squares
  - Structures
  - Prisoners' Dilemma
  - Conflict Resolution

- **Norming to Performing/Transforming**
  - Fishbowl
  - Brainstorming
  - Nominal Grouping
  - Stranded on the Moon
  - Lego Man
  - Force Field Analysis

- **Mourning**
  - Our Group
  - Symbol

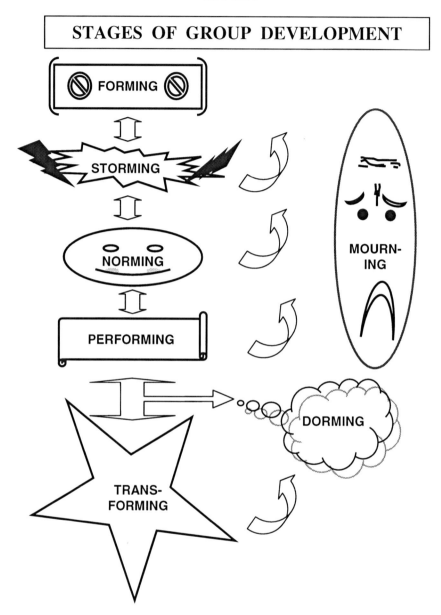

Figure 8. Stages of group development.

ICE-BREAKER

Goals

1. To provide an opportunity for participants to give information about themselves and to receive information about others.

2. To help a new group mix.

Use

1. Any age group.

2. Very appropriate for a new group and at the beginning of a workshop.

Group Size	Time Required	Materials Required	Physical Setting
Any size	Approximately 30 minutes	A card approximately 15 cm x 10 cm and a pen for each participant. Tape or pin to attach the card	A room large enough for participants to move around and talk to each other.

Process

1. The facilitator introduces the exercise by suggesting that:

   a)   as we enter a group, we are usually curious about the others in the group; and

   b)   this exercise will help identify individuals with similar or different interests.

2. Each participant is given a card and tape or a pin to attach it to him/herself.

3. The facilitator draws on the board a diagram of the card and asks the participants to write the following information on their cards:

   a)   in the middle, in large letters, their first name;

   b)   in the bottom left hand corner, their job;

   c)   in the bottom right hand corner, what they expect to get out of the workshop or group;

   d)   in the top left hand corner, their place of birth and the name of their favourite place;

   e)   in the top right hand corner, something interesting they have done in the past twelve months, and something they can look forward to in the next twelve months; and

     f)   anywhere on the card, three adjectives that describe themselves.

4. The facilitator then asks the group to mingle and using the cards to meet with at least five other participants.

5. The exercise should continue for as long as the facilitator thinks is valuable for the group.

6. The cards can be kept on the wall for the entire workshop so that participants get a chance to follow up.

7. The facilitator can check the cards early in the workshop in order to respond to any inflated expectations and/or return the cards at the end of the workshop to check whether expectations have been met.

Variations

1. Ask participants to look at the cards silently for 5 to 10 minutes and then go to someone they would like to talk to.

2. The information asked for can be varied according to purpose and age level, e.g., favourite TV show, favourite novel, hobbies, area of specialisation.

INTERDEPENDENCE

Goals

1. To explore the effects of collaboration and competition in group problem-solving.

2. To study how task-relevant information is shared within a work group.

3. To observe group strategies for problem-solving.

Use

1. Upper secondary school age onwards.

2. May be used to demonstrate the nature of co-operation in a task-related group, e.g., school curriculum and/or review committees.

Group Size	Time Required	Materials Required	Physical Setting
Groups of 6 (plus 1 or more observers to observe all groups)	Approximately 45-60 minutes	• A set of 6 Interdependence Basic Information Cards for each group • An Interdependence Observer Sheet for each observer • An Interdependence Answer Chart • Pencil and paper for each participant	A room large enough for the groups to work without influencing each other

Process

1. Before the session, the facilitator prepares a set of **Interdependence Basic Information Cards** for each group.

2. The facilitator distributes an **Interdependence Observer Sheet** to each observer and asks them to read it.

3. The facilitator distributes a set of **Interdependence Basic Information Cards** to each group, one card to each member. Three minutes is allowed for members to study the information.

4. Groups are instructed to begin working.

5. When there is agreement within a group that the solution has been reached, the group can check with the facilitator to see if it is correct. If is not correct they may elect to continue the problem solving process or to debrief.

6. Depending upon time constraints, each group should be allowed to continue until it has completed the task. However, facilitators should make sure that **at least** 15 minutes is left for debriefing.

7. When a group reaches the solution (or the facilitator asks the groups to commence debriefing), observers should make their comments. Groups then discusses how it organized to accomplish their task.

8. The facilitator may then call all the groups together to elicit some general comments on how they went about problem-solving and how this relates to their "real life" situations.

9. If any group has not reached the correct solution, it can be announced by the facilitator (See Interdependence Answer Chart overhead).
   He/she can inform the members that the solution can be reached by:

   a) Making a blank chart similar to the one displayed.
   b) Filling in the names of the teachers who are known to be in certain rooms during certain class periods from information provided on the **Interdependence Basic Information Cards.** (This process is aided by using the clues to make one list of teachers and another list of aides, in order to differentiate between the two.)
   c) Using deductive reasoning to fill in the names of other teachers in each of the spaces, so that each teacher is in a different room during each of the four periods.

Variations

1. Additional participants can be accommodated within the groups by duplicating information cards. For example, if there are 8 members, two participants receive the card with one dot at the end of the first sentence, and two receive the card with two dots.

2. The problem-solving phase can be interrupted several times for processing. Participants can be instructed to rate their confidence in the correctness of the solution and their satisfaction with the work style of the group.

3. The facilitator may give any of the following hints:

   > Discover who the teachers' aides are.
   > Discover who the teachers are.

   Deductive reasoning should be applied to the problem.

Interdependence Basic Information Cards

The six information cards below should be typed or glued onto cards and then placed in separate envelopes for distribution to group members in step 3 of "Process". A set of six cards will be needed for each group.

Each card is coded by the number of dots (from 1 to 6) following the first sentence on the card. Each of the six cards contains different data from the other cards.

You may tell your group what is on this card, but do not pass it around for the others to read.   .

Information:
Room B2 has Mr Pearson for a teacher during the third period.
Mr James and Ms Carr do not get along well, so they do not work together.
During the first period, the team leader, whom Harry likes, teaches Room B3.

You may tell your group what is on this card, but do not pass it around for the others to read.   .   .   .

Information:
All teachers teach at the same time and exchange groups at the end of each period.
Each teacher likes a different group best.
During the second period, each teacher teaches the group he or she likes best.
Each teacher teaches each group during one of the first four periods of the day.

You may tell your group what is on this card, but do not pass it around for the others to read.   .   .

Information:
Willowvale High School has two teachers' aides, four teachers and four groups of students.
Ms Martinez is the team leader for the Intermediate Unit.
Mr Pearson likes to work with Room B1.
James teaches Room B2 during the fourth period but he likes Room B3 best.

You may tell your group what is on this card, but do not pass it around for the others to read.   .   .   .   .

Information:
Your group members have all the information needed to find the answer to the following question:
In what sequence are the teachers (by name) in Room B4 during the first four periods?
Only one answer is correct and you can prove it.
Some of the information your group has is irrelevant and will not help solve this problem.

You may tell your group what is on this card, but do not pass it around for the others to read.   .   .   .

Information:
Ms Carr and Mr Wilson disagree about how it would be best to handle Room B3, in which there seems to be a history of abusing substitute teachers.
The team leader has been at the Willowvale High School for 5 years.

You may tell your group what is on this card, but do not pass it around for the others to read.   .   .   .   .

Information:
The team leader teaches Room B2 during the second period.
Harry works with Room B3 during the second period.
Ms Martinez has been at Willowvale High School for the shortest period of time.

Interdependence Observer Sheet

General

1. How did the group share its information?

2. What group strategies were employed for problem solving?

Specific

1. Some common errors in information sharing that reduce the effectiveness of problem solving include:
   - failure to agree on a common frame of reference (e.g., a chart)
   - attempting to work in pairs or trios rather than staying as a single group
   - passive listening
   - silent acceptance of non-understanding

The last three errors result in full information not being used—with a consequence that the solution is usually wrong.

2. Does one member take over the problem solving? If so, does he/she involve or ignore the others once he/she has all the information and how does this affect the morale of the rest of the group?

3. Do group members withhold information from their cards? Why?
   - because they have decided that it is irrelevant without first checking with the group?
   - because they are upset with others in the group?
   - because of competition among group members to be the first individual with the correct answer?

4. What does the group member with the problem directions (card 4) do after reading out his/her information?
   - retire from the exercise?
   - get frustrated with other members for not solving the problem (particularly if the exercise "drags on")?
   - is the irrelevant information used to boost the morale of the group or is it totally ignored?
   - are any members frustrated with having to rely on others for information to solve the problem?
   - is there a tendency, especially when difficulties arise, to "blame" individuals for withholding information, for not cooperating, etc.?

Interdependence Answer Chart

Room	Period			
	1	2	3	4
B1	*James*	*Pearson*	*Martinez*	*Wilson*
B2	*Wilson*	*Martinez*	*Pearson*	*James*
B3	*Martinez*	*James*	*Wilson*	*Pearson*
B4	*Pearson*	*Wilson*	*James*	*Martinez*

TRADING

Goals

1. To become aware that individuals can react differently to exactly the same stimuli.

2. To become aware that a person's view can be affected by the position taken by the group and to examine how group support and competition can affect the accuracy of individual perception.

Use

1. Any age group.

2. Very appropriate for a new group and at the beginning of a workshop.

Group Size	Time Required	Materials Required	Physical Setting
Any size	Approximately 45 minutes		A room large enough for participants to move around and form groups.

Process

1. The facilitator introduces the exercise by creating a "test" atmosphere by indicating that each individual is going to be asked to solve a piece of mental arithmetic.

2. The facilitator slowly and clearly reads the following story asking the participants individually, without discussion, to note their answer to the question asked:

> "A poor farmer comes into money – $60. He decides to buy a horse to help with the plowing. With the plowing done, he sells the horse for $70 and uses the money for seed. After the harvest, he buys another horse, but this time for $80. However, he is soon forced to sell the horse to pay for medical bills. He receives $90. How much does the farmer gain or lose as a result of all these transactions?"

3. Participants are asked to raise their hands when the facilitator announces an answer that corresponds to their answer (start at minus $20 and increase by $10s each time but be prepared for other answers) and then form a group of all those with the same answer in one part of the room.

4. Facilitator announces that a number of rounds (depending on the time available and usefulness of the interaction) will be held containing the following sequence:

   a) discuss the group's answer (5 minutes);
   b) select a representative of the group (2 minutes);
   c) this representative tries to convince members of other groups to join his or her group (2 minutes per group);
   d) when all representatives have spoken, participants have an opportunity to change groups.

5. The experience is discussed. Questions such as the following may be explored:

   a) Did individuals react differently to the same initial stimuli?
   b) Did the "test" atmosphere (mental arithmetic) affect answers and/or confidence about them?
   c) Why did individuals stay in groups?
   d) Why did individuals change groups—convincing arguments, size of other group, someone who is known to be good at arithmetic/ accountancy, lacking confidence in one's own mathematical ability, other?
   e) How did the group representatives emerge?
   f) Were the group representatives amongst the earliest or latest to change groups (if they changed at all)?
   g) Was it found that the longer the experience continued the more difficult it became to convince others to change groups—because of factors such as group solidarity or pressure, self-justification for a decision already made, a feeling of competitiveness, public defence (for spokespersons) of a position, other reasons?

Variations

1. Allow pen and paper to help work out the answer.

2. Step 4 can be shortened with the group simply given the task of gaining consensus on the answer.

SECTION 3:

THE PROBLEM-BASED LEARNING PACKAGE

CHAPTER 4

WORKSHOP PROBLEM/SITUATION OUTLINE

FORWARD

This problem-based learning project reflects the values embodied in the following quotations:

> Leadership. Everyone talks about it, everyone wants it. But who are the people who will lead us into the new millennium? ("Leadership," 1998)

> You drive your car. It is a machine that you control, with the aim of getting where you want to go. The car takes you there. You do not 'drive' a plant to grow. Nor do you 'drive' your teenager. Nor, we would argue, do leaders 'drive' their organization. The organization is a human community. It is a living system, like the plant or the teenager. There is no one driving it. But there are many tending the garden. (Senge et al., 1999, p. 21)

> A manager's position is analogous to that of a gardener: the gardener cannot make the plants grow; he or she can only create the optimum conditions under which the plants' natural self-organizing tendencies can function. The gardener has to *allow* them to grow. (Hurst, 1995, pp. 136-137)

> As for the best leaders, people do not notice their existence,
> The next best, the people honour and praise.
> The next, the people fear.
> The next, the people hate.
> When the best leader's work is done, the people say, "We did it ourselves."
> (Lao-tzu, trans. 1986)

This problem-based learning package consists of five chapters. This chapter (Chapter 4) outlines the situation or problem, its product/performance specifications, learning objectives and resources, as well as providing some guiding questions. The following chapters (Chapters 5 and 6) each contain a case study (Appendix 3 an 4 contain shorter versions of the case studies) and, for easy reference, a summary of that case. Chapter 7 details the results of the student and teacher surveys from the two case study schools as well as the State averages for comparison purposes. Some other evidence from the two schools is also summarized. Finally, two supplementary readings about leadership and organizational learning can be found in Appendix 1 and Appendix 2.

SITUATION/PROBLEM

The principals of Altona and Heronwood High Schools (see Chapters 5 and 6) have both been promoted out of their schools. You are the new principal of one of those schools.

Both schools have a reputation as school restructuring success stories. Staff and the Superintendent are worried about the principal departures but see the need to keep the good work going. A number of teachers have stated that without their previous principal, the school "would never be the same." Although the superintendent is aware of those teacher sentiments, and has mentioned that the staff might have difficulty adjusting to you, the new principal, she had been crystal clear that her number one concern is the continued demonstrable improvement of the schools.

With the advent and subsequent involvement of the state Principals' Institute in principal selection and ongoing principal accreditation, you are aware that the principalship is much more rigorous than in the past. Early in their tenure, principals are expected to develop, present and defend a succinct school development plan based on their understanding of the school and its potential.

The Superintendent and her school review committee are scheduled to visit your school 2 weeks from today. As other principals have told you that these visits are "very serious business," **you and your planning team have decided to start immediately on your plan and its presentation**. You have also decided to use the data and results generated from the recent Leadership for Organisational Learning and Student Outcomes (LOLSO) project (see Chapter 1 of this book), of which Altona and Heronwood were a part, and the additional reading in Appendix 2 to help in your understanding of the school's past success and the opportunities for the future under your leadership.

PRODUCT/PERFORMANCE SPECIFICATIONS

1. **Prepare a 3-year action plan** (maximum of five pages) that reflects you and your planning team's solution to the situation/problems at Altona or Heronwood High School. Remember, you will be sharing this plan with the Superintendent and her school review committee. As well, remember that the Superintendent has been crystal clear that her number one concern is the continued demonstrable improvement of the schools. Your plan should be a group product and include the following sections:

   1.1   Definition of the situation/problem as you view it at Altona/Heronwood and the data that led you to your conclusions; if you identify more than one problem, please prioritize those that you chose to address.

1.2   A plan addressing the important components of the situation/problem; the plan should include sample activities, the sequence in which you intend to proceed with them, and your rationale for the selection and sequence. You may wish to consider your strategy for gaining the support of key actors and for overcoming potential obstacles you will face implementing your plan.

2. **Prepare a 15-min presentation** to the Superintendent's school review committee in which you describe your plan and discuss the solution to the situation/problem(s) at Altona/Heronwood. One member of the planning team will be chosen by the group to be the person to give the presentation. The planning team, however, will be responsible for assisting in the defence of its proposals.

LEARNING OBJECTIVES

The first stage of the LOLSO Project described in Chapter 1 required these phases of data collection conducted over 3 years. In Phase 1, in 1997, surveys of Year 10 students, their teachers and principal were conducted in 96 secondary schools from two Australian States, namely, South Australia and Tasmania. In the second phase of the study (1998 and 1999), cross-sectional case study data were collected from schools selected from the sample to triangulate and enrich the information generated by the survey data. In the third phase in 1999, a second survey of students, teachers and principals was conducted in one of the states following the original Year 10 cohort of students to Year 12. In this way, the project allowed for iterative cycles of theory development and testing, using multiple forms of evidence.

By using data gathered for the LOLSO project and participating in this exercise you will:

1. acquire knowledge and insight into how to:

    1.1   **identify conditions** inside and outside schools that account for variation in OL;

    1.2   **describe** those **leadership practices** that make the most significant contributions to OL in schools;

    1.3   **determine the extent** to which **OL accounts for** variation in students' participation in and identification with school (both good predictors of student achievement as well as retention); and,

    1.4   **determine the extent** to which **leadership accounts for** variation in students' participation in and identification with school.

2. develop skills in:

    2.1   **applying** your **knowledge** and **insight** on leadership for organizational learning and student outcomes to further develop a school;

    2.2   **coping** with **vast amounts** of information in a **short time frame**;

    2.3   **working collaboratively** as a member of a team; and,

2.4   **presenting** your **knowledge** and **insight**, and its application, to others in a succinct and convincing manner.

3. come to appreciate the **value** in leadership of:

3.1   **allowing others to grow**.

RESOURCES

For this project you will have the following resources (see summary overhead projector master – Figure 9):

1. **Case studies** and case study summaries of two high schools

   - Altona
   - Heronwood

2. **Survey data** from two high schools

   - Altona
   - Heronwood

3. **Reading material**

   - Chapter 1 of this book.
   - Two readings focusing on leadership and organizational learning (Appendix 1 and Appendix 2).

   Other readings found in the library and/or on the World Wide Web (the Web). The reference section at the end of this book provides a good starting point for those wishing to explore further.

4. **Group members**

   As often is the case, members will have read about the topic or will have had first hand experience with it. Hence, we encourage you to exploit whatever resources exist within your group.

   Others will have links to resources that lie outside of the group whether these be readings, survey data, case studies, and/or others who have knowledge or experience of similar situations. Again, we encourage you to use such resources within the time constraints of the project.

5. **Instructors**

   Instructors will be available during the sessions to answer questions.

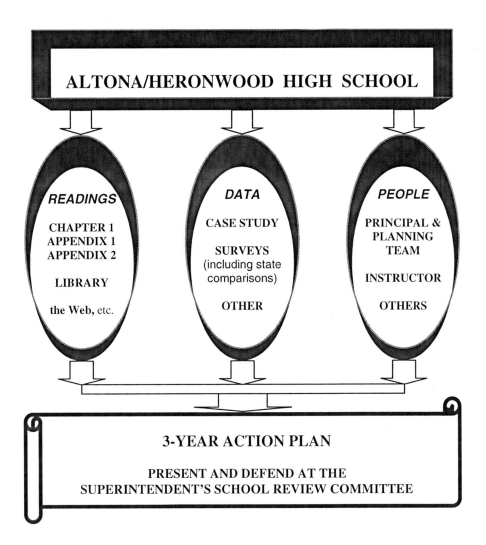

Figure 9. Resources for developing the 3-year action plan.

GUIDING QUESTIONS

The exercise seeks to address the following kinds of questions:

- How is the concept of organizational learning defined in schools?
- What conditions inside and outside high schools account for variations in organizational learning? That is, why are some schools seen as learning organizations and others are not?
- What proportion of organizational learning is accounted for by school leadership?
- What kinds of leadership practices promote organizational learning in schools?
- Does the level of organizational learning in secondary schools contribute to student outcomes? (In this project, these outcomes are both academic—university entrance scores—and non-academic—retention until Year 12 as well as student self-concept and the extent of students' participation in and engagement with school.)
- Does the leadership in schools contribute to student outcomes?

CHAPTER 5

THE ALTONA CASE STUDY

SETTING THE SCENE

Altona High School is a Grade 7 to 10 (ages 13 to 16) government school in a state which has a three-tier schooling system, primary (Kindergarten to Grade 6), high (Grades 7 to 10), and college (Grades 11 and 12). The school drew its name from the suburb in which it is based. Like most parts of the State, the suburb is not divided by a railway track—yet many regard Altona as being "on the wrong side of the tracks." Typically, the statistics for Altona show extremes: the suburb scores the highest and lowest on numerous social indicators. The area records amongst the highest on elements of social disadvantage and near to, or the lowest, on social indicators which point to privilege.

Whereas just over a decade ago, there were equal numbers of men and women living in Altona, now there are only 83 males for every 100 females. Limited job opportunities in the suburb mean that many teenage and adult males leave Altona in order to find work. Premature deaths, gaol terms, and partner separations also account for the low number of men living in the town. Four in every 10 Altona households have no men in them, compared to a nearby affluent suburb where only two households in 10 have no men in them.

In one sense, Altona is a young person's place. More than 35% of its population is less than 15 years old, and fewer than 7% of its citizens are older than 64 years. The median age of Altona citizens is 24 years. Most residents of Altona completed up to 4 years at high school. However, as a place, Altona has the lowest proportion of people with post school educational qualifications. No resident has a higher degree; 31 hold a Postgraduate Diploma; 212 hold a Bachelor Degree; 91 have an Associate Diploma, and 333 possess a skilled vocational qualification. In effect, only one in five Altona citizens aged 15 years and over has a qualification. Two and sometimes three in five residents in affluent nearby suburbs have qualifications. Given the shifts in industry and labour market patterns, it is thus not surprising that Altona residents have been particularly affected by unemployment.

More than 30% of those who are eligible to work are unemployed, which is about three times the unemployment rate experienced by residents in more affluent nearby suburbs. In addition, only 16% of Altona residents work in a government sector, as compared to 21% of residents in many surrounding suburbs. Of the 320 Altona residents who are employed, most work as either Labourers and Related Workers (67); Intermediate Production and Transport Workers (51); Elementary Clerical, Sales and Service Workers (32).

Whereas the median individual income of residents in nearby suburbs is $13,451, an Altona resident's median income is $9,547. Similarly, whereas in a typical nearby suburb the lowest median family income is $32,260, in Altona it is $20,320.

The cost of owning or renting accommodation in Altona is less than in most parts of the State. The median monthly housing repayment in Altona is $476, which is about $110 cheaper than loan repayments in nearby suburbs. Similarly, rental properties cost around $248 monthly compared to $416 in towns close to Altona. Despite the relatively cheaper nature of housing stock in Altona, less than one third of occupied private dwellings are owned or being purchased. Typically, affluent nearby suburbs have a home purchase or ownership rate of 67%.

In most places within the state, the population is largely made up of people who were born in the country. People born in the country comprise 95% of Altona's population, which is 6% more than that typically found in nearby towns. One hundred and twenty two native people are residents of Altona.

Altona has one of the highest proportions of Anglicans amongst its citizenry, with 41% identifying as Anglican. At the same time, Altona has one of the highest proportions of people who follow no religion. Around one in five residents follows no religion.

Although there are 1649 Altona residents, Altona High's student population is drawn from the suburb in which it is based as well as suburbs immediately adjacent to Altona. These "feeder" suburbs have a similar social profile to Altona's.

THE LEADERSHIP TEAM: CREATING INTERGENERATIONAL LINKS

In his eighth year as principal at the school, Davidson is synonymous with Altona High. It is an association that Davidson is proud of because of "the importance of what we are doing here." Schools, according to Davidson, do enormous good for students, their parents, and society. But schools often adopt a narrow focus, as he did in his first few years at Altona. "I probably had a fairly narrow focus and it was to do with kids coming into a school and kids going out of a school and what we did to them while they were here." These days, schools need to be more adventurous in what they do and more conscious of the links they can create for students between business, training, and further education. Not to do so is to sell kids short. In Davidson's opinion, "the pressures on these students are absolutely mind-blowing."

Job opportunities which were freely available less than 20 years ago are now non existent or have, as they then were, to be accessed through personal contacts and networks. The contacts and networks which many families used to draw on when a son or a daughter wanted an apprenticeship are now not easily found amongst Altona families. "We have had to step in and replace a lot of that." Davidson is acutely aware of the harsh labour market that awaits many of the young, especially those from less materially-privileged areas. His descriptions of the personal and social dislocation which can come from being unemployed are supported by a wealth of statistics and "seeing so much of it."

In the suburb of Altona, there are grandparents and parents of students who have been unemployed throughout the last decade. Davidson is keenly aware of the implications that can flow to students in such situations. He is also aware of the enormous effort required to arrest some of the problems which flow from, and often attach to, unemployed families. In Davidson's view, the proportion of the problem provides no grounds for schools to ignore or temper their responses to the situation.

When Davidson talks about the challenges facing Altona, his voice takes on a surer tone. The plain words which Altona's articulate principal employs in conversation, symbolize the preference Davidson has for straight-talking and straight-dealing. He has little patience for politicians who criticize teachers and schools. "They would not have a bloody clue. Any politician who has ever had the gall to make critical comments about what teachers do, doesn't deserve to remain paid by taxpayers . . . teachers ought to be admired, thanked, and appreciated for what they do." Before politicians resort to criticizing teachers, Davidson claims they should be "self-critical and ask why the society that kids are growing up in has all the problems it has . . . it is my generation that has created this world that young people are going into." Many of the glaring social problems which confront or await students have led Davidson to "a passionate belief now that we have got to do a bit better and turn that around."

Davidson's impatience with politicians who deflect criticism about society and young Australians on to schools is matched by his contempt for a minority of teachers who are not committed to teaching. According to Davidson, Altona has only a couple of poorly motivated teachers amongst a full-time staff of thirty. The limited number of teachers who appear unenthusiastic about their work provides little salve for Davidson. Poorly motivated teachers are an impediment to Altona "because we want a good deal for our kids."

In a similar vein, any centrally-located departmental bureaucrats who are unhelpful to the school's efforts are deemed as having little to offer. By contrast, edicts and personnel from central or district office who evidence a willingness to talk with, rather than only talk at schools are appreciated. "In my district office, particular people have been very supportive over time—they have developed an understanding of what a school like Altona is trying to do."

"When Ian Davidson gets one of his ideas, he becomes driven," said June Syme, the Grade 9 coordinator of Altona High School. "He can get an idea at four in the morning and, by the time he gets to school, that's all he wants to talk about. He isn't easily put off." When Davidson corners Syme, in the middle of an English lesson, she is in no doubt as to who is boss. "I get along well with Ian and, in terms of ideas, I don't think there would be a better principal in the State. But in terms of organisation, it's fortunate that there are other people around at times. And in terms of the implementation of his ideas . . . I'm not sure that it has always been by a process of consultation or democracy."

Despite Syme's concern with her principal's often single-minded efforts to improve Altona High, she considers the school benefits from being led by Davidson. "While he expects a lot from the staff and is very focussed on advancing the interests of students, Ian can also see the humorous as well as heart-rendering aspects of school life. For staff, that sort of leadership is important because, sometimes here, if you didn't laugh or crack a joke, you'd cry. Here, kids come from low socioeconomic backgrounds. They have massive problems in their home lives. A lot of it affects their learning abilities and their prospects. I think my expectations of what I could deliver have been lowered on the basis of my contact with these students. So the challenge is tremendous. There is only so much you can do. There is no point hitting your head against a brick wall. It is a matter of setting realisable, achievable goals. But you also have to maintain some perspective, keep some humour about life—and Ian does that as well."

Increasing years at Altona have provided Davidson with greater understandings about teachers' work and the principal's role. In the early years of his principalship at Altona, Davidson was authoritarian, a style which, when employed, frequently failed with both teachers and students. These days, Davidson's greater knowledge of teachers' qualities and motives translates into support and encouragement for those teachers who are keen to offer interesting and unique learning experiences to students. Despite his heightened understanding of teachers, Davidson believes the teaching profession is not sufficiently understood. "We are never aware enough about the capacities of teachers and their desire to really be creators and to, as far as possible, be independent," he said. Because most of the teachers at Altona are highly motivated employees and the school places high priority on meeting and anticipating students' social and educational needs, Davidson says he enjoys his work. The long hours that he devotes to the job, both inside and out of school, are, in part, able to be sustained because of what he believes has been and continues to be achieved. For Davidson, his contribution at Altona forms part of a long-term mission that is underpinned by beliefs about humanity, community, and social justice.

A deeply religious man, Davidson's sense of satisfaction with his colleagues and the school is apparent in conversations about the extent and sources of achievement at Altona, "this is a school that really cares about its kids. That is reflected very much in general talk amongst staff and the way they approach things. I think we are on a good direction which is the result of a number of things. It is very much to do with the people I work with." Davidson rarely talks of development having been the result of only his efforts. Davidson's pride with the school's progress and his contributions leave him convinced that Altona can create further successes for their students. Yet, despite his unswerving loyalty and commitment to Altona students, he cautiously accepts that the school will not be able to adequately assist many students. Literacy problems, for example, are severe amongst many students. "We do magnificent work in improving their language skills. Huge commitment to it. The problem is solvable, but not by the education sector. The problem is solvable by a turn-around in community attitude. The community has got to take responsibility for it."

Davidson's interactions with students' parents and home visits he has undertaken during his 20 years in the education system have convinced him that society needs to reclaim ownership of key educational and socialisation issues. "The community has got to say 'we own everything in this town including the levels of disadvantage and we have to look at strategies for dealing with these things'. If you had that sort of context where the community had genuine ownership, it would not be too hard to get up programs where there were interventions in the homes . . . volunteers and professionals all combining resources and really dealing with that problem." Altona's principal believes that affluent, as well as struggling Australians must play a part in owning and attending to educational and social problems.

In an era when politicians are increasingly focussing on student outcomes and league ladders of schools' literacy and numeracy achievements, Davidson bristles at the notion of all schools being compared to one another in this way. Such comparisons underplay the nature of many students' lives. "You have a proportion of students who are so far behind the eightball when they begin school—there has never been a book in their house, parents have not been able to read to their kids. There is not a culture which values that sort of thing. With all the intervention programs under the sun, the research has shown that those students never, never get up onto a level playing field."

Narrow State wide comparisons also omit a wealth of achievements that schools like Altona make to students, their parents, and the community. "In a lot of cases, schools are providing a lot of nurturing and fixing up." Davidson is convinced that many schools are unable to focus on purely educational matters because of the depth and breadth of "baggage" which surrounds some students' lives. The complexity of many students' out-of-school experiences is frequently reflected in their practices at school. Although Altona High has made enormous strides in assisting many students to achieve success at school, Davidson realizes there will be an enduring need to provide additional support for troubled students.

By and large, the extent of what Altona currently achieves with students is limited by time and money. Most teachers are fully occupied with their classroom and additional responsibilities. The priority which Davidson and his staff place on meeting each student's "individual needs" often leaves teachers with insufficient time for adequately attending to everything the school would like to do. Moreover, like many within the profession, Altona teachers are better at embracing new elements of programs than they are at then correspondingly removing a program component. One up-shot of such attempts to improve what is offered to students is that teachers rarely feel they have adequate time in which to do work to their satisfaction.

For Davidson, the volume-of-work challenges often are met by putting in further hours. He frequently addresses fraternal organisations in a bid to promote the achievements and profile of the school and liaises with the local business community. He is constantly hunting for extra monies for Altona in order for some additional school-based initiatives to be funded. Although in no doubt about the importance of searching for extra resources and community liaising, Davidson is conscious that it often reduces his instructional leadership. "I have some insecurities and some concerns that I do put a lot of energy into global issues which sort of distance me from that aspect of the work." In the absence of being able to provide detailed instructional leadership to staff, Davidson relies on Sally Green, whose office is based next door.

Davidson's deputy and stand-in is, he says, "this principal next door, Sally Green, an outstanding teacher and outstanding lead teacher." Green's way of working allows Davidson to "have every confidence that my staff is being provided with good instructional leadership." The close proximity of offices assists Davidson and Green's efforts to complement their leadership work. Green, who is fit, 15 years younger than the 55-year-old principal, and always immaculately dressed, has a productive working association with Davidson. Although staunchly loyal to her principal, she does not refrain from telling Davidson—or anyone else at Altona— how she feels if something important at the school is dysfunctional or unsuitable for implementation. On occasion, Green's frankness has extended to dismissing some of Davidson's "unrealistic" ideas as "unworkable" in one-to-one or senior staff meetings. Yet, this no-nonsense leader also acknowledges those initiatives of Davidson and others which have, against considerable odds and her good sense, sometimes succeeded.

In the main, Green believes her principal's ideas over the past 4 years have been sound and ultimately resulted in favourable improvements for the school. Regardless of personal doubts about the aptness of specific strategies which are ultimately adopted at the school, Green is in no doubt that her role is to support her principal and staff on agreed policy and program matters. One of the myriad ways in which she does this is "by providing a link between what happens in the trenches." Like many school administrators, Green has a regular teaching load. "I don't ask a teacher to do what I'm not doing. So, if I say to teachers that students' reports are due in on a certain date, I need to have mine in then too. They need to see I am doing that."

Opinion across the staff at Altona echoed Davidson's view that Green was highly competent as a teacher and assistant principal. Moreover, teachers claimed that troublesome students or other problems that they presented to Green were dealt with thoroughly and effectively. In the relatively short time that Green has been the assistant principal at Altona, staff have come to appreciate her leadership. In marked contrast to her predecessor, Green is uniformly regarded by teachers and Davidson as being committed to the school and what it is attempting to achieve in the interests of Altona students. Sandra Miere, who was in her ninth year at the school, reflected a widespread staff view when she claimed "our previous assistant principal couldn't relate to these kids and had agendas that were not directly connected to the kids. Sally Green cares about the students and teachers and isn't self-serving. She puts in 100%—you know where you are with her."

Another way in which Green supports the Altona staff and principal is via her time use. "Once my day begins here, I give 100% absolutely, until the end of the day. I like to work in this type of school setting." While Green's energy is highly productive, she knows that time is the enemy of much else that could—and should— be done at Altona. By and large, the hardworking staff and principal are, Green claims, limited by the constraints of time. One casualty of time is discussion with staff as well as with Davidson. "We don't have a lot of discussions, and when we do it is usually on the run. Because there is not a lot of time to do that." Detailed discussions between Davidson and Green are usually reserved for their once-a-fortnight meetings, at which any lengthy school matters can be detailed. Despite the strategic shortcomings which inevitably arise due to the perils of time, the complementarity of Altona's two administrators is highly productive. It is a working synergy underpinned by a belief in one another's competencies and intentions. In this sense, it is not surprising that each has invested considerable trust in the other, and both believe the trust has been warranted.

Time challenges in schools invariably privilege the immediate and the practical. At Altona, classroom imperatives, individual student crises, and, to a lesser extent, timetable and bureaucratic routines continue to demand much of administrators' and teachers' time. Documentation of the school's education policy and, in particular, the curriculum policy have not kept pace with the changes that have occurred at Altona over the last 4 years.

Green accepts the need for the school to review and update its curriculum. She is sceptical, and unconcerned about the absence of working documents which outline the school's mission. "You could have it written down with a magnificent chart, which I've seen at other schools, but it means little. I think Altona's staff and principal know where they are going, know the things that are important. But if you were to ask them to give you a mission statement, there would only be a vague notion."

Despite her sceptical view of policy documents which do not cohere with a school's practices, Green acknowledges the potential value of the state Department of Education's Assisted School Self-Review process. "It will give us a chance to write down our goals and it will be concrete. That will be a good thing because they have been floating around in the air for far too long. So if it can do that, that will be good."

Like Davidson, Green is intolerant of any individual's or group's actions which interfere with the school's efforts to assist students in ways that are legitimate educationally, and in keeping with how things are usually done at Altona. Teachers who choose not to fulfil their professional obligations to students are not regarded favourably. Indeed, she describes such teachers as "slack." A failure by teachers to properly apply themselves is, Green asserts, "unacceptable." No school deserves teachers who do not commit strongly to students. But in Altona's case, Green believes that students cannot afford such a situation. The out-of-school personal and social circumstances of many students, plus their slowly emerging learning culture require enormous and persistent support from teachers. In Green's view, those teachers who fail to offer such support either should change their ways or find another occupation.

Like Davidson and almost all her colleagues, Green does not live in Altona. Irrespective of where one lives and which students one works with, Green considers that teachers "must do the right thing by students, their colleagues, and the system." Her disdain for uncommitted teachers lies in marked contrast to her empathy and support for those teachers who, whilst at Altona, have experienced difficulties with student behaviour. "There is no blame because a teacher can't handle little Johnny. It isn't a case of the teacher being hopeless." Instead, Green claims, most colleagues and the administration provide those teachers with coping and teaching strategies as well as, when necessary, helping to deal with a difficult student or grade. "In this school, you help each other. Here, if a student has been sent to the office because of poor classroom behaviour, my response to the student is to say 'right, you get in here, sit down and do some work.' Here, you work as a team. People pull together."

Green's clear and simple instructions to students who misbehave echo her colleagues' way of communicating both in classes and with one another. "At this school it is a case of calling a spade a spade. It is probably a legacy of the environment," she said. Underpinning the direct–talk is, Green suggests, a message to students and teachers of "for God's sake get in and have a go." Green is grateful that, by and large, the Altona staff is a highly committed team. "It is a combination of people who happen to work extremely effectively individually, and in groups. There is a sense that you're all in this together," she said.

Being the assistant principal in such situations is of little relevance to students generally and, in particular, to those who misbehave. "You might be the deputy, but it does not mean students treat you any differently from other teachers. From the time I first came here and many times since I've said to colleagues 'it does not matter what tag you're wearing, the kids are going to give you the same treatment. They see you as a teacher, they don't see the tag you carry'," said Green. Altona High is one vital institutional means by which students can be assisted so as to enhance their life chances. According to Green, "it is crucial for some students who are up against the odds." Hence, for that reason alone, Altona teachers have to experience success in what they do.

CONTINUING WITH THE STATUS QUO NO LONGER AN OPTION: A RATTLING OF CAGES

In an important way, most Altona teachers feel they are fortunate to have two administrators who are genuinely committed to advancing the interests of students, work well together, and, at the same time, are strongly supportive of staff. Many teachers have experienced life under less cohesive and less trusted leaders, particularly in other schools. Yet, the synergistic relationship between staff and administration has only been achieved during the last 4 years.

In 1993, Ian Davidson vacated the Altona principalship for a year in order to take up an interstate fellowship, as part of a professional development initiative. It was an appointment that Davidson enjoyed and learned much from, especially because the fellowship allowed him to mix with a range of educational leaders who were committed to improving schools and, in the process, themselves. The year was also made memorable because of what Davidson found, once he returned to his principalship at Altona.

Davidson returned to a school in which students' cultures prevailed. For teachers, that meant chaos reigned, for much of their working week. Classes and the school grounds had become battlegrounds for a significant number of students. Teachers, many of whom were long-serving and highly experienced in dealing with a range of student needs, frequently found themselves unable to teach effectively. To many students, educators had become another problem, in much the same way that some of their parents, and other adults in their lives had. In addition, the principal of Altona had left the school which, despite his return, was not dissimilar—in the eyes of students—to what many parents in Altona households did. Students were used to seeing or experiencing directly, adults leaving or moving away from them. Although few could articulate their depth of feelings about such departures, they could, with greater ease, display their reactions. To many students, being left by adults represented a type of rejection. The failure to have explained, or understand the reasons for adults leaving, whether parents or school personnel, left students to make their own meanings of such events. When rejection was felt, students' efforts to make sense of the situation were neither comprehensive nor generous. Instead, feelings of rejection and misunderstanding became the developing grounds for alienation and anger.

Overlying widespread feelings of disenchantment by students was their inability or unwillingness to find classes meaningful. Few of the students had an intimate knowledge of the national, state or local labour market. Yet most of them lived in, or knew of, households where someone was unemployed. As well, many students saw acquaintances or ex-Altona students who were unemployed around town. They knew enough about unemployment to be bewildered by or concerned about their own futures. Rather than school being a means of achieving employment, school had become a place where students had little choice but to attend. In the face of what seemed to many students to be meaningless and pointless learning and frustrated associations with most adults, school nonetheless could be both a place of action and one from which to escape.

Absenteeism was unusually high in 1994, but it was ultimately an individual action which often involved small numbers of "wagging" students meeting together elsewhere during school hours. From their perspective, creating havoc within school was, ultimately, a much more powerful way for students to use their time and energies. Although many students were not, of themselves, unruly at school, few were able to avoid being embroiled in class and schoolground disruptions. Invariably, teachers also were drawn into daily school-based manifestations of a disenfranchised student population. Margaret Evans, who in 1994 was in her eighteenth year of teaching, recalled being in a staff meeting after school had finished one day and being interrupted by the sound of breaking glass. As it turned out, she said, "there was a student who was going around the school and just breaking windows down, smash, smash, smash. An ex-student, who had had a bad time at school was with him, and she also was smashing windows."

Peta Reece, who at that stage was in her sixth year at Altona, recalled that "we were in chaos. It was a crisis and the school was walking away bit by bit. It was being trashed. Student behaviour was totally unacceptable . . . spitting, swearing, slagging off at people and there was a general lack of respect plus a lot of graffiti around." Inside classrooms, "there was no teaching, just survival. Entertaining and survival. No teaching. No teaching subject matter. Really, it was a case of how to get students into a room without them murdering or maiming each other."

Edith Grange, who had taught at Altona during the early 1980s for 6 years prior to being promoted to another school, returned in 1994. Grange claimed "the student population had changed so much. What we were able to teach them then was completely different. By 1994, the kids were a lot harder and more street-wise. They knew their rights more and tested out new teachers in particular." In Edith's case, she was ultimately not seen by students as just another new teacher. "What put me in good stead was the fact that I had been at the school before, and I had taught older brothers or sisters. In some cases, I had actually taught their parents. As soon as the kids knew that, instead of being, if you like, right down the bottom of the ladder, I was sort of put a few rungs up."

The often hostile learning culture of students contributed to a growing sense of frustration and tiredness amongst Altona teachers. Many of them had been teaching at the school for more than a decade during which time, according to Terry Faine, they had witnessed first-hand, a continuing deterioration of the students' learning culture. "When I started here 10 years ago, students had a different attitude to staff and the school. In those days they were far more open as students, far more willing to admit their sins, and accept the punishment. The kids were very honest. Over that time there has also been a deterioration of the work ethic amongst many students," said the Grade 10 coordinator.

Added to that, various structures which at one stage had worked effectively and complemented teachers' work, no longer suited the school's circumstances. In particular, the four part sub-school system which had been most viable in those years when there were as many as 800 students, had become dysfunctional. The absence of a "critical mass" of students in each sub-school plus their failure to operate as a symbolic, rallying-identity for students left Altona with an outdated structural system. Yet, for many longstanding teachers in 1994, sub-schools were synonymous with Altona and had been recognized nationally. The prospect of their formal demise was unacceptable.

Sub-schools were, at least, familiar to and understood by teachers. The student learning culture, like the sub-schools which were designed to augment it, was certain—if unproductive. In this way, the possibility of disbanding sub-schools represented to many teachers, a potential heightening of an unsatisfactory school environment. Moreover, the architecture of the school had been designed around the concept of sub-schools. Phillip Reid, who joined the staff at Altona in 1986, said "when I first came to the school, the sub-schools were very autonomous. I was in Cosgrove House, and only taught Cosgrove students. Whereas Cosgrove had their own timetable and taught 7 periods a day, when other sub-schools only taught 6, Cosgrove teachers did exactly what they felt their students needed." The artificial boundaries between sub-schools which had originally been introduced to foster a sense of identity and belonging had, by 1994, been translated into a siege mentality by some students, according to Reid. "I saw Cosgrove kids sitting outside a classroom saying 'we're not going in there, there are Lawlor House students in there,' even though they desperately wanted to do, say, typing which Cosgrove did not offer. They wouldn't mix with students from other houses."

In a similar vein, teachers on yard duty often experienced difficulty in being accepted by students. "If you gave a direction to students, which was consistent with school rules, but did not teach those students, they would just abuse you. Because they didn't know you. And so the response would be 'you can't tell us what to do', plus a few words in-between!," recalled Mary Lempriere. Whilst students worked in classrooms that belonged only to their sub-school, there were no such boundaries in the school grounds.

In addition to being able to move freely in the school grounds during lunch and recess periods, a culture of aggression amongst students had developed to a point where bullying and physical violence had become daily events during break times. At its zenith, two students who had been suspended, returned to the school to fight each other during a lunch break. "The police were called. Big packs of students followed those boys around the school, pushing the boys together, egging trouble on. Then two police came and they too were followed by students and we ended up in an area where the boys were arrested, with all the students standing around in a circle just watching. Pretty scary stuff. 'Just kneel on this lad's back while I help the other officer with the hand-cuffing' one said to me. It was awful to go on duty," said Lempriere who had been on duty that day. Yard duty had become so difficult for teachers that "staff would pair on duty. They didn't feel safe on duty. Staff hated being at Altona," said Margaret Evans.

Although Altona still had some students who actively wanted to learn and who avoided being drawn into disputes in the school grounds, teaching at the school usually meant confronting an overwhelmingly negative work environment. Teachers were used to handling difficult or troubled students. However, they had not previously experienced such an extent or intensity of student alienation and resistance.

In the first few months following his return to the school, Ian Davidson's response to what he found was to adopt a domineering style, particularly in relation to students who misbehaved. It was an approach that he thought was, ultimately, of limited value. Used more sparingly in the past, the approach had worked. Yet, for many students, it was a style of interaction that differed little from what they experienced in their homes, to which they had become immune. Davidson believed that he needed to better understand the difficulties being experienced by teachers and reconsider not only his own role, but that of the school's. "It was a really demeaning, challenging job, I was trouble-shooting, problem solving, and trying to keep myself together, let alone the school together."

Teachers' disenchantment with the school plus what they then saw as unhelpful leadership responses, characterized many of Altona's collegial conversations during break times. As a result, Joanne Little, who was highly respected by teachers and had been at the school for nearly 7 years, finally spoke with Davidson about changing the restrictive nature of his leadership style and the importance of remaining open and positive to finding solutions. The conversation involved a degree of risk for both Davidson and Little—there was a chance for offence to be taken and a possibility of their professional association suffering. Little was confident that her messages were sound and believed Davidson could ultimately provide the school with outstanding leadership. Davidson trusted Little's motives for approaching him as well as her leadership and teaching capacities. Almost immediately, Davidson attempted to temper his style by becoming more collaborative and encouraging of teachers, especially those who were canvassing new ways of improving the school. "He did change the way he operated, for which he must be given credit," noted Michael Morrow, a Grade 9 Science teacher.

Despair and experiences which, in hindsight, appear to be the opposite to what should have occurred, are sometimes a catalyst to making radical changes in life. At Altona in 1994, some teachers believed school life could not get worse. Others feared that, without major change, it might deteriorate further. Still others were more concerned about their survival strategies being eclipsed by personal exhaustion, especially if they were to take part in significant organizational change.

As an outcome of the professional development undertaken a year earlier by Altona's principal, Ian Davidson learned about "middle schools" which had been successfully introduced into several Australian secondary schools. Following discussions with staff, in mid 1994, Davidson suggested that a few teachers, including Wayne Falls and Joanne Little, should visit various schools within the State which had middle schools in operation. Falls, like Little, was widely respected as a teacher by colleagues and regarded by many as having a high profile amongst staff. In response to their investigations, Little, Falls and others reported their findings to colleagues, one afternoon at a staff meeting.

Falls and Little spoke strongly in favour of implementing a middle school system into Altona's organizational structure. At a subsequent staff meeting, further discussions took place to determine whether a middle school system would be adopted. Numerous queries and concerns were raised regarding the implications which would flow from a change to a middle school—resources, funding, and equipment to existing sectors of the school would inevitably be altered. The implications of the inflexible design of the school into sub-school buildings also worried several teachers who were unsure the change would be worthwhile. Three quarters of the staff voted in favour of making the structural change. Most teachers hoped the end result of the change would be to achieve a dramatic cultural change amongst students.

At the end of 1994, 17 out of a total of 30 teachers transferred to other schools. "Several of those who left thought that if they moved to a different school, the job would be easier. Some found it wasn't," claimed Edith Grange who occasionally met ex-Altona colleagues "around town." Included amongst those who left the school that year were many teachers who did not want to be part of the middle school initiative, which was to be implemented at the start of the 1995 school year.

CHANGES EVERYWHERE: TRUST, PERSISTENCE, AND RISK-TAKING

Just as principals, central education authorities, and parents are dependent upon teachers to work productively with students, so too are teachers dependent upon students to willingly attempt to learn. In this sense, schooling is a risky enterprise. The decision of Altona's administration and teachers to respond to students' negativity towards schooling by setting major organizational changes in place, including dismantling the highly reputed sub-school system, represented further risk-taking. At the start of the 1995 school year, Altona's middle school was formally put in place.

One key purpose of the new structure was to provide students with a reduced range of teachers, for 22 of their 30 class periods, so as to build more productive teacher-student relationships. Historically, "teaching out of area" has been an unattractive proposition for specialist-trained, secondary teachers. At Altona, few middle school teachers relished the opportunity to break with such a tradition. Indeed, most teachers feared the prospect. Yet they also recognized the need to restore productive working relations with students and to build a positive learning culture. In turn this meant that they had to embrace teaching unfamiliar subjects, and ultimately becoming more multiskilled.

Because of the difficulties wrought by students' behaviours during 1994, relatively little time was found to prepare middle school teachers for the following year's work. Hence, for most teachers, much of what they could develop in advance for those classes was done during the summer holidays. "Initially, it meant teaching on-the-run," said Joanne Little. The lack of teacher knowledge in new subject areas and inadequate curriculum preparation plus continued negative learning culture across the school resulted in rowdy Year 8 classes, especially during the early part of the year. Although Year 7 classes consisted of students who were new to the school, many Term 1 periods were characterized by student rebellion and resistance to learning. "In one class, it was total bedlam," said Margaret Evans, who had observed the class on and off over the first term. "But the teacher of that class didn't mention to others that it was bedlam," she added.

The difficulties which teachers encountered in the middle school were, however, accepted by most Grade 7 and 8 teachers as an interim legacy of the changed structure. Importantly, according to Joanne Little, the middle school coordinator, the new structure "shifted the behaviour management focus to the class teacher." Hence there was a greater chance for interaction and on-going engagement between a teacher and a student who misbehaved. As well, such interactions allowed other class members to observe, and hear their teacher's expectations of how students should behave. Moreover, the middle school system enabled those teachers to adopt a long-term approach to building a positive learning culture amongst students.

The inability of middle school staff to be well prepared in advance for their classes in the early implementation phase of the structure was, to some extent, offset by several strategies. "Middle school teachers had high energy levels and great commitment to the initiative," said John Westbrook, who was a member of the team. "So we put in extra time and effort as well as having two timetabled sessions where we could all meet to share ideas and plan," recalled Westbrook. According to Westbrook, the preparedness of middle school teachers to give additional time to the job was made easier because of the ongoing support and encouragement they received from Joanne Little. Westbrook regarded Little's leadership as "terrific. It brought out the best in me as a teacher."

When middle school teachers were presented in class with questions from students which they could not answer due to a lack of knowledge or skill, they referred the inquiring student to another middle school colleague, in a nearby class. "It was important to appear credible in the eyes of students, so if one of us didn't know, we knew who did and confidently told that to the kids," said Westbrook.

In order to build the skills and knowledge of middle school teachers, many planning sessions were held that involved teachers explaining to one another how they would conduct a lesson on a specific topic, so that it could be adapted or followed by colleagues in a subsequent class. "That helped a lot because it gave us new insights and, if something didn't make sense or seem a viable way to teach, we could make a joke about something and discuss it amongst ourselves," said Joanne Little. In the course of those sessions, teachers shared resources which they had cobbled together or developed themselves. "Over time this meant we built up stacks of resources and became more structured. Initially, we had no Maths or English resources," noted Little. During the course of 1995, middle school teachers took part in various professional development activities, which were held at locations outside the school. A disparate range of professional development activities were intended to augment teachers' knowledge and skill shortfalls. However, within the year, most middle school teachers stopped attending many, if not all external in-services because of difficulties they subsequently encountered in their classes once they returned. "It just wasn't worth it. The students reacted so badly if we were away. They were so unsettled by their teacher's absence that it took days or sometimes weeks for us to get them back into some semblance of order," said Peta Reece.

In response to students' reaction to teacher absences, the school then occasionally brought professional development consultants into the school and arranged for them to meet with teachers either after school or during non-teaching times. Because most middle school teachers arrived at school about an hour before the first class began and stayed back about an hour after the last class, there were additional opportunities for collegial collaboration. "Very few of us were ever away due to being unwell. If we didn't feel terrific, we still came to work, because we knew what would happen with the kids and what that meant for everyone else, and what we were trying to achieve," said Little.

By taking into account Altona students' prior experiences, attitudes towards learning, and their need for consistent rather than uninterrupted or broken associations with adults, the school's learning culture showed modest but noteworthy improvement over the course of 1995. In particular, there was a noticeable decline in middle school students' resistance to learning in classes. Nonetheless, most students evidenced a continuing inability to quickly adapt to change such as accepting teachers who were unfamiliar to them and accommodating teachers' class–specific or subject–specific expectations of them.

Reaction to the middle school structure by Grade 9 and 10 teachers in 1995 varied. At that stage, most were eager for the initiative to succeed and confident of the abilities of the middle school teachers. Several remained unconvinced that the new structure could lead to improved student outcomes. Few wished to operate a similar system with Grade 9 and 10 students. Despite the varied views about Altona's middle school, all teachers actively implemented new procedures for dealing with student behavioural problems—especially those which occurred in the school grounds. The heightened attention to discipline was intended to complement the middle school initiative and more generally signal to Altona's student population that "the ways things are done around here have changed."

As with most attempts to change cultures within an organisation, the strategies adopted at Altona did not produce uniform or instant results—either in the middle school or Grades 9 and 10. Carl Thomas, who joined the teaching staff at Altona in 1995, reflected on an early encounter with one Grade 7 class. "It was a bit like a scene from the Wild Bunch. I had previously worked with some pretty disturbed kids but . . . I mean, there were all sorts of anarchy. There was one particular class, and it was termed "the zoo." Teaching the zoo class resulted in several sleepless nights for Thomas, while he worried about his students and his teaching performance. As he mulled over what to do and what was wrong in his class during the early hours of one morning, Thomas recalled asking himself "Is it me or is it them?" He resolved that the problem belonged "to them." So, for Thomas, "it was really then a question of developing relationships with the kids."

"Being aware of their backgrounds and what led them to their very obvious behaviours" helped Thomas experiment with and learn ways of effectively interacting with the students. The use of classroom discipline strategies, relying on the support of colleagues for ideas and encouragement, plus trying to make lessons stimulating enabled Thomas to feel that by year's end, his efforts had contributed to favourable student progress at Altona. In addition, Thomas joined with several other teachers to put forward and have accepted by staff and administration, a case for having a "Time-Out" room for students whose classroom behaviour was best responded to by separating them for up to one period from their classmates. The room was supervised on a rostered basis by staff. "I knew in many ways it wouldn't solve the problem with those kids but it was a symbolic thing for them. The message to students who really misbehaved was 'we don't accept you in the class when you behave like that'," said Thomas. During its first year of operation, the Time-Out room itself became a site for student rebellion and aggression. Thomas indicated "it wasn't pleasant because the kids were not used to it and they used to play up a lot in there and we didn't know what to do."

Over time, and mostly as a result of continually trying to understand the students, trial and error use of strategies, and dialogue with colleagues, teachers learned which ways of handling Time-Out students worked. Students also slowly learned to follow the procedures which came with attending the Time-Out room. At the same time as many teachers were attempting to shape the ways in which they and their students worked in school, Altona's principal was developing another initiative.

"Work Plus" had emerged as the title of what was soon to be presented to Altona's staff as the latest initiative which required school-wide acceptance. As a result of Ian Davidson's frustration in "seeing youth leaving school without anything else to go to," he approached many business and community leaders in order to discuss ways of responding to the problem. The outcome of those discussions was Work Plus, a scheme devised for all of Altona's Grade 10 students. The scheme was to be operated from Altona High but have the ongoing involvement of various business and community representatives. The scheme was intended to ensure that, once Grade 10 students had successfully completed their final year at the school, they would go on to either a job, further education, or job training. Altona High, with the assistance of business and community networks, was to act as the students' broker, organising each student's "transition contract."

In a routine that was familiar to Altona's staff, Davidson addressed teachers at a staff meeting in mid 1995, and outlined the need for Work Plus. Davidson wanted—and knew he needed—staff support so that at the school level, the implementation of Work Plus would be a success. The proposal was, to many teachers, another impost. It was also an initiative that did not evolve from a widely-felt need for it amongst staff, and, hence from the outset, was not fully "owned" by teachers. Nor was it an initiative that would have a direct impact on what happened on a daily basis in classrooms. But it was one that few strongly disagreed with. "Ian was and continues to be the big picture, ideas person at Altona. I haven't agreed with everything he has done or the way he has operated, but his heart has always been in the right place," recalled Paul Robertson, an English and Social Science teacher who had been at the meeting.

Whilst the "bulldozing" through of Work Plus at the staff meeting was helped by an impassioned speech from Davidson about its anticipated benefits to students, it was also helped by a staff-wide belief that their principal's motives were worthy and student-focussed. Moreover, teachers understood that on a daily basis, and due to the school's leadership, they had considerable freedom to teach in ways which they deemed appropriate. Davidson trusted most staff to make caring and highly competent decisions in their classes. Only rarely did he challenge the nature of teachers' interactions with students. However, when he did, a teacher was left in no doubt that Davidson rejected a teacher's right to denigrate students or put in a half-hearted teaching effort at the school.

The empowering faith which Davidson had in Altona High and its teachers was, in turn, reciprocated by staff when they endorsed the Work Plus initiative. "I was happy go along with that. I was given free rein and that happened with other teachers too. That is the way it happened here," said one of the teachers who not only supported but actively assisted with the implementation of Work Plus. "We have constantly been encouraged by Ian to initiate things for the students. He was happy if he could see it benefited the kids," said Carl Thomas.

Davidson's habit of acknowledging teachers' capacity to make their classes, and the school, ultimately operate in a highly productive way through being encouraged to make context-specific judgements, assisted teachers' sense of empowerment. It also enabled Davidson to gain the support of specific teachers to help implement Work Plus, and thereby freed him to again develop other key initiatives for Altona. Brad Ames, who was approached by Davidson to become actively involved in Work Plus recalled "in other settings I had worked with unemployed people and so perhaps I was an obvious choice for Ian to approach. Ian said he couldn't allow me much time and there wouldn't be any resources to assist, but that was par for the course. And we did make Work Plus happen." At the end of 1995, almost every Grade 10 student left Altona to undertake further study, job training, or employment.

Just as school leadership that succeeds in creating a coherent environment for teachers to work in is highly complex, so too is the challenge of teaching which fosters meaning and understanding amongst students. Inevitably, both require an ongoing capacity to analyse situations and improvise, as well as extraordinary skill and commitment to democratic, school-based learning.

At the start of the 1996 school year, most Altona teachers and their administration returned to begin what was the second year of the middle school operation. According to Bob Sykes, who was then a middle school teacher, students settled into classes more quickly than they had done at the start of the previous school year. Nonetheless, teachers across the school again found themselves having to deal with considerable numbers of students who did not want to actively learn.

With the benefit of the previous year's experience behind them, most middle school teachers and some Grade 9 and 10 teachers responded to the situation by continuing to develop their relationships with students and continuing to provide curriculum through class topics which were developed by building on students' interests.

Carl Thomas again found that "there were problems and discipline was difficult. But I still needed to talk to the students. I called on my experience, the places I had been, the things I had done. I talked to them about my experiences and challenged them with regard to their future." Thomas recalled that there was "a lot of bitchiness amongst the Grade 10 girls and a lot of disenchantment amongst the boys." Some of what he attempted to achieve in class worked but some fell short of what he had hoped for. "I did not feel I was making headway, so I said to the students, 'let's do something totally different'. I rang up a local primary school's principal and said: 'I have a class and I want them to make some kind of contribution and to take some kind of responsibility'. The principal said 'fine', so we arranged for my class to go to the Grade 1 and 2 classes, once a fortnight." The students wrote stories and typed poems on computers for the primary students and hosted a visit by them to Altona for a barbecue.

Of the initiative, Thomas said "that worked well and it enhanced my relationship with my students. It gave them a sense of responsibility and it was amazing to see the difference. Students who were really difficult in class here, at Altona, were different people inside the primary school classrooms. There was not one kid in a class of 26 who did not take responsibility for one or two primary kids and do a good job."

In another attempt by staff to connect interpersonally with their students, all Grade 9 students and teachers organized a graffiti-cleaning day at Altona. Parents and school cleaners also joined in to help remove graffiti from walls and paint inside several classrooms. "We had a catering group provide us with muffins for morning tea and a barbecue lunch. It was just tremendous," said Margaret Evans. "Of course we got feedback, like 'it sucks', but you expected that. Overall, it was a great success," she added.

On a day-to-day basis, much of the focus of middle school teachers' efforts was on laying the foundations for productive student learning. According to Barry Meadows, "knowledge was probably not so important. Instead, it was teaching kids a few of the social skills plus reading, writing, and maths." As well as emphasising "the social aspects of life and school," Joanne Little indicated that Grade 7 and 8 teachers heightened their promotion of a culture of work with students. "We worked very hard on being productive, attending school, and being proud of being part of a team."

Teachers who, by 1996, had been working at the school for several years, claimed they had gained and learned from their experiences of working with Altona students. Although the learning culture was changing for the better, teachers were convinced that further improvement was still required. Nonetheless, the poor student behaviour they had experienced in recent years provided them with a benchmark and means by which to gauge, and remind themselves, how far the students had progressed. However, for teachers who were new to the school, there were no such benchmarks. Instead, many new teachers' perceptions of Altona students' classroom behaviours were influenced by comparisons with students from their previous school appointments.

For Greg Panetta, first term in 1996 was a memorable experience. "At the end of the first week, I went home and spent the weekend looking at the walls in my house. At the end of my second week, I was still fairly shocked but I didn't think it was as bad. My wife said to me 'Are you coping?' because apparently I spent most of the weekend just watching television programs that I don't usually watch, and sitting around just flicking through books, just staring at the pages. But by the end of the third week I had started to readjust to different expectations of the children here. That 3 weeks it took, and then, by the end of Term 1, I think I had really come to terms with the students."

During Panetta's first term at Altona, he spoke with other teachers who were new to the school. "We talked about those things happening. It was interesting that they were experiencing the same things." Panetta, who worked in the middle school, found the learning culture of students to be poor but resilient. "The avoiding behaviour of students surprised me, both how well they had learned to avoid work, and their techniques. For example, the getting up and getting a biro, the 'have lost the sheet?', 'I don't have a ruler,' 'I have lost the book' and 'what notes?' lines. Those comments seemed to be constant at the beginning of every lesson. It was continuous—you could be in the same room all day and students would want the same books and materials at the end of the day that they said they needed in Period 1. Also, the bickering and arguing amongst the students. There could be a good fight, disagreement, or conversation so as to be off task. That seemed to be a fairly standard way of avoiding work."

Like many teachers who were new to the school, Panetta was forced by circumstance, to change how he operated. "I learned to monitor students more. You didn't expect anything to be completed. Whereas in other schools, it was assumed the students' work would be done and it actually was done, and done on time, and put in the mark basket. Here the expectation was something I had to work out, and devise techniques to get around the problem, and change my behaviours completely in the classroom so that the students' avoiding behaviours couldn't be carried out." As a result of postgraduate study and professional development undertaken during school holidays and weekends, Panetta gradually introduced a range of cooperative learning activities, including mind maps visualisation, into his classes. "The students initially enjoyed them so much that I then developed those areas."

One of Panetta's colleagues who started at Altona in 1996, also found several professional development sessions helped to increase her teaching strategies. "Barrie Bennett's mind mapping ideas were excellent," she said. Despite the difficulties students had adjusting to teachers being away from school for their own learning purposes, Janice Greenway, a Grade 9 English teacher, indicated that the in-school time allocated to Altona's professional development program in 1996 had been insufficient and thus the school had lost an opportunity to provide support and "lift staff. People in different schools have different emphases; for example, at my previous school there was an emphasis on understanding learning differences and developing different teaching strategies. At Altona, we couldn't get to that level of learning, because people were simply trying to cope with the situation. It was more or less a grinding-down process."

Panetta and Greenway were pleased to have joined the staff of a school where, Panetta indicated, "there was very little frustration with the administration. From day 1, it was very open and if something needed to be said by anyone, it was said." The key sources of staff frustration in 1996 were student and resource-related problems. "We seemed to be losing our capacity to keep pace with technology changes such as updating library and classroom computers and software," indicated Peta Reece. A then widely-held staff view sheeted responsibility to the government for the shortage of funds to purchase such equipment. "Ian was always very good at obtaining extra funds for special initiatives which benefited the school, but in the end, there was only so much he could do regarding the overall funding. There just wasn't enough for us to do what we needed to do. In the 1990s computers, for instance, became a basic rather than luxury item," said the school's technology coordinator, Elle Rainsford.

Ongoing problems with student learning which Altona staff attempted to respond to also continued to be seen as relating to larger social problems. "When I started here in 1996, one of the first things that struck me was the number of students who came from broken homes. Fathers weren't present. If there was a male at home, it was usually a stepfather and there were relationship problems with that. A lot of the boys in the school had trouble coping with authority," recalled Greg Panetta.

"Ian got an At-Risk campus program going that year and it was designed to deal with anger management and help students to cope when parents left home," said Panetta. As with all innovations, the At-Risk campus, which was located about a kilometre away from the school, had shortcomings as well as many advantages attached to it. One of its chief limitations was the lack of communication between those who initially ran the At-Risk campus and mainstream class teachers. "The problems associated with a student who attended the At-Risk campus for part of the week never got back to the mainstream teachers and so we didn't know what the specific problems were and couldn't compensate for them," indicated Margaret Evans. In that sense, according to John Westbrook, it was not surprising that the At Risk campus, like the Accelerated Learning initiative was not "strongly supported by most staff."

Even though the effectiveness of the At-Risk campus was initially limited by the inability of staff to adequately share information about students' problems and progress, Ian Davidson was in no doubt that the venture had been worthwhile and "a good way to respond to diverse student needs." Louise Griffin, who started at Altona in 1996, recalled one of the first key difficulties she encountered with school life at Altona. "Not having sufficient time, time was a big thing. Wanting to do things or seeing a need to change something but not having the time to be able to do that." An additional problem which, in part, related to time, concerned teachers taking risks or experimenting with new ideas in classes. Griffin was not convinced she had seen widespread examples of teachers attempting to adopt innovative approaches in classes. "It came back to having the time to think about those whole new approaches or new ideas to be able to actually implement them. If you didn't get that time or that motivation to do it, then the risk was fairly minimal, because you stuck to what you knew."

Conscious of the need to cater for the educational requirements of Altona students who were highly capable and motivated learners, in 1996 Davidson determined that the school should provide an Accelerated learning curriculum. Due to space constraints at the school, Davidson decided to find an external location for the proposed accelerated campus. As had occurred with all of his major initiatives, Davidson sought and obtained staff support for the venture. However, as with the At-Risk and Work Plus initiatives, whilst staff supported the proposal, many saw their endorsement of the Accelerated campus decision as a fait accompli. "Again, the idea was good. But it wasn't seen like the middle school initiative, which most teachers felt they owned. With the middle school concept, it was investigated, debated, and implemented by staff members. Everyone had a say, whereas with the other initiatives, we knew it was a case of Ian really wanting them to go ahead," said Jenny Warner, who was then in her ninth year at the school. With the benefit of some additional funding that Ian Davidson obtained, as well as monies from Altona's school funds, a five year lease was taken out on a property in order to house the accelerated campus, and the program was staffed with a full-time teacher and started in 1997.

Curriculum initiatives which are introduced into schools as a matter of priority, or in haste, often leave teachers unclear about what should be deleted from their existing programs, as a way of accommodating such changes. At Altona in 1997, teachers overwhelmingly sought to accommodate the demands brought about by student involvement in the At-Risk and Accelerated campuses through their school and class programs. Despite this practical support for the external campuses, many teachers questioned the impact on mainstream school which flowed from having an extensive range of programs.

Mary Lempriere claimed "the logistics of so many ongoing initiatives created all sorts of headaches." However, when one-off activities such as excursions also had to be adjusted for, but only involved some students, extra difficulties were created for class teachers. Usually teachers who were left with only some of their classes had to choose between not introducing new concepts on those occasions or repeat-teaching them on the following day.

Altona's successful efforts at embracing multiple initiatives also meant that, during 1997, less time and energy was available to evaluate and further develop the school's core curriculum programs. The inability to systematically review mainstream curriculum on a school-wide basis left some teachers wondering whether or not Altona was offering the best possible whole school program. "Teachers' doubts about the appropriateness of Altona's core programs were often shared with one another over coffee in our break times," said Jenny Warner. Indeed, Altona teachers regarded their brief break periods as important for regaining, and hence sustaining, their energies as well as maintaining positive relationships with colleagues. Staffroom conversations frequently involved good natured teasing of one another and humorous, self-deprecating "stories from the trenches." In the main, however, most teachers used such shared times to talk with colleagues about student-related issues, including concerns about curriculum matters. Yet, despite continuing staff doubts about this aspect of Altona's school program, during 1997, no review of curriculum was undertaken.

RE-CREATION, LESSONS, CHALLENGES

Schools are never fully functional education settings when students' socialisation and learning are starkly inadequate. Yet, for schools like Altona which are genuinely committed to developing close affiliations with their students and providing a breadth of ways for them to learn and demonstrate their competence, the journey of renewal is often a long, fractured and arduous one.

By 1998, staff who had witnessed first-hand the improvement in Altona students' attitudes towards their learning, teachers, and school friends were convinced that the school had achieved much in the previous 5 years. One telling feature of the school's success was evident from students' attendances. Carl Thomas claimed that "one of the important things in a high school such as Altona is actually getting kids to come along. It is not what we can shove down their throats, it is showing them how to learn and making them willing to come to a place to learn. That is fairly noticeable now. Also, the fact that some of our previously worst middle school kids have gone on in subsequent years to never have days off school. To me, that is us being successful—we are a bit of stability for students."

A check of school records supported Thomas' impressions about student attendances having improved. Whereas in 1994, 10% of students were absent at least once during Term 2, in the same period in 1998, only 8% of students had been absent for one or more days.

Nonetheless, despite fewer student absences, records for 1998 continued to reveal disturbing facts about attendances amongst sections of Altona's student population. The rates of absence from school of native girls and boys as well as non-native boys remained, in relative terms, especially high. For example, in one week of an Attendance Survey period, every native student was away for one day. Half of the native student population was away for two or more days. Amongst non-native boys during the same survey period, patterns of absences were as high. Moreover, typically, 60% of students' absences and early departures or late arrivals at Altona were "unexplained." That is, no notes of explanation from parents about the reasons for such student absences were received by the school in 60% of cases.

At a superficial level, the failure of many Altona parents to provide the school with explanations about student absences suggested that providing such information was not considered important. However, Carl Thomas suspected that there were many deeper reasons behind why some parents failed to provide such information to the school. Illiteracy, depression, and time shortages amongst adults in some Altona students' households were factors that may have contributed to no "absence" notes being written. As well, in a few instances, parents may have been unaware of their children being away from school.

All schools have students who, for health reasons on some occasions, invariably cannot attend school. However, student absences which are due to an inability to identify with or engage in school are especially problematic. In this sense, the attendance records suggested that the section of the student population that the school had been most successful at engaging with was non-native girls.

On the basis of stories which colleagues had told, Clare Thornton, who at that stage was in her second year at the school, accepted that Altona had strong grounds for being pleased with those developments. Nonetheless, for Thornton, students' limited skills and understandings were a source of great concern. "Students in my class who are 14 years old, can't even read a dictionary, let alone comprehend some of the set literature texts," said Thornton. The disparity between what the students could actively engage with and the grade level, pre-set curriculum left Thornton believing "that the curriculum here is somewhat irrelevant in a lot of cases."

The contrast for Thornton between Altona and her own private high schools years as a student during the late 1970s was, she said, "massive. What I experienced is just not happening here." According to Ann Hinze, who also teaches English at the school, "You don't want to discourage the kids but, really, at one time you could leave a school and know you could read, write, spell, and put a sentence together. That, I've found, is now a real problem and I don't think it's the school's fault. I think that it is just the evolution of modern education, really."

The pivotal need for students to be ready to learn was understood by Joanne Little. Little, who was one of several colleagues whose advice was frequently sought by Altona staff when they needed teaching or learning ideas, accepted that the difficulties many students continued to encounter would not easily be overcome in the short or medium term. "Although many students have made enormous progress, most of us realize that we still need to get to know our students, try to motivate them, and somehow engage with them."

Like all Altona teachers, Little was well aware of the often overwhelming difficulties some students faced in trying to regularly and productively participate in classes. Because of the disruptions which those students created in classes, since its inception, the Time-Out room had continued to be a well-used means of creating a place for troubled and misbehaving students. Yet, in the main, the withdrawal process merely shifted students from the mainstream class setting rather than remedying their underlying problems. Furthermore, the difficult behaviours which had led to students being removed from their classes in the first place sometimes continued to be transferred to, and replicated in, the Time-Out room, as extracts from supervising Time-Out teachers' records indicated (see Table 1).

The successes with students which Little and most of her middle school colleagues experienced were many, but required teachers to remain persistent and adaptive. As well, Mary Lempriere, who had worked in the middle school since its inception, claimed teachers needed to continue to share ideas and resources amongst themselves. "In my case, I have excellent rapport with Joanne. She can work with anybody and she never judges. She has never prejudged anyone and gives you so much support and assistance if you are not sure of something. Also, she readily listens to any ideas that you have and so you feel valued."

Table 1. Time-out room records snapshot (Altona High school).

Date Time Student name	Details	Notes
Friday 20 March 1998		
Ben	Was the only person doing the right thing for the entire lesson	
Tony	Attempting to communicate with others.	
Alan	Rude at end of lesson – told Ben I "suck" when I wouldn't let him go to the office. Everyone bolted at the end of the lesson – what a horrible, horrible lesson.	
Monday 23 March 1998		
Period 1		
Sandra Jones		
Alexandra Maher		
Molly Smylie		
Dick Andrews		
Dough Fallshore		
Tony	Thanks to Special Ed for lesson	
Period 2		
Ian	In at 11.03	
Erin	In at 11.15	Over extending break
Sandra	In at 11.12	Over extending break
Doug	In at 11.13	
Brett	In at 11.15	
Tony	In at 11.25	
Erin	Working system still making noises trying to disrupt and maintain/establish control	
Period 5		
Ben Caruthers	To lunch @ 1.30	
Tony Charles	To lunch @ 1.45	
Erin Hipwell	To lunch @ 1.30	
Bonnie Geeves	To lunch @ 1.40	
Jill Emerson	To lunch @ 1.40 return from lunch @ 2.30	
Sally Anderson	To Library 1.33-1.40	
Alan Evers	Returned from library @ 1.30	
Tony Charles	To Special Ed	

(continued)

Table 1 — continued

Date

Time

Student name	Details	Notes
Sally Davidson	To toilet @ 2.05	
Erin Hipwell	Will need to spend an extra day learning to demonstrate the appropriately settled behaviour in the internal room.	
	People distracted when I arrived settled briefly, then WENT OFF!	
Erin	Constantly disruptive, attention seeking noises,	
Bonnie	picking arguments with others, (teacher) arrived at	
Andrea	2.25 and took Bonnie and Erin to library – Andrea	
Sally	extremely disruptive prior to this. Sally rude, uncooperative, produced no work. Ran out of room in front of (class teacher), was told by (teacher) that she would have another day of internal. Eating.	
Jill	No work, talking to other inmates, eating.	
Tony	Returned from Sp.Ed 2.30pm. Read newspaper as he had no other work.	
Sally	Still chewing after being told to bin it.	
Alan	To library at 2.15, back 2.30, making distracting and strange noises for remainder of lesson.	
Sally	Extremely rude and silly for entire lesson – needs more time in here!	
Erin	Then asked to go to toilet and was refused because she wasn't doing as she had been asked to, but, of course, got up and went anyway.	
Linda and Erin	Wouldn't shut up!	
	Recess very calm and it would need to be!	
Erin	Has heaps of work which she must do to catch up.	
Period 4		
Maggie	Quiets and working.	
Tim		
Linda	Talkative.	
Elsa Porter	12.43 lunchtime detentions.	
Anne Gregson		
Betty William		
Erin	Removed to Fainey's office 12.45 wouldn't shut up.	
Linda	Toilet.	
Linda	Break lunch 1.05 pm.	
Dave	Lunch break 1.10 pm. All very quite.	
Period 5		
Erin	Noisy, refusing to work OK. Others settling down.	
	Noisy towards end of lesson. NO work.	
	Arrived at 2.00pm (Year 9 teacher).	

(continued)

Table 1 — continued

Date

Time

Student name	Details	Notes
Erin	To special Ed 2.05.	
Maggie	A bit talkative.	
Linda		
Tim	Good.	
Maggie	Settled down quickly.	
Erin	Avoided work at beginning but settled down after about 10 minutes.	
Linda Simpson	Arrived at 9.10 apparently from Grade 9 assembly; began working without direction.	
Tim Masterman	Arrived at 9.15 and began work immediately. All were generally excellent – Erin struggled having to concentrate for so long.	

Monday 23 March 1998

Erin	Still wasting time . . . and broke her biro. The boredom wasting time starting to get to them all at about 10.15 off task but no one was disruptive except Erin and her broken pen! I offered her new one but the novelty of having a new "toy" was too much. Her insistence on getting a pair of scissors to fix her biro started to disrupt others. She informed me that she just had to get a "bloody" pair of scissors and was not satisfied with my negative reaction so she spent most of this period fiddling and complaining.	
Linda	Passed a note to Maggie whilst borrowing her ruler! Offered Erin a new biro.	
Erin	Went to the office to buy a biro at 10.20 and returned (yippee!) and did nothing but suck the ink end of her biro. It's just *so* exciting in here!!! I asked her not to and informed her it would make her SICK which seemed to amuse her. She then wanted to chat with me (help?!!) and read her book aloud.	

Lempriere's effective working relationship with Little greatly contrasted with that of the new subject coordinator. The end result of the ineffective collaboration was that she resolved to, as much as possible, work by herself in that subject area. "For that subject, I developed all my programs for the middle school. Initially I didn't see the coordinator much, but I knew he was specifically trained in the subject and I was not. But because of my lack of formal training, I tried to teach in a way that ensured that any kid who came out of my class would understand the subject. Surely that is better than just being able to whiz bang in your head and not know why. However, when I discovered the coordinator had no program, I lost faith in him. I just went on my own merry way."

The tensions from Lempriere's subject coordinator not having developed his program but nonetheless teaching the subject, stood at odds with what most Altona teachers considered to be a key collegial requirement. Because of the school's teacher culture, there was a widespread view amongst staff that colleagues' professional commitments extended beyond students to take account of Altona teachers and the school. For most staff, the class and curriculum freedom allowed them by Davidson was reasonable only when it was honoured through substantial preparation and implementation by all teachers. Not being hamstrung by imposed, tightly prescriptive curricula enabled teachers to better tailor programs to the specific social as well as intellectual needs of students. In 1998, the need for context–responsive teaching remained noticeably different to, but as important as that which prevailed in 1994. Just as in 1994, by 1998 teachers, like their principal, still believed that Altona personnel owed it to everyone at the school to demonstrate commitment, adaptability, and hard work.

Over the course of 4 years, Altona students' learning culture had most noticeably impacted those students who, in 1995, had started in Grade 7. "We are reaping the benefits of all the effort attached to the middle school initiative. You still get the odd student who is not going to do any work but they are a real minority and, in most cases, they are not the disruption in classes that they were last year or in previous years," said Terry Faine. Moreover, longstanding teachers across the school commonly acknowledged the favourable contrasts between the Grade 10 students in 1998 and the Grade 10 students of 1995. Although the school had, over the previous 4 years, altered many of its organizational and enforcement procedures, the key means by which Altona maintained its impetus for cultural change amongst students was through classroom interactions and developmentally attentive teaching.

Sustaining developmentally appropriate teaching can be as or more difficult than the beginning efforts required by such an approach. Invariably, most teachers needed substantial, ongoing professional development in order to maximize their theoretical understandings and build a repertoire of classroom strategies. Yet, like most public schools, in 1998, Altona's professional development funds were modest. Less than $20,000 was available for the school to use and professionally enhance its 30-strong full-time teaching force plus part-time employees. Limited funds plus a perpetuation of the negative classroom reactions of students toward staff who undertook professional development outside of the school figured in many teachers' decisions to continue to not develop themselves in this way. As well, some teachers were unconvinced that "outside" programs would necessarily provide the quantity and quality of information to warrant the time required. By contrast, a few teachers chose to undertake university courses as a means of providing themselves with additional and current understandings about learning and teaching. Nevertheless, for most Altona staff, professional development in 1998 comprised their own and colleagues' school-based efforts at sharing expertise and ideas, drawing on the gains from particular individuals' postgraduate studies plus occasionally being addressed at the school by an "outside" speaker.

For teachers who were new to Altona's staff, only a limited formal induction program was provided. Despite the intentions of administration to provide an extensive induction process for incoming teachers, time impediments resulted in, at best, only one or two meetings being held between senior staff and new staff at the start of each school year.

Given the pressures of time, few teachers were strongly critical of the failure to provide such a directed learning opportunity to new staff but many believed it would have accelerated their acculturation and provided valuable information about the school and its operations. One way of getting around the time shortages of senior personnel, according to Margaret Evans, was to develop a staff mentoring system, which may end up being implemented at the school. "Recently I gave an article to Sally Green, which mentioned pairing a senior teacher with an incoming person. If we end up doing that here, it would add even further to the camaraderie and support amongst staff," said Evans.

Despite the constraints on teachers enhancing their professional learning at venues beyond the school, teachers' school-based learning was developed on a daily basis. Collegial conversations in the staffroom and other rooms where teachers gathered for a meeting or during break-times still usually focussed, in large part, on school, curriculum, or classroom matters. The extent of formal and informal exchanges about teachers' work and the practical support colleagues offered one another were two of the reasons why an overwhelming majority of teachers regarded the Altona staff and administration as the most supportive school team they had worked with.

Indeed, prior to being appointed to the school in 1997, Daniella Overton had heard from "teacher friends in other schools" that Altona was a highly collegial, collaborative school. "When I came here, I had a fairly strong impression of the school as a supportive environment. Mostly it has lived up to that reputation. The staff are extremely friendly and willing to discuss student cases, and personal or professional development on my part. I have been offered a lot of help with resources for subject areas. Sometimes I seek help if I need it. But mostly it has been offered to me by other teachers, like an open invitation. And in some cases they have even followed up to make sure that I am getting enough help, even if I haven't asked for it," said Overton.

In the relatively short time Ellen Arnott had been teaching part-time at the school, she had also found staff to be student-focussed and highly collegial. Most days she travelled to and from Altona with one, and sometimes two, of the middle school teachers. They use much of their travelling time to discuss work matters. "That time continues to be especially important at the end of the day—we both use it as a debriefing session," said Arnott. The benefits gained from sharing ideas and experiences in the car pool were complemented by conversations with other staff during the day. Her interactions with staff have convinced Arnott that, despite the difficulties which confront Altona High, the school operates successfully in two important ways. "You don't have people barking at you all the time saying 'do this, do that.' So you are able to develop your own style and that is recognized and celebrated. Here, staff put the kids first, regardless of other considerations. For instance, when a teacher does not get along with a student, there is always another teacher who does. The one who does get along with the student will always step in to help the teacher who is having trouble interacting with that student. Conversations between staff about students are constant at this school."

Like most of his colleagues, Allan Grey appreciated the supportiveness of Altona's staff, which was especially noticeable to him shortly after he transferred to the school, several years ago. "The staff needed to be, and were, particularly supportive when we started the middle school system. Everyone worked together and there were good interactions between staff. I noticed how different that was to my previous school. A lot of the soul had gone out of that school. Whereas here it was very friendly and open and staff were only too willing to assist. And that is still the case."

One way of supporting colleagues at Altona in order to sustain the staff's collective efforts and energies continued to be through conversation. "By discussing, for example, a problem kid with other staff members you know you are not the only one who has that problem—that others experience the same. Just being able to sit down and have a bit of a laugh about things and not look on the too serious side of things. You have to have a sense of humour otherwise you'd go around the twist. Yes, it's a case of just getting together and talking things through and supporting each other, realising you're not the only one with a problem kid or problem class and being able to do that is great," said Grey.

Although Graeme Black was also grateful for the support provided to him during his 2 years at the school, he did not like the regular practice of teachers discussing work matters in the staffroom during break times. As well, Black considered it was a habit which was related to teacher stress. "A lot of the time it is stress that people talk about and much of that is self-imposed. Instead of treating the staffroom as a place to get away from the kids, they treat the staffroom as a place to come and conduct their post-mortems. They need to leave that outside. You go to the staffroom to get away from it, but it's there. The way I look at it is, you shouldn't spend every waking hour worrying about the kids. We all have bad days—you just need time away from it. Sitting there, discussing the ins and outs of what has just happened and mulling over who you have in the next class is counter-productive. That is where all the stress comes from." Although Black's view of what should happen in Altona's staffroom was at odds with most of his colleagues, the prevalence of teacher stress at the school was widely acknowledged amongst staff.

Jane Bannon, who was in her third year at Altona, echoed the observations of many teachers when she claimed "the stress level of the staff is pretty high, due to the nature of the students. You can say 'okay this is what I am going to do today' but there are so many things that crop up during the day, that you find that you either don't do them or you cram so much in, that you end up physically exhausted. Also, usually your class efforts are not viewed by students in the way that you would have hoped they would be. In another school you might get students who would react differently to things that teachers planned."

Within Altona's administration, both Davidson and Green were conscious of teachers' stress levels. Green maintained a regular personal exercise regime and, in combination with Davidson, endeavoured to operationally support staff across the school so as to partially offset the demands of teaching. In addition, her reputation for thoroughly and quickly following through teacher complaints about excessively unruly behaviour by individual students left most teachers feeling they were given responsive, helpful support when required. Davidson's appreciation of the classroom difficulties and consequent stresses which teachers continued to face influenced his overwhelming respect for the profession and continuing efforts to gain extra resources for the school. In addition, he indicated that many teachers had temporary or lasting personal difficulties to contend with, yet chose to do justice to their work. "I personally know about teachers who have all sorts of things to contend with and they come to work every day and do their best. You would not know half of what some of these people are putting up with, yet on a daily basis some of them are working their guts out."

While evidence of stress has been apparent amongst teachers in most of the country's schools during this decade, it was not a phenomenon at Altona that was only confined to adults. Many students also experienced stress. One way a minority of students reacted to their negative life experiences was to escape through regular "substance use." Lyn Harper, who strongly supported Davidson's efforts to establish an At-Risk campus and taught music in the upper school, claimed "there is a lot of drug use in this suburb. At this school the kids are pretty open about their drug use. Many of them have two or three cones before they come to school and then another at lunchtime. Every weekend a few of them have a bottle of Jack Daniels—and they are 11-year-olds. The use of such substances is celebrated, it's part of their culture." The extent of substance abuse was, Harper indicated, "horrific." However, she constantly sought to understand rather than be punitive toward those "using students," as a precursor to efforts by herself and the school to reduce or eliminate drug taking.

Five years at Altona had convinced Harper that, in most cases, students' had longstanding problems that emanated from outside the school and were influential in triggering such activities. "They use to feel normal. If they are not stoned, if they are not drunk, they don't feel normal. They put alcohol in their plastic drink bottles and bring it to school—it's regular behaviour for those kids. Most teachers can't tell because that's what those students always look like," she said.

At the At-Risk campus, one way that coordinator Gillian Anderson has responded to students' concerns was through her emotional and mental health education curricula. "I use activity manuals that have been written specifically for the 'different needs' area. Those materials are very important guides and focus on students' feelings. So the idea is to help students to identify their feelings. And I also promote the idea that it is okay to feel what you feel and look at healthy ways to express that. A lot of students have never done that. They have got stoned or drunk since the age of 6, and for many, it worked. They did not feel pain any more. We're trying to get them out of that downward slide," she said.

Although Anderson was not based at Altona when the At-Risk campus first began, her efforts at creating worthwhile programs as well as effectively communicating with, and advocating for, students who attend the campus, have impressed staff. Despite a view of the At-Risk campus having dramatically increased the effectiveness of its operation, many staff remain unsure about whether the advantages which flow from its existence outweigh what could be achieved by mainstreaming those students and thus supporting all students in the course of their daily classes, plus spreading the funds that are used by the At–Risk campus across the whole school. Anderson was aware of a perception amongst some staff that the quality of the initial at risk program did not justify the outlay of school funds continued to be held at Altona. She also realized that teacher frustration and doubts about the campus were heightened when, as had happened in recent years, many subject-based budgets had been reduced or were manifestly inadequate. "I think without Ian Davidson's fierce protection and support of the At-Risk campus, much of what happens here, couldn't happen. This campus is very much to do with Ian Davidson's philosophy, which is that kids learn in lots of different ways and that we need to respond to that positively." Most of the students who attend the At-Risk campus have, according to Anderson, "considerable mental or emotional mental pain," as a result of years of leading deeply troubled lives. The depth of those students' anguish and disenfranchisement is such that even the most talented teachers would have difficulty in trying to consistently attend to such need as well as provide for more common student requirements in classes. "There are far more kids at risk than just those who identify themselves with behaviour," said Anderson.

The At–Risk setting provides an opportunity for more intensive interactions between the students and Anderson, and "gives the kids the chance to learn that they are okay as people, that they can develop a good sense of self, and that what they believe and feel is important." Anderson added: "It *does* matter and it *does* count." By respecting and recognising students, including those who were at times quite resistant to Anderson's efforts to acknowledge their worth as individuals, her programs sought to improve communication, and formally address issues such as anger, blame and control. "We look at how to cope with different situations. One of the biggest issues for students is controlling things, and getting them to see that the only person they can control is themselves—that they can't make other people change what they think or do. Also, that it is a student's choice to get on better with other people, and to be able to communicate their needs and feelings. As well, we consider strategies for dealing with stress and developing better attitudes toward school, teachers, and their family."

Although few teachers were steadfastly opposed to the At-Risk campus when it was originally proposed by their principal, and few were vehemently critical of its current workings, there was not widespread, active support for the initiative. A consequent pruning of specific budgets and the ongoing challenges teachers faced in Altona classes left many teachers more concerned about the nature of their immediate and own work.

The classes which Barry Meadows took varied in number, with the largest having 27 students. "In my biggest class, around 20 of the students have some form of learning problem." Not surprisingly, the nature and extent of learning problems continued to shape both the content and teaching of Meadows' classes. Often times Meadows was left weary from what seem to be enduring battles with students about completing class work, especially if exercises required demanding literacy skills. "On a Thursday I have them Period 6, which is a case of just shutting the classroom door and waiting for the bell to ring. It is not working, and once again it is very much a work sheet oriented thing. I have started to side step that for the time being and I have got them doing projects that they are interested in. With projects, they can draw- and they will do that- which I guess is for my benefit too, because I'm then not constantly fighting to get them to do something," said Meadows.

Not all of Meadows' classes were deeply troubling to him. "In another class I design work sheets that have a range of difficulties and I say to the kids 'just do the ones you can do'. The ones who I know are good, are going to do them all and do them well." Meadows indicated that many students followed those instructions and did only what they could do. "There is another stream of kids whom I have never come across before, in my 20 years of teaching, and they do absolutely nothing." Despite the shortcomings of using work sheets regularly, Meadows claimed that they provided students with some structure. "That is why these things are good for them and they will have a go and do it page after page. Whereas if I try to have a class discussion, it just degenerates, because someone gets distracted and then will distract someone else."

Teaching which is framed on behaviourist notions of learning reinforces classroom roles "teacher" and "student." As well, it results in teachers producing highly teacher-directed class activities for students. In the course of being attempted by students, the activities effectively cull those learners who are unable to grasp the nature of what is required of them. In so doing, such lessons embed the teacher's power as well as the standing of those students who "succeed" because they are adept at, or can adapt their learning, to the activity. However, for those students who regularly fail in such settings, feelings of disempowerment and disengagement usually prevail. In this sense, behaviourist—informed teaching often inhibits the extent of what teachers can learn about their students and the disparate learning processes they employ. Yet this transmission-oriented practice of teaching was the means by which most teachers learnt when they were school students and undergraduates.

For Barry Meadows, teaching at Altona was both frustrating and valuable. It was personally upsetting because he wanted all of his students to succeed in school, but on a daily basis, he was confronted with classroom situations which convinced him that would not occur. Meadows chose to work at Altona because of his beliefs in social justice and a keenness to contribute to the education of a socially disadvantaged group of students. In broad terms, he believed a key factor in Davidson and most staff being drawn to and staying at Altona was the value they placed on social justice principles. "What the school is trying to offer, I guess at times, is a bit of a losing battle. I still don't think that is a reason to either change it or give up. If I ever got to a stage where I thought 'as long as the salary is there', then I would give it away, because that is not the purpose of the exercise. Someone in the community has got to deal with this situation."

In a continuing effort to learn how to better adapt his teaching strategies in order to engage students, cater to disparate learning capabilities amongst students and provide a modicum of skill-based content, Meadows frequently sought ideas from Joanne Little and other middle school teachers. Their knowledge, experiences, and stories of success and failure were freely shared with him and provided a further impetus for persisting with his efforts, even during extremely frustrating class sessions. Meadows was appreciative of his colleagues' support and impressed with their enduring commitment to the well-being of students. "People in my staffroom are pretty job-satisfied. They are very motivated and extremely conscientious. And that is important because what we are doing is serving a purpose, and hopefully, in the end, we can serve a better purpose."

Ever conscious of the need to promote a greater alliance between the school and the parents of Altona students, in 1994 Davidson set out to inform and "invite" parents into the school. It was a strategy he continued to develop over subsequent years. "My own personal agenda was always about trying to get the community involved in doing various things. That started to happen on the issue of disbanding the sub-schools. Late in 1994 we had a big public meeting at which our community had the chance to hear the arguments and then say 'yes we will abandon the sub-school system we have had for 20 years and we will get into a new way of doing things in the school'." As well as holding numerous award and information sessions for parents and Altona citizens since then, Davidson ensured that various achievements by students were celebrated formally. Those events contributed to a growing sense of partnership between the school and most parents. Davidson also expanded the role and membership of the School Council so that it took a more active part in determining Altona's forward planning.

"I believe what we are doing here is very strongly supported by our own community. In 1998, parents are our greatest advocates," reflected Ian Davidson. It was now only on rare occasions that parents of Altona students would express wholesale concerns about the ways in which the school was endeavouring to educate their children. "There is a lot of really good stuff that is happening here, like the launch of Work Plus, where the whole school gets together. The assembly hall will be packed to capacity for the Work Plus Award Ceremony this year. And every Grade 10 kid has been placed. Plus the Middle School initiative, Accelerated, and At-Risk campuses. And the quality of the staff—sometimes, for instance, there has been a staff meeting where there has been a lot of humour and people throwing in anecdotes, and I've left there feeling we are a great lot of people."

In reflecting on the quality of staff contributions to the school during the past 5 years in particular, Davidson claimed that the willingness to remain open to new ways of improving the school as well as holding on to what was educationally important helped the school to make much progress. Amongst what Davidson had learned during recent years was the high value teachers place on helping students. "My awareness has been heightened regarding the extent to which teachers warm to agendas which they know will enhance the outcomes of students and the outcomes for themselves in terms of their ability to do their work and teach effectively. I have always known that but the changes that we have undergone have reinforced that view. As time goes on and we look to make further modifications to what we are doing, I can see that view will continue to be ingrained into the way we go about things."

The practice of teachers viewing critically many of his ideas and any which might, in future, be imposed on schools from federal or state governments was, according to Davidson, a healthy feature of Altona. "Because at the end of the day, teachers will run with agendas that they believe in. They will be dismissive of the agendas that are imposed where they can see that it is not going to make a difference to them and their work and the outcomes for their students."

On rare occasions some of Davidson's change proposals had languished shortly after he floated them with individual teachers or the entire staff. Over the past 5 years Davidson had learned not to concern himself about such results due to the realisation that "they don't waste their time doing things that they don't believe in, that they don't believe will help kids. Because they respect me and so on, they have given some things a go, but not for long if they saw it wasn't going to help."

Davidson's confidence in much of the staff's "critical eyes" was underpinned by an enduring belief that he was leading a team of "committed, high energy, positive teachers. Teachers here have an ongoing agenda which is more about finding every way in which to enhance the opportunities available to their kids, homing in on the individual needs of students within this context. Because of that, Altona teachers will have a much more profound effect on the life chances of the students than, say, a group of teachers that functions—and there are plenty of them—without too much regard for the context in which they are situated."

The achievements of Altona, and especially the breadth of student outcomes, had to continue to be considered in light of context, Davidson suggested. In so doing, a chance was provided to evaluate progress within the realities of circumstances which the school, and in particular its students, faced. "The general level of motivation of kids is currently not anywhere near perfect but it is ahead of where it was before. Their general work ethic is greatly improved. They are taken on trips to the mainland, and given access to all sorts of activities. These are real outcomes, where students are getting a type of premium on top of what has been the traditional sort of curriculum," said Davidson.

The emphasis on understanding a school's context in relation to gauging its outcomes and progress remained especially important given that, according to Davidson. "In 1998, 30% of students entering Grade 7 are coming here with a reading age of less than 9 years." In addition to wanting educational authorities to grasp the contexts in which schools like Altona operated, Davidson was aware of the mammoth challenge such statistics presented in terms of communicating with local constituencies. "How do you deal with that issue when it is so important for the community out there to regard the school highly?," he asked. Unpalatable and potentially unsettling as those figures can be, Davidson argued that the school should not shirk from the findings of his school's reading assessment results. "I don't think you can hide behind them. We need to be able to tell the community what we are doing here," he added.

Although Davidson was less sure of precisely what messages the community had gained from or assumed about the school on this aspect of student achievements, he was convinced that "somehow or other we are able to convey the message that anything any other school is doing, we can do. And because of the calibre of our staff, our particular current level of energy, and the range of things we are doing, we can actually do a lot more than a lot of other schools can."

One message Davidson suggested parents of prospective Altona students should accept was the school's invigorated capacity to respond to a variety of learning requirements. "It does not matter what category a youngster fits into—whether they are the brightest of bright or the ones who need fixing up, the ones who need intervention because of problems that they are currently experiencing in their learning. Or those whose parents may need motivating and switching on to their kid's education. We can demonstrate that we do all of that very, very well," he said.

In 1998, Altona High had become a school where, Davidson believed, "Youngsters are provided with experiences that they understand can be of benefit to them." Rather than the school providing a planned formal set of experiences on the basis of a traditional curriculum, Davidson urged teachers to be creative and adventurous in crafting "a whole platter of opportunities for students which relate to helping these young people to be able to achieve their potential, be fulfilled, and lead productive lives."

Amidst the considerable progress which has been achieved in the past 5 years in particular, Davidson realizes many problems remain and some have only been partially overcome. The combined efforts of administration and staff to provide authentic schooling which ultimately connected with a guaranteed transition pathway at the end of Grade 10 has laid a firm foundation for students who can, or want to, learn. Nonetheless, he acknowledges that a vocal minority of students continue to resist making the most of their learning experiences at Altona. In the main, it is those students who, due to their past or some current experiences and what they observe around them, are unable to find school sufficiently meaningful. For the overwhelming majority of Altona students, school in 1998 plays a positive role in their lives.

The extent to which many students identify with being from materially poor families remains strong. On numerous occasions teachers have observed students criticising particular classmates and friends who have given an impression of being from a materially privileged or middle class family. Jane Bannon, a Grade 9 teacher who is in her fifth year at the school, said "if you are a student who is clearly from a family that has money, sort of a middle class income, you try to downplay that. Those students try to look poor or else they get teased and described as being snobby or a 'richo'. So the prevailing identity is that you are from a low socioeconomic group. I come across that situation quite a bit. You don't look wealthy if you are a student from here."

Practices which foster acceptance or marginality of students by other students on the basis of appearance or apparent wealth act as a control on, and way of endorsing, the mainstream Altona youth culture. The intolerance and fear which underpins such practices and notions of "difference" continue to extend to student interactions with teachers who are newly-appointed to the school. When Jim Lewis joined the staff at the start of 1998 he immediately noticed "a heightened sense of suspicion towards me from students. It was as if I was an outsider, to be kept outside. But once they found out that I had taught here about 7 years ago, my standing improved a fair bit. Students wear thick skins here a lot of the time but, at heart, they are sensitive about being rejected and others appearing to be better than them."

The prevalence of peer group pressures to conform to particular ways of being both inside and out of the classroom remain considerable, especially for those students who do not have a strong sense of self. However, in 1998, the pressures are not so great within classes that those students who are able and keen to do well, cannot succeed.

One initially successful contribution the school has made to student identity has been through Work Plus. The scheme, which now annually succeeds in its aim to place 100% of exiting Grade 10 students each year, has provided students with "real grounds to believe there is hope and a chance to get a job in the near future," said Mary Lempriere. The actions of the school in securing a transition to work, training or further education have been especially important to students whose parents and or grandparents have experienced long-term unemployment. Davidson remains adamant that Work Plus is vital for those students in particular. "It is no good sitting on your hands and saying 'these poor people have just got nowhere to go.' I think you have got to do the opposite and encourage them."

By and large, students are more actively, and productively, learning in classes. Yet, when teaching is highly abstract, lacks a context, or students are unable to relate their learning to practical life matters, they quickly become disheartened by the experience. In that respect, there is not a collective perspective across Altona in relation to a uniform way or commitment to actively engaging students' learning.

Some teachers continue to place considerable emphasis on pre-packaged curriculum in order to respond to their own or central authorities' view of what students need to know. A greater number of Altona teachers continue to adapt what they teach as an outcome of their understandings of the types of students they have in class. The former strategy requires much more student adaptability, confidence, and tenacity than the latter. The latter strategy has a greater, yet still difficult, prospect of leading to in-depth learning.

Both Ian Davidson and Altona staff remain keenly aware that the learning culture needs to further improve at Altona. However, he continues to rail at unfair comparisons of Altona students with students from schools where, traditionally, there have been strong learning cultures. To underplay the nature and complexity of where many Altona students were when they entered the school, compared to what they had subsequently achieved over 4 years, is to unfairly downplay the school's achievements. It also fails to adequately comprehend the profound impact which students' prior personal and learning experiences have had on them. As well, it obscures the manifest contributions which an administration and staff, as a team, have made on behalf of, and in the interests of, students. "It is important that we understand what has been and continues to be, achieved. Professionals have to be given credit for understanding what needed to be done in the best interests of students," said Davidson.

While Altona's administration and staff have made considerable gains in rebutting negative images of the school and its students, many prejudices remain throughout the surrounding non-Altona community, in particular. These limited, stereotyped views of the suburb, the school, and Altona's youth still imply that the area and its people are on "the wrong side of the tracks." It is likely to take many decades, and numerous celebrations of further achievements, before such stereotypical views will be largely ameliorated.

Amidst the many broad-based achievements that have occurred at Altona over the past 5 years, the most compelling one is that many students have given effect to their right to learn, regardless of their individual circumstances. It is unclear how long- or short-lived will be the transition arrangements which Grade 10 students have been contracted into, as a way of supporting their immediate employment hopes and galvanising their later life prospects. However, it is unequivocal that Davidson and his staff have refused to allow circumstances and the harsher aspects of Australian society to extinguish the learning opportunities which they believe Altona students deserve.

ALTONA HIGH SCHOOL CASE STUDY: OUTLINE

Setting the Scene

Altona community on the "wrong side of the tracks":

> absence of men in households
> young person's place
> lack of post school qualifications
> high unemployment
> blue collar emphasis
> low income levels and home ownership

The Leadership Team: Creating Intergenerational Links

Principal:

> wants schools to be more adventurous
> aware of situations faced by students and role of school because of straight talking and dealing
> contempt for those who criticize schools and poorly motivated teachers
> gets ideas and becomes "driven"
> expects a lot from staff
> passionate about advancing interests of students
> sees the humorous as well as heart-rendering
> questionable organizational skills
> previously authoritarian and still not always consultative
> enjoys work, including long hours
> gives others the credit
> bristles at notion of all schools being compared on a narrow set of criteria
> realistic about situation, sees a need for the community to reclaim ownership of its own destiny, aware of time and financial constrains
> works very hard in community, at expense of instructional leadership
> a one-year professional development (PD) interstate fellowship

Deputy Principal:

> provides instructional/complementary leadership

frank, calls "spade a spade"
supports principal and staff
sees herself as "linker"
sees need to lead by example
committed
not self-serving
high energy, always giving 100%
principal and deputy principal trust each other
lack of time, e.g.,
 gives privilege to immediate and practical
 agrees documentation not kept in place
 curriculum policy not kept up with actual changes
 sees need to review and update curriculum
 believes mission "known" but not written down
intolerant of uncommitted, slack teachers
believes more needs to be demanded of students
supports teachers/teams including those experiencing difficulties with students

Continuing With the Status Quo No Longer an Option: A Rattling of Cages

Altona in 1994:

student culture prevailed
alienation, anger, violence, chaos, battleground
student feelings of rejection, seeing little meaning in school and facing a future
 of unemployment
absenteeism high
growing sense of frustration and tiredness amongst many long-serving teachers
the previously highly reputed sub-school structure now dysfunctional
inappropriate principal response i.e., authoritarian
respected teacher successfully risked confronting principal
despair and exhaustion catalyst for change
Middle School seen as the appropriate response
 idea from principal's PD
 discussions with staff
 respected teachers visit other Middle schools
 staff meetings, leading to a 75% vote in favour
17 teachers transfer at end of 1994

Changes Everywhere: Trust, Persistence, and Risk-Taking

Middle School:

structural change

risks for teachers but willing to go along with for promise of improved learning
culture
little teacher preparation for
high teacher commitment to and interaction about
support and involvement of respected teacher opinion leader
PD initially outside but later inside the school
things get worse before they get better with modest improvement by end of
1995
Year 9/10 teacher scepticism
teachers new to the school experience problems, especially with little induction
importance of professional development

Time-Out Room:

teacher initiated

Work Plus

principal's initiative
staff support because of principal's student-focussed motives, but "bulldozed"
in staff meetings
principal trusts teachers, e.g., one or more teachers coopted to champion
teachers constantly encouraged by the principal to initiate things that have
benefit for students, e.g.,
Year 10 class visits a local Primary School
Year 9 graffiti cleaning day
Some changes did not have majority staff support:
At-Risk Off-Campus program
Accelerated Learning curriculum
Having so many initiatives creates its own problems, e.g.,
lack of time, coordination, and energy for program evaluation/curriculum
review

Re-creation, Lessons, Challenges

Middle School:

Middle School, with its attention to classroom interactions and developmentally
attentive teaching took 4 years, i.e., one cohort to move through the school,
for noticeable success.
Results for the overwhelming majority of students included improved
motivation, work ethic, and capacity to respond to a variety of learning
environments. The school is now seen to have a positive role in their lives
and to provide "a bit of stability."

Lessons:

cultural change a necessary first step BUT can be a long-term process.

being open to new ways as well as holding on to what is educationally
important

teachers continue to share—collegial discussion and support are very important

having a place and time for the sharing e.g., staffroom, school-based
professional development induction of new staff, travelling together

staff humour

school/teachers being able to choose, to have critical eyes, especially in times of
multiple demands including from governments

empowered teachers not hamstrung by imposed, tightly prescribed curriculum.

understanding and working within the context of the school e.g., 30% of
students at Altona with a reading age less than 9 years

administrators need to be aware of teacher stress and act in a timely way to
alleviate it

teachers need to be aware of student stress and act in a timely way to alleviate
it, especially with cooperation of parent(s) and the community

Challenges:

learning culture needs to continually improve

given limited funds and difficulties created when out of the school, PD mainly
school based

negative stereotypes of Altona and its community persist

as the changes bring order, concern needs to turn to lack of student achievement

CHAPTER 6

THE HERONWOOD CASE STUDY

SETTING THE SCENE

Just over 10,000 people resided in Heronwood in the mid-1980s. In terms of the town's history, it was a relatively prosperous period. However, it was an era that, in some respects, was drawing to a close. The once burgeoning population of mostly working class townspeople had not escaped several key changes which affected almost all who lived in the state's regional localities during the 1980s. As a result, by 1991, the town was annually losing about 30 citizens—as, for example, individuals relocated in order to find work or resettled elsewhere due to marital or partner separations. Indeed, by 1991, 2 in 10 Heronwood households (with children) had no men in them. Not only had the town's population peaked in the previous decade, but the proportion of the labour in the full-time workforce had gradually reduced since the mid 1980s.

One in 10 Heronwood citizens between the ages of 25 and 64 years was unemployed. For those aged between 15 and 24 years who were able to work, the unemployment rate was twice as bad. Whilst unemployment in Heronwood in 1991 was least likely to be experienced by those who occupied professional positions, fewer than 250 of the town's citizens held a university qualification. Furthermore, whilst many professionals worked in the town, a significant number of them lived in neighbouring towns. The most common post-school level of attainment amongst the town's people was a skilled vocational qualification. The dominant industries in Heronwood were wholesale and retail trade, manufacturing and community services. Together, those industries employed nearly two-thirds of the town's employees. Nonetheless, for every adult in Heronwood who held a post-school qualification, there were two who had no qualifications.

While the median income of families in Heronwood in 1991 was $24,680, one in four families survived on a total annual income of less than $16,000. Also in 1991, median individual income in Heronwood was $10,680. Those income levels were markedly lower than nearby more affluent towns. Although 70% of dwellings were owned or being purchased by those who lived in them, the median monthly mortgage payment was, at $375, relatively expensive. Yet rental costs, by comparison, were even cheaper and typically cost about $290 a month. Whereas

23% of the population comprised children aged less than 15 years, the town also had a significant number of older citizens—with 16% aged 65 or over. The median age of Heronwood citizens in 1991 was 34 years.

As was the case in most rural parts of the State, church attendances at Heronwood were typically poor despite the fact that nearly 80% of citizens identified as Christians. Of those, most were Anglican, Catholic or Uniting Church in denomination. Ten percent of the population held no formal religious identity.

In a similar vein to many towns nearby, 90% of Heronwood's population was born in the country. Moreover, a majority of those not born in the country emigrated from New Zealand, the United Kingdom and the Netherlands. Overall, by 1991, Heronwood was characterized by a population that was qualified for a manufacturing era. With the onset of an Information Age, which was heavily geared by technology, the town found itself with increasing unemployment, poverty, family breakdowns and alienation. For the first time in its history, it was becoming evident that many young people would not achieve the favourable standard of living or labour market conditions that either their parents or grandparents had, for most of their adult years.

By the time Andrew Ingram took up the principalship of Heronwood High, a Grade 7 to 10 (ages 13 to 16) government school in a state which has a three-tier schooling system: primary Kindergarten to Grade 6), high (Grades 7 to 10), and college (Grades 11 and 12), in February 1991, more than half of the school's 47 full- and part-time teachers knew to expect considerable change. Ingram, who had been notified of his promotion in December of the previous year, talked with any teachers he came across in the township of Heronwood over the summer holidays. That Ingram managed to discuss his aspirations and plans for Heronwood High with nearly 30 teachers was a measure of his local networks and leadership commitment to ushering in an era of positive change at the school. Whether at a sports venue, fraternal association, community health centre, the Heronwood shopping strip or through sheer chance meetings, Ingram talked with teachers and listened intently to their often lengthy comments about the school. The exchanges not only provided Ingram with a detailed insight into the workings of Heronwood High but also left him convinced that most of the school's teachers were deeply committed educators.

Equally apparent to Ingram however, was an impression that the school's progress in the previous decade had, at best, been incremental and founded on delivering "more of the same." Indeed, Ingram learned that, under the previous principal, no teacher had been promoted out of the school in 11 years. "That was an incredible statistic. It wasn't that there weren't good teachers, it was just that the principal was keeping them at the school. There was a very, very strong teaching staff—many of whom should have been promoted in order to develop their skills, learn more and grow," said Ingram.

The damning fact of teachers' non-promotion at Heronwood under the previous principal proved to be costly to those individuals and the school. Not only had teachers missed out on the rewards and challenges that can come from accessing promotions and working in different settings, it also meant that staff turnover had stagnated. As a consequence, internally, the school had not benefited from the diversity of experiences, ideas and standpoints which often accompany the arrival of new staff. Moreover, a culture of repetition rather than renewal characterized much of teachers' work. "Initially what I saw was staid, conservative, functioning classrooms—but not much innovation," said Ingram. Of particular concern to Ingram, once he started at the school was that, by and large, he "wasn't seeing kids turned on by their learning." By contrast, Ingram's observations of classrooms in his early days at the school resulted in him seeing "a lot of really good, positive interactions between teachers and kids. That was the strength of the school—the quality of the teaching staff and their interactions with the kids. They were extremely strong, indeed. So their foundations were strong."

Although Ingram had lived on the outskirts of Heronwood for 15 years, he knew much about "what happened in town and how things ticked." Helped by being an avid and extremely astute "people watcher," Ingram had noticed several of the troubling changes to life in Heronwood in the late 1980s and early 1990s. Job losses, in particular, were increasing as more and more businesses were either being closed or taken over by larger companies and the work of many employees was being done by technology.

With greater frequency, Ingram was also seeing young adults—and their parents—unemployed or engaged in casual and part-time work. Not surprisingly, the 37-year-old principal was also hearing about or noticing greater alienation amongst Heronwood youth, increasing family breakups and a heightening intolerance toward change and diversity.

CHANGING LEADERS, CHANGING TIMES

Just as life at Heronwood High was shaped indirectly and directly by the experience and circumstance of the town it served, Ingram believed that the school needed to change dramatically in order to improve the learning and, ultimately, the life chances of its students. Heronwood High needed to better capitalize on the strengths of its teachers if students were to become active, engaged and adaptive learners.

At one of his first addresses to staff in 1991, Ingram expressed his confidence in the capacities of Heronwood teachers. "I trust you to do the job," he told them. As well, Ingram promised to provide an open style of leadership that was characterized by consistency and fairness. Part of the transparency, on his part, would include "opening up all those lines of communication and an open sharing of information." In the same meeting, Ingram flagged his desire to both improve the learning culture of students and actively negotiate with teachers in order to increase the school's effectiveness.

Even though Ingram broadly outlined his vision for the school to staff, he believed teachers needed to be significantly involved in both "imagining" and redrawing any vision that was ultimately to be documented and acted upon. To achieve widespread staff involvement in this process, Ingram, in conjunction with staff, negotiated a planning structure which would enable teachers to develop, "own" and implement the school's new vision. He also signalled to staff that collaborative and transparent processes would characterize all future planning processes at Heronwood High: while particular members would make up specific committees and groups, any staff member could attend any meetings and—with the exception of confidential, need-to-know matters—participate fully in their decision making.

Whilst Ingram's stance represented a marked and refreshing difference to his predecessor, "many staff were cautious about having a new principal," said Francis Sullivan, who had been at the school since 1984. "The previous principal was completely different in a whole lot of ways. He was a very shy man and, like many shy people, they cover it up with arrogance and remoteness. This was his way of dealing with people. Really, for many years, he continued to function fairly independently of what teachers did, and the assistant principal and staff generally ran the school. The school was supported in that way, and I think that was one of the reasons why it was such a good staff—that we had a lot of very confident teachers who really ran the place. Nonetheless, the man was an excellent science teacher, there was no doubt about that."

May Somerville, who was in her fifth year at Heronwood when Ingram took up the principalship, recalled "when staff knew Andrew was coming, there were initially some reservations, partly because staff felt they'd managed well under a principal who had an entirely different style of leadership, and partly because of a fear of the unknown. This fear was compounded by a rumour that went around suggesting Andrew had been 'marked for rapid promotion'. Whether in fact this was true, I don't know. The staff had been very, very, settled plus many had been here 20 years, and only known one or two principals."

Charles Preston, who had worked with the principal whom Ingram replaced for 4 years, welcomed the change. "The differences were vast. When I look at leaders in a school, I look for three qualities. First of all I look for their personal qualities in terms of the way they deal with colleagues and students. Then I look to see whether they've got an 'educational' brain. Thirdly, they've got to have an 'administrative' brain. Unfortunately, the previous principal rated fairly low on all three qualities." Within a year of working with Ingram, Preston had concluded that "Andrew was the only principal I'd worked with who achieved a big tick on all three criteria."

Somerville's memory of her first Heronwood principal being distant from staff and difficult to interact with, matched the recollections of many colleagues, including Pierce James. "He was very aloof. He wasn't an easy man to talk to socially or at any other time. In fact, he had a social problem. Staff found him very aloof." Yet, like Somerville, James recognized several positive attributes in the former principal, including a capacity to keep a confidence. "You could go and talk in confidence, complete confidence to him. And you knew if he was on your side, or if he agreed with you, then you had his full support, and things went well. He was a good man and really helped out a lot of students' families who had difficulties. He was a compassionate man."

Despite a widespread perception amongst staff of the inadequacies of the previous principal, his leadership had, by default, contributed to teacher empowerment. The leadership vacuum had been responded to by the assistant principal and key teachers initiating those actions considered necessary for the functioning of the school and classrooms. With Ingram's appointment "several teachers were concerned that their capacity to keep initiating would be restricted," said John Evens, who had joined the staff of Heronwood High in 1987.

Conscious of the micropolitics both in and beyond schools, Ingram also chose, in his first staff meeting, to outline the mutuality that contributed to trust between staff and a principal. "We talked about trust, more loyalty, I guess. I said to them 'right, I expect you to be loyal to the school' and by that I meant if they had anything to say about the school that was derogatory or detrimental, that I should hear it first and someone in the community second. I extended that to talking about colleagues as well. So I expected them to be loyal to colleagues, and, if they had interpersonal issues they needed to take up with other members of staff, I said they 'ought to do it face-to-face'." In addition, Ingram told staff he disagreed with staffrooms being used to discuss frustrations about colleagues, including himself. "In effect, I said 'it's no good getting into staffrooms and talking about the issues that concern the leadership of the school and me, in particular, without me being informed about it as well'."

Because of what Ingram had been told about the school and its leadership, he believed that staff needed considerable additional support. One form of support he promised at another staff meeting again related to trust. "We talked about trust, so that from then on, they could trust me to do the things I was going to do and follow up things I said I was going to follow up."

"At the start of 1991 school year, staff memories were still fresh concerning the type of leadership we'd had and the dampening impact that had created over a long period for many teachers," said Alison Gavin, who at that stage was a subject coordinator at the school. "But teachers wanted to see whether Andrew's promises would be fulfilled, and so there was an air of caution amongst some of the staff for a fair while." Gavin's attention was drawn to Ingram's "outstanding interpersonal skills" during the first week of school. "He knew my name instantly," she said. Ingram's early dealings with Gavin registered strongly because, in the 3 years of working with the school's previous principal, her name had rarely been mentioned when they interacted. "He had trouble with names. Actually, with him, I didn't exist really."

Ingram's quickly established, daily habit of being in the school and being available to teachers at short notice provided a sharp contrast with the style of the previous principal. It also helped to build connections with staff who sought clarification of issues or required assistance of some sort. By walking around the school at least twice daily observing classrooms along the way, Ingram rapidly built up a dense understanding of the school's culture. In turn, his roving presence was interpreted by many staff as early evidence of the priority Ingram gave to teaching and learning in the school. But not every teacher was immediately impressed by Ingram's "visible" leadership, according to Greg Davey. "Some staff were sceptical about Andrew's appearances in classes and the corridors and a few clearly disliked them," recalled Davey. "They didn't know how to interpret them or what they might lead to," he added.

Aware of the prospect that such a presence might be threatening to some teachers who did not know him well, Ingram consistently maintained a positive and low-key approach when entering classrooms. Just as in his first few staff meetings with teachers he sought to establish relations with teachers by offering a leadership style that few could disagree with, Ingram tried to defuse any insecurities and tensions teachers had when moving into their "turf," through affirmation. "What struck me was not only the fact that he was in and around classes but that he was genuinely interested in what teachers and the students were doing," said Doreen Woodley, the then Grade 8 coordinator.

At other staff meetings early in 1991, Ingram raised the matter of teachers' professional development, "because the amount of professional learning that had been occurring here was almost nil. If there was a desert at Heronwood, in terms of teachers' learning, that was it," he said. Most teachers realized that, in the preceding decade, there had been scant attention to either individual or staff-wide professional development. As well as denying them access to learning beyond the school "it also meant that teachers had to draw on their own or their colleagues' reserves as a way of generating new ideas. And that could only go so far when everyone was in the same situation," said Jane Allsop, who had transferred to the school in 1986. Also during term one, Ingram clarified with teachers what professional development they'd undertaken and would like to undertake. "As well, I asked what areas of school they'd like to be involved in, where they saw their opportunities with promotion, how they felt about teaching as opposed to administrative tasks. We covered a whole range of issues concerning teachers' professional lives. That gave me a really clear picture of where they were going. It also established a lot of trust, because it meant I had a profile of the staff that I was then able to acknowledge to them."

The readiness, and in many instances keenness, of staff to access further learning soon resulted in teachers frequently undertaking professional development activities both within and beyond the school. "The school was literally saturated with professional development—I had teachers going everywhere. It got a bit out of control in many ways, but I needed to get the lifelong learning message across to staff," said Ingram. Criticisms of the initiative were known about and acknowledged by Ingram—especially in relation to the number of times it took teachers away from their classes. Yet, for Ingram, professional development represented a keyway in which teachers not only could develop their knowledge and skills but also become more open to different ideas and values. The encouragement and material support Ingram provided to teachers who took up professional development opportunities "helped some of us feel that he was committed to teachers as well as the benefits which would flow to the kids," said Debra Hyams, one of the school's English teachers who attended a series of out-of-school language workshops. Apart from providing teachers with new learning experiences, the act of attending a seminar or visiting another school during the day was a marked departure in teachers' work practices. Hyams found "being able to identify and attend something that was professionally relevant to be invigorating."

Not all of Hyam's colleagues found the professional development opportunities to be wholly worthwhile. "Some of it was good, but often I found the students were unsettled by my absence and played up a lot when I was away and initially once I returned," claimed Ralph Hipwell. The disruption to students was a factor in several teachers' decisions to curb or discontinue professional development activities that took them away from the school. Like a majority of the staff, Hipwell continued to identify and attend externally-provided professional development, especially in the early part of 1991. "In relative terms, students misbehaved less during the warmer weather and so I made some planning decisions around that—plus I knew Andrew was wanting teachers to grow and alter some of what we did," recalled Hipwell.

During subsequent staff meetings in term one, Ingram elaborated on the commitment he had originally given to open leadership and governance within the school plus his expectation of staff honouring the arrangement. Typically, once a major agenda item came up, Ingram firstly endorsed the principle of "communicating really openly with teachers, indeed to the entire school community, so that there were no secrets." Aware of teachers' perceptions that, in prior years, the school had been "pretty secretive," Ingram reinforced his opposition to autocratic leadership and restricted communication by fully detailing the agenda item and openly responding to teachers' questions or comments. "The other thing I did was really push the notion of professionalism, with things like confidentiality, and made sure that teachers were aware that, with the increased flow of communication, came increased responsibilities as well."

The combination of hearing Ingram's commitment to openness and subsequently seeing him "deliver as promised," according to John Evens, helped build teacher confidence in Heronwood's new principal. "It also reduced some of the fears amongst staff that related to the unknown—the unknown which comes with any new principal," said Evens.

In the course of having worked in schools for 15 years, Ingram had interacted with thousands of individuals. Amongst the educators he had mixed with, many had impressed him. Those he had admired most were appreciated because, amongst other qualities, their manner was consistent "in good and difficult times." It was a quality Ingram believed excellent teachers demonstrated and one that was essential in effective leaders. It was a feature of his leadership that he valued and "what teachers looked to me for—how consistent and fair I could be. I was always both consistent and fair, which was 90% of the battle, on two fronts. If the people who walked through my door found the same person every day of the week at any time of the day, under any circumstances, I figured that was of real value to the people who worked in the school." As well, Ingram believed it was especially important to students that they have an approachable leader who had a consistent manner. "So that, when the kids came in to my office, they didn't have to decide whether I was in a good or bad mood, they'd find the same person. And just as with staff, students then needed to be able to trust me, confident that I would listen to what they said, provide the information required and, when appropriate respect confidentiality."

The more teachers saw of Ingram consistently being a caring, attentive and responsive leader, the more teachers continued to consult with him about initiatives they wanted to pursue. Louis Stedman said his one-to-one dealings with Ingram were particularly productive because "he seemed to have his finger on the pulse. Anything that related to the school, or remotely related to benefiting the school, he seemed to know enough about to either point you in the direction for further information, provide practical support or give you an opinion on it." With the introduction of school-based autonomy over their budget in 1991, Stedman claimed

Ingram supported his many requests for monetary back up with student program initiatives. "Depending on the request, Andrew would say 'Yep, I'll find some money, we'll cover that little hole there or we'll patch that up.' It was good, and good to know that there were no sanctions if I took a risk with something and it failed. I knew pretty early on that he was supportive of what I was trying to achieve, even when things went wrong."

Coinciding with schools gaining greater decision-making capacity over their budgets, was a heightened capacity for autonomous planning. To take advantage of greater decision making powers "we established a Planning Group," said Ingram. Within the umbrella Group were many smaller committees that focussed on feeding back recommendations about specific issues. One of the key offshoots of the Planning Group was a committee that "looked at ways we could better involve ourselves in the community, and have the community involved with us." Through newsletters and by communicating through personal and local networks, staff and active members of Parents and Friends Association, and Ingram "spread the message that there were ways in which Heronwood parents could play a part in kids' schooling," said Debra Hyams. Initially there was little response from parents: "They held out, but as soon as the community saw a change in Heronwood, they started to give a little bit too," said Ingram. Hence term one of Ingram's first year at Heronwood resulted in pronounced efforts to further develop staff professionally and enhance the involvements of parents in both the school and the education of students. The initiatives were underpinned by leadership that was predicated on trust and mutual responsibility. For Ingram, it meant that by the end of first term he and the teachers "were one staff."

THE SECOND YEAR – 1992

Although most staff and Heronwood's new principal believed they had good grounds for being optimistic about the changes that took place in the school in 1991, not every teacher agreed. By the end of that year, several teachers had applied for transfers to other schools. As well, a couple of teachers gained promotions to other schools which took effect in 1992. Hence by the start of the 1992 school year eight new teachers joined Heronwood High's staff of 46 full-time and part-time teachers. Most were pleased with the transfers and immediately impressed by "Andrew's relaxed style," recalled Anthea Andrianopolous, who had moved to the area "for pretty much personal, lifestyle reasons." Daniel Wade, who also shifted to the outskirts on Heronwood because he "wanted to settle on an acreage," was equally impressed with his new principal's welcoming and supportive "interpersonal approach." But it was not long before Wade "heard grumblings. There had been an old guard here for a long time and Andrew represented change. A lot of the grumblings were about student discipline, problems with discipline and that sort of thing. Some teachers were saying it had 'gone down the drain' and that discipline 'was not the way it used to be'."

Shortly after Anthea Andrianopolous joined the staff of Heronwood, she frequently found herself in conversations with several teachers who were not only concerned about student discipline but also critical of their principal's level of empathy with "difficult students who misbehaved. Many staff believed that Andrew was too supportive of students, especially in relation to students who played up. They also felt that Andrew needed to be more pro-teacher."

Ingram was acutely aware of the disappointment felt by some teachers who had sent students to him to be further disciplined—and subsequently discovered their principal "hadn't read the riot act." Their frustration with him rarely resulted in Ingram changing his response strategies when dealing with students who misbehaved. Ingram consistently sought to engage troubled or troubling students in an honest conversation, identify mutually acceptable or reasonable behaviour and endorse their teacher's efforts. When students had been sent to him because of apparent misbehaviour, Ingram considered that it was vital that he tried to understand the student as well as the incident that triggered the problem, rather than simply or uniformly adopting a punitive response. For Ingram, the strategy was put of an overall effort "to reset the kids' expectations of what the school ought to be like." In the course of students reporting to Ingram over behavioural difficulties, their principal wanted them to know that they had a right to state their case and have it considered. The process also provided Ingram with a chance to learn about the values and attitudes which both prevailed amongst many students, and were revealed through their conversations.

As well as gaining insights into the reasoning and worries of students, the interactions often enabled Ingram to "turn their arguments around so that students could see why their teacher had become so annoyed with them. While that was good for those students, it frequently fell short of teachers' expectations. Some of them wanted a more autocratic approach," said Betty Palmer, who joined the staff in 1992 and had come to the school with a reputation for "helping troubled students and slow learners." Palmer's observations of Ingram's interactions with students were not confined only to those who misbehaved. "When I arrived, it was clear that the children saw him as someone they could go to easily. Not as a friend, but kind of like that. Whenever I heard them talking about him, it wasn't with trepidation or fear. It was like 'I'll talk to him about this'. So the relationship between the principal and students was one of ease."

Ingram's efforts to affirm students by being open to their viewpoints, even if he challenged them, "helped his standing in the eyes of many teachers as well as the student population," said Palmer. "His regular presence in the school grounds during break times plus the fact that he taught—and taught extraordinarily well—added to his credibility," she claimed. Previously Palmer had taught in a school where the principal "rarely taught and wasn't effective in the classroom. There was a lot of indecision from the top and there wasn't a great deal of respect from kids or teachers towards him." The contrast between Palmer's previous principal and Ingram was made even sharper "because Andrew was so keen to improve the teaching and learning at Heronwood." The emphasis which Ingram placed on the classroom was apparent to most teachers—including his detractors and those who did not see the need to change their teaching practices.

Although Ingram was aware of ongoing "pockets of resistance" amongst staff concerning the need to expand teachers' knowledge and use of more teaching strategies, he continued to encourage colleagues to "take up professional development opportunities." "Teachers who were sceptical about the need for change plus those who were open to it often came back from a professional development session quite enthusiastic," said Daniel Wade. However, for those who were unconvinced or wary of the need for teachers to be better able to engage student learning, "discontent remained. With some staff it was about being scared to go out on a limb and to try something new, in case it all come back in their faces," recalled Wade.

At the same time, many of those teachers who were reluctant to embrace the heightened emphasis on classroom practice had accepted that Ingram had kept his pledge about open leadership and active collaboration in school-based decision making. The latitude to initiate, which staff had crafted amongst themselves due to the previous principal's lack of instructional leadership in particular, had not been erased by Ingram. Thus whilst fears about being disempowered under Ingram's active leadership had dissipated in one sense, in another way, some teachers' sense of control continued to be challenged by the prospect of having to adopt a greater range of teaching strategies. "It was a time at Heronwood when there was enormous change. Not only in terms of what Andrew was trying to achieve, but also in terms of the political interfering, from the outside—the Centre, basically. Principals were told which way to push us. Usually it wasn't for the better. There seemed to be a lot of people out there trying to justify their jobs, pushing change for change's sake," recalled one senior staff member.

A traditional antipathy toward non-school-based personnel and externally-developed policies existed across much of Heronwood staff. It was quickly drawn on to delegitimize or at least dampen Ingram's persistent efforts to improve professional practice—as a precursor to improving student engagement and outcomes. "At the time, it seemed like another instance of unnecessary change. You would be half way, two-thirds of the way through a bright new program which had lots of potential and into which you'd put a lot of hours, and somebody else would come along with a new direction and you were thrown back into the melting pot, having to head off in another direction," said Louise Stedman.

Stedman claimed Ingram was not immune to the influences of Central or District edicts. However, with any such key demands, "Andrew sat down and made judgements with the staff or Planning Groups about the suitability of many of those initiatives. Sometimes they would reject an initiative, other times they would modify it. In that sense, Andrew took account of what Heronwood was aiming for and tried to minimize the impact of imposed initiatives, as much as was possible." According to Stedman, Ingram was "always politically astute and learnt early that if something was being pushed that we—the people who were applying it—didn't want, that was to be accepted. He knew that without sufficient support, anything implemented under those circumstances would be only given a half-hearted attempt. So some things were put on the back burner."

Though occasionally disappointed by the scepticism which some staff attached to change initiatives that evolved either externally or from within the school, Ingram continued to embed his collegial relationships through actions which reflected optimism and tenacity. Not only was he optimistic about what could be achieved if a large number of staff improved their practice, he was confident that ultimately most would do so. Because of his unremitting belief in the need to improve what students achieved at Heronwood, he was prepared to accept some time delays in the course of working toward the greater goal. For Ingram, such delays were "understandable." They were also a minor trade off in comparison to not proceeding with any attempt to improve the school's teaching and learning. In 1992, those considerations contributed to Ingram spending "90% of my time on teaching and learning."

The honesty which was apparent in Ingram's dealings with staff was appreciated by most teachers, according to Charles Preston. "Even those who were uncomfortable with Andrew's change agenda were grateful for his frankness—we knew where we stood with him. Staff were a lot happier on that level. Plus he put a lot of things into perspective, especially when staff felt a bit overloaded or up against it."

Ingram claimed he injected "a lot of humour, a lot of good natured stirring into relationships, in order to help staff maintain a balance. Teachers could often be their own worst enemies in terms of getting things out of perspective. Sometimes I reminded them of their achievements because they didn't get their heads up long enough to actually see what had happened, what they had achieved. I also reminded them that school life wasn't as bad as they thought it was."

When Adele Arnold transferred to Heronwood High in 1993, she was aware of "the poor reputation it had around town during the late 80s." The reasons attached to "the gossip weren't clear or based on anything in particular," she recalled. But because she had lived in Heronwood for most of her life, she'd "heard the negative comments plenty of times." Sometimes the idle chat had come from parents, other times from townsfolk who, amidst their deepening alienation with a changing social and economic environment, saw Heronwood High as somehow "falling short of the mark." Arnold's "inside information" about the school, which she had gained from colleagues just prior to transferring to Heronwood, proved to be more reliable and current than the casual observations she'd previously heard. "Under Andrew's leadership, the school had grown. When I arrived, it was clear that Andrew didn't purely base his leadership role on the education of the child. He cared about the whole development of children. It was great."

Arnold's early perceptions of the leadership were complemented by what she saw as "generally, an excellent staff. They were very caring and tried hard to make everyone, including newcomers, feel comfortable. It worked quite well."

Tom Jackson joined the Heronwood staff at the same time as his English faculty colleague Adele Arnold. Like Arnold, Jackson was immediately struck by "the quality of the principal and staff. In terms of getting along together, they were a pretty cohesive group." In sharp contrast to the school Jackson had come from, "there was active leadership from Andrew where he supported staff and was prepared to take risks in order to improve things. He encouraged staff to experiment with new ways in classes and wasn't deterred when things didn't always work." Despite Jackon's positive early impressions about the school's leadership and staff, he found difficulty "in being accepted by the students. I was seen as an outsider."

The resistance and suspicion toward incoming teachers from much of the student population had long been "part of the scene at Heronwood," according to Catriona

Lorimer. However by 1993, it was also difficult for some new staff "because they came into a very student empowered school—and that wasn't typical of many high schools." Lorimer, who was widely regarded on staff as being one of Heronwood High's outstanding teachers, claimed that the empowerment of students had occurred, in large part, because of and during Ingram's leadership at the school.

"From the outset, it was obvious that Andrew liked kids, and the kids knew that. And with each year that just grew. For example, if there was an injustice between a staff member and a student, the student would feel quite empowered to go to Andrew and put their view. Not that he would necessarily agree with them but everyone, including students, knew he was very much an open-door person."

Having an open-door policy, however, did not mean Ingram accepted or endorsed everything that was told to him in his office. Indeed, as a result of hearing about the marginalisation of some students by other students one day, Ingram organized a special assembly, which was attended by nearly 700 students and staff. "The kids from Room 45 always got a hard time. They were our Special Ed. Kids. As you'd expect, there was always a bit of a thing amongst the kids and the Special kids were targeted," said Ingram. Tolerant as Ingram was, he had tired of the bullying and harassment Room 45 students had received. At the time, the volume of it seemed to be at fever-pitch level. The abuse deeply angered Ingram because nothing got him more upset than seeing "kids not being able to live their lives and not being accepted for what they were."

At the assembly Ingram "ran it with just those kids and got a few of them to say what it meant to be ridiculed in the way they had been. It was a bit of a tear-jerker really, but it had a significant impact on the way the student population subsequently accepted others into the school."

One offspring from the heavy investment in teachers' professional development ushered in by Ingram was an increasing effort by teachers to negotiate with students on curriculum matters. Lorimer believed it was an effective avenue for engaging students and providing them with meaningful learning experiences. "A lot of staff started to use interactive Barry Bennett type stuff, and focussed tasks as well as accounting tasks. Students in my classes were expected to negotiate the curriculum. I would also suggest topics and we would sit and talk about topics. If students didn't say 'I'd like to do this . . .' I would be disappointed. However, for teachers who were unused to this type of student involvement, it could be very threatening."

The difficulties new teachers to the school experienced in being accepted by students were ultimately reduced over the time they were there provided it became clear that, in classes, teachers cared. "Students could tell when teachers cared about them," said Lorimer. An ethic of caring was an ongoing feature of Lorimer's classes and a means she used to connect with and engage students. "I think students have always felt positive in my room. And cared for. I've made a point of trying very hard to speak each kid's name every lesson." With quiet, shy, discouraged, or only partly engaged students—as well as those who actively asserted themselves— Lorimer employed a series "of games where, in effect, I kept looking at them until they said 'hello', just stupid little things, little tricks, juvenile things." Lorimer's efforts to make her classes inclusive, affirming environments were, according to

Louis Stedman, as successful with students as were her professional development sessions with colleagues.

Despite the widespread respect for Lorimer's work with students which Francis Sullivan claimed "characterized her teaching from day one at Heronwood," it took an enormous amount of cajoling by Ingram, and others to convince Lorimer to lead a series of staff development exercises on literacy. Irrespective of the praise she had often received from Ingram and numerous colleagues in relation to her classroom teaching, plus her strong sense of achievement with students, Lorimer regarded teaching as "one of the biggest mysteries and most frightening gifts on the planet." Her extraordinary teaching talents did not prevent her from recognising and reflecting on "the power I had over kids." Because of Lorimer's weighty sense of responsibility to students, the school and her profession, she found teaching "a pretty daunting job."

The literacy workshops run by Lorimer for staff were, by and large, enriching and uplifting. Teachers who had not been into her classes saw, for the first time, that she was "brilliant," said Alison Gavin. Although she had been aware of Lorimer's teaching capacity "because I had been to Catriona before the literacy thing and she helped me to show students how to write good essays," Gavin valued being on a staff with "so many committed colleagues." However, it was important to be able to draw on the talents of highly skilled teachers like Lorimer because, "at Heronwood, literacy was an area that people continually found hard to tackle. Going to Catriona's literacy program was a lifesaver. She really made a difference to me."

Not only did many teachers find assisting students in literacy and numeracy a challenge because of a lack of specialist skills in those areas, but Heronwood had a significant number of students who entered the school at Grade 7 with core learning difficulties.

In addition to using Lorimer to expand the understandings and skills of colleagues, Ingram provided "an enormous range of PD in key and specific learning areas for staff." Believing that "good PD with special needs kids in mind is the best PD you can do for all kids, ultimately," Ingram was conscious of not only the needs of students with specific learning disabilities but also "a large group of students who were disengaged from the mainstream curriculum."

Whether students had social, intellectual or specific learning disabilities, Ingram increasingly encouraged staff to identify the "ghost population." The ghosts were those students who "were there, teachers knew they were there, but didn't know who they were, nor did they know how to deal with them once they found them," said Ingram.

THE THIRD YEAR – 1993

Ever conscious of the ongoing and constricting economic and social changes that were taking place in the township of Heronwood, Ingram realized that students required even greater assistance from the school in order for their future life chances to be maximized. What Ingram was seeing "more and more of" on the streets and in the houses of Heronwood was greater numbers of young people—youths and adults—encountering unemployment. By 1993, more than a third of individuals between 15 and 24 years of age in Heronwood were out of work. As well as creating social frustration and disharmony amongst those young people, the unemployment contributed to a growing "underclass" within the town.

In committee and staff meetings, Ingram frequently shared with staff his observations about the changing nature of the township. To Ingram, the town's social and economic shifts meant that the school needed to ensure students who needed to be supported, were helped in increasingly disparate ways. Numerous interactions with parents and checks of the school's records added to Ingram's picture of the township. Increasing numbers of families were experiencing economic difficulties whilst, at the same time, their employment contacts and networks were evaporating. Whereas, a decade before, individuals who lost jobs could pick up unskilled or semiskilled work nearby or in Heronwood, by 1993 that rarely occurred.

As a consequence, the period of unemployment experienced by individuals "between jobs" had extended greatly. For some teenagers and young adults the break time was six months, whilst for others it was usually longer.

Increasing numbers of those in unemployment were parents or siblings of Heronwood students. More and more, the frustrations from pressurized home lives showed through in the playground and class behaviours of students at Heronwood. Fights in the school grounds during breaktimes and "rudeness in classrooms" were becoming a more common feature of school life at Heronwood. One of the responses to this problem from Ingram and Heronwood teachers, in keeping with their efforts to develop a more supportive school environment, was to undertake professional development which expanded staff understandings of student behaviour management.

Most teachers considered those professional development sessions provided staff with more explicit and coherent strategies to use, and given the perceived need for them, they were ultimately more consistently applied by staff in an effort to improve student behaviour. However, several staff believed "Andrew remained too pro-student, at the expense of teachers," recalled Clara Phineas, who had noticed that "there was a more unsettled student population at Heronwood by then, compared to the late 1980s." The "less regimented style of Andrew's leadership" was appreciated by Phineas, in part, because she "saw him as one of us, really." Ingram's leadership, Phineas claimed, had contributed to the school being "a more relaxed place to work, where teachers were a lot happier." Nonetheless, the capacity of teachers to grasp the benefits of and reasons behind Ingram's leadership style were much greater than students' understanding of their principals interactions with them. "In those days, Andrew's expectations of students weren't that high," said one staff member.

According to Phineas, it led several staff who had worked with both Ingram and his predecessor to conclude that student behaviour "was slipping under Andrew." Those staff claimed the previous principal "had higher expectations of students' behaviour."

Phineas believed Ingram's responses to student behaviour were influenced by "the big picture. Andrew looked at that and saw what was happening to those kids out there—in their homes and society. As a result, he thought we needed to look after those kids at the school." Many students "were bashed at home or had drunk parents, so Heronwood High was their safe environment," said Phineas. Knowing that, meant staff, including Phineas, accepted it was the principal and teachers' responsibility to "keep the school safe and pleasant for students."

Amidst the recognition that many student lives were troubled and that much of their behaviour was a reflection of that negative experience "in the home," teachers continued to expect "reasonable behaviour at school," said Alison Gavin. Classes were increasingly characterized by students rejecting instructions from teachers "if it was about their behaviour," said Gavin. Often times "it was hard to work out just what had triggered the really bad behaviour of a class. But you knew they were off! And it made for a bad day for teaching and for me," Adele Arnold recalled.

Ingram's own outstanding record as a teacher had convinced the Heronwood principal that the better the interpersonal relationships between students and their teacher, the less problematic were discipline problems in classes. It was a key reason why teachers continued to receive ongoing encouragement and financial support from Ingram to attend seminars which focussed on improving teaching and learning. It was an initiative that teachers who agreed with Ingram's reasoning on student discipline strongly endorsed. Catriona Lorimer's successes in the classroom led her to believe that Ingram's promotion of "practical professional learning for teachers was both effective and proactive. When teachers got on well with kids it was terrific." Lorimer believed that students talked to other students about their teachers who worked well with students "the word spread, and so with the next class you'd have, the students' expectations were positive. The discipline issue was cut in half."

Amongst those teachers who were unconvinced about the need to expand their teaching strategies, there was often a deeply-held view that students needed to behave well, irrespective of who was teaching them or what was being taught. Although Ingram broadly concurred with the theory of that argument, he also believed that it was unlikely to produce productive change in the classroom or with student behaviour. For Ingram, the changing nature of children's lives plus the poor learning culture amongst much of the Heronwood student population meant that teachers needed to adapt what they did if students were ultimately going to respond more positively within classes.

Although Ingram was convinced the weight of responsibility for adapting rested with teachers ahead of students—he also knew the challenge was particularly threatening for some staff members. At staff meetings throughout the year, and in many one-to-one interactions with teachers, Ingram encouraged colleagues to use their initiative and experiment with new ideas and practices in the classrooms. Often he reminded them of several risks he had taken which failed within the overall context of many more things that succeeded in his teaching and leadership work. Failures, to Ingram, were part of the process of school improvement and potentially instructive, because of the chance to learn from them. However, Ingram refused to be burdened or held back by mistakes or failures.

Occasionally at staff meetings teachers would tell Ingram of unexpected or undesired problems that had arisen in relation to school initiatives which had been geared to improving student learning and outcomes. Typically, when straightforward solutions could be identified, an immediate decision was agreed to. In other instances, the matter was referred to the Planning Group. Sometimes Ingram reminded colleagues to "move on," rather than be preoccupied with disappointments or "hiccups."

Ingram also occasionally used staff forums to remind "teachers to not take things too seriously, when the going gets tough." As a majority of the staff did at various times, Ingram continued to use humour and engaged in "good natured stirring" as a means of connecting with teachers and "encouraging them to put things in perspective."

When it appeared that staff were feeling daunted by their workloads or particularly frustrated with an aspect of school life, Ingram ensured he "made them aware that things are not as bad as teachers think they are." Citing recent achievements of the staff and individual teachers, Ingram also nominated aspects of teachers' work lives that were a cause for optimism or appreciation—especially by comparison with some occupations.

While highlighting the relatively high incomes and lengthy holidays which the teaching profession enjoyed may have been dismissed outright by some staffs when relayed by their principal, at Heronwood many teachers "at least noted the point Andrew was trying to make," said Louis Stedman. Ingram's arguments about "keeping a balance continued to be taken on board by many because of his standing amongst most teachers," recalled Stedman.

"In my eyes he had integrity, credibility and a high intellect. His people skills were outstanding. I admired him as a school principal and a teacher. He showed us that he was an excellent teacher—so he had the requirements to hold that position with credibility," said Deane Jennings, who joined the school mid-way through 1993. While Ingram's leadership had produced positive changes at Heronwood which were "too numerous to mention," Jennings indicated that her "classroom practice had not been changed in any way" by her principal. "But he did affect my performance professionally in the sense that he encouraged a few teachers, including me to run professional development sessions for the staff, and that was hugely successful."

Jennings, who was seen by her departmental colleagues as an "outstanding social sciences teacher" believed that, across the staff at Heronwood, teachers were "much happier" working under Ingram. "Given how supportive staff were of each other, and especially any teacher who was having problems," said Jennings, Ingram's empowering leadership "complemented many key values and expectations of Heronwood staff."

Like Jennings, Ingram considered his leadership had an indirect, yet highly productive impact on the classroom practices of most teachers. "I knew there was a strong relationship between the interpersonal skills of the leader and the things a leader did, and staff's happiness in school. As well, I knew the relationship between the leader and teachers influenced how staff felt about school in terms of the positives and negatives." Indeed, as he had evidenced at the beginning of his principalship at Heronwood, Ingram believed "the relationship between myself and teachers was of critical importance to their happiness and performance in the school in terms of their willingness to accept new ideas, to accept challenges that were put in their way and to change practice."

Ingram's belief in the importance of a principal and other leaders having highly effective interpersonal relations with others in the school continued to be evident with the student population. "The same link existed between myself, in particular, and the kids." Once Heronwood students had developed a rapport with Ingram "the kids were not just happier, but were more willing to try things differently too." Just as students talked amongst themselves about the teachers they most enjoyed in classes, Ingram's teaching continued to be an effective means of connecting with and engaging students. Ingram also found that he achieved a "fair bit of credibility amongst the kids because they saw me as a teacher."

Whereas Ingram's consistent manner and the transparent structures he had collaboratively introduced added to many teachers' sense of empowerment, several teachers remained unconvinced about the need to change their teaching practices. In particular "they expressed doubts about whether all of the content that needed to be covered, could in fact be done when new teaching strategies were used," said Louis Stedman.

Not only had those concerned teachers talked with colleagues about the risks to content and coverage from, for example, facilitating more group work in classes, but a few had voiced their concerns in Planning Group committees.

By late 1993, a minority of teachers continued to regularly voice such concerns even though they failed to sway other colleagues who had accepted the need to expand their teaching strategies and more actively engage student learning. Nonetheless, one of the issues which the coterie of concerned teachers raised in support of their arguments was the matter of time. It was an issue that few teachers could dispute—regardless of how they operated—shortage of time was a perennial enemy within schools. Added to that, was a culture amongst Heronwood teachers which accepted diversity of opinions. The degree of collegiality amongst staff that had seemingly always characterized their interpersonal work relations enabled most teachers to acknowledge differences of opinion on particular issues. Deeply-held opinions by some teachers that did not accord with or sway the rest of the staff were, even when hotly contested, rarely proved to be a cause of enduring friction between individuals.

As with most of the thirty-something-year-old teachers, Ingram had witnessed the introduction of many system-wide initiatives which, amidst great promise, had failed to live up to expectations or had, "at the classroom door," been shunned by teachers who were unconvinced of their worth. This organizational "memory" provided a healthy reference point for Ingram. In his view, such memories underscored the legitimacy of school-based personnel critically considering requests from within or beyond Heronwood to heavily invest time or energy into new initiatives.

"The scattered bodies of young teachers who had been left after the dust cleared" from the efforts of one principal who insisted his staff "did things his way" also served to convince Ingram that any dissent at Heronwood on prized school matters should not be crushed. Rather, as well as hearing but only selectively challenging the claims of teachers who saw insufficient reasons to change classroom practice, Ingram sought to better use their talents. It was a practice that did not go unnoticed or unappreciated by many teachers. "He led with wisdom. To do that, he empowered every bastard in the place he could, just like we tried to do with our students. He picked up and brought every talent of every person with whom he worked," said Catriona Lorimer. In that way, Lorimer observed Ingram "wasn't a one-man band." The demonstration of Ingram's commitment to workplace diversity—whether or not he agreed with different teachers' viewpoints—reinforced his largely favourable standing in the eyes of many trenchant critics of change. By providing avenues for all teachers who wanted to share or further develop their talents, Ingram's action "reminded some of the most sceptical teachers of the positives that could come from change," recalled Pierce James.

THE FOURTH YEAR – 1994

For a few teachers, however, Heronwood was no longer a school that they were keen to remain in. With the support of their principal, by the end of 1993, most of those teachers had gained transfers or promotions out of the school for the subsequent year.

The key attraction that drew Celia Warne to Heronwood High in 1994 was the fact that "the general consensus around the district was that the leadership at the school was about as good as it got." Because she lived within half an hour of the school, Warne considered herself "lucky, as a lot of the people on staff were my personal friends out of school. So I had all those contacts to begin with, and that was another reason why I transferred to Heronwood."

Despite her pleasure at being appointed to Heronwood and "the quality of the staff and, particularly, the principal," Warne was surprised by much of what she encountered at the school. "I had some pretty awful times," she recalled. In her early interactions with students she found a dispiriting culture. "They struck me as pretty small-town minded. There wasn't a desire to get out of or beyond Heronwood. There was a lack of inquisitiveness, a lack of motivation to know anything much about what existed apart from in their immediate little world. That may have been the case in other schools but it seemed very pronounced at Heronwood. The kids were very conservative. There wasn't a questioning approach to life, where you question everything and everyone's values. They were very conservative, very accepting and saw their lot in life as pretty much meaning they would remain in the area."

While students did not critically question in the course of exploring class topics, Warne soon regularly experienced an avalanche of questioning about the legitimacy of her instructions to students. The nature of students' comments left Warne feeling that being a new teacher only partly accounted for what she experienced. "Females copped and dealt with more flack, with more resistant student behaviour than did the male teachers. Certainly compared with the people who had the status of principal or assistant principal, those of us at the bottom of the pile had a lot more student resistance to contend with each day," she said.

The more Warne got to know her students, the more she believed much of the resistance was related to "the way women were treated in their families." The disrespect for their mothers which many young male students evidenced when they talked in class of "telling their mothers where to go," said Warne, betrayed an attitude that culminated in "female teachers being tarred with the same brush." Warne also observed similar attitudes at play "in their relationships with girls of their own age group. They were pretty awful."

The regularity with which Warne was confronted by such attitudes was so great she "ended up being selective in responding to them. It wasn't worth challenging them on all the relatively insignificant things or I'd never have made it through the course of the day." Warne also understood that amongst many students' families "there were quite high levels of unemployment. As well there were a lot of single parent families, break-ups with high levels of conflict and the kids were pretty much caught up in that." From Warnes' observations around the town and listening to some of her students' comments, she knew a large number of "families experienced considerable financial difficulties." Against the hardship in which many students lived and the narrow, ingrained attitudes which characterized some families, Warne hoped "to make a little contribution along the way."

Not long after Bob Muscat joined the staff of Heronwood in 1994, he realized his colleagues "were probably the most supportive staff that he'd met." Like Warne, Muscat soon noticed some "anti-social attitudes and behaviours amongst students." Moreover, after teaching at Heronwood for a couple of months, Muscat was convinced that "many students who would be capable of going on to university would not be," due in part to the culture of the town and many families within it.

Muscat's conclusion came as no surprise to the principal of Heronwood— Ingram had personally estimated that "the school was capable of producing about 50-55 graduates out of a cohort of 180 Grade 10 students a year. Yet, the nature of our intake and the fact that like much of regional Australia, the town held the kids in the area—meaning we produced about 20 graduates."

Within a relatively short period, Muscat had actively joined forces with Ingram and other staff who were trying "to put educational solutions in place" which would more actively contribute to Heronwood students learning and life chances.

As one of the school's three assistant principals, Muscat shared Ingram's view that schools needed to be conscious of the futures awaiting students when they reviewed curriculum. The need to be forward and outward looking was of itself a vital challenge to Heronwood, which Muscat knew had begun "at the top" when Ingram started at the school. The urgency for this had, in the intervening years, accelerated as economic and social changes etched more sharply into the life of Heronwood township. While the pace of change in society did not surprise Muscat, he was alarmed by what he "suspected" was an all increasing development amongst some Heronwood families. "When students needed parental support, it just wasn't there for some students. The kids were, in effect, on their own." It was a phenomenon that Muscat had not observed during the two decades of his teaching career.

In Elysia Regan's first term at Heronwood she found herself teaching "mostly pretty good, nice kids and just individuals who were challenging." Aside from her empathy with students, Regan was also disturbed by "the home lives of many students." In Regan's view, most of those students who were "challenging in their class behaviour had inadequate home situations and few aspirations. They didn't feel they needed what school had to offer. So they were off doing their own thing or wanted to challenge me or other kids."

The nature of Heronwood students resulted in Regan attending several evening PD sessions on Social Skills curriculum development later that year. The professional development enabled Regan and other colleagues "to slowly introduce classwork that dealt with sharing, cooperation and helping students to get out of an argument." In her department, the traditional emphasis on purely subject-based skills eventually gave way to an emphasis on "developing people skills—being able to work with people, and in a group, those sorts of skills." The thrust of Regan's efforts initially focussed on gaining widespread "student participation." Teachers in Regan's subject area subsequently echoed her comments to students in their classes. "We all told the students it was their 'participation we wanted'. We wanted them to enjoy classes more. We also told them 'being the best at something but having the worst people skills wouldn't get very many marks'."

The growing difficulties many students were experiencing "at home" were accelerating concerns about negative class and school ground behaviour from new and long-standing Heronwood teachers. While there was an emerging consensus about the difficulties that teachers—and many students—were experiencing due to poor behaviour, there was disagreement amongst staff about what could or should be done about it.

One solution, which achieved the support of staff, led to an increase in the number of excursions and "special event" activities that were organized for students. Another response saw additional professional development being provided to teachers who wished to expand their understanding of student discipline strategies. As well, student opinions were actively sought in the course of further refining the school's discipline policy. Once amended, the grade level coordinators ensured that all students were told of the changes and what that meant, in terms of "acceptable" behaviours.

As part of the school's continuing effort to identify and adequately respond to disparate student learning requirements, teachers were provided with "further reskilling opportunities so that, over time, most staff became greatly familiar with, for example, attention-deficit, vision-impaired, conduct-disordered kids' needs," recalled Ingram.

A further strategy which was initiated from Heronwood's Planning Group resulted in the appointment of counsellors to each grade level. Augmented by a professional guidance officer, teachers on staff met weekly with interested colleagues to talk about "kids and the problems kids were having," said Trevor Warburton, one of the junior grade counsellors. Despite "enduring concerns about student lives and the behaviour of a number of them," Warburton claimed that the counselling system "put out a lot of spot fires very early at Heronwood." During Warburton's 22 years of teaching, he had seen "only a couple of other schools do anything like that." Because a summary of the counsellors' meeting was briefly relayed back to staff the next morning, Warburton claimed it meant "there were no communication problems. Teachers were kept up with the general detail of what was happening." The extent of structural support at the school for initiatives "that, in the end, were for the benefit of students" was, according to Bob Muscat, "amazing at Heronwood."

One additional key advantage of having counsellors concerned the additional insights—which they gained—into the lives of students. For counsellors in particular, as well as for grade level coordinators and teachers in general, it enabled staff to look at issues more comprehensively from a student perspective. The chance for students to talk about problems, from their points of view, ultimately added to the quality of decision-making in the school. Moreover, it reinforced to students that their views had a place, and could often influence what happened, at Heronwood High.

Ingram's consistently applied practice of allowing anyone to attend all but confidential meetings resulted in new staff very quickly developing "a sense of ownership with the structures," said Warburton. In that respect, Ingram considered honouring agreements was an ongoing part of his trust-building with staff that "showed them you did what you said you were going to do."

At the same time further initiatives were being developed to galvanize the learning opportunities of students in general and, more specifically, to assist those with special needs, Muscat started work on reframing the school's curriculum. By talking informally with teachers who had indicated an openness to reviewing curriculum and, after subsequently raising the matter with Ingram and at Planning Group, Muscat and several staff met regularly on the issue.

That Muscat saw the need to review curriculum was, given their many conversations on students, of little surprise to Ingram. Indeed, he welcomed Muscat's determined interest in better equipping students to "think critically" whilst, at the same time, realising that core learning areas needed to be adequately addressed.

The prospect of Muscat finding the necessary time to undertake a curriculum review was, in part, made possible because of the highly effective leadership team at Heronwood. In particular, Assistant Principal Ben Fraser, who coordinated the timetable, "was known for working miracles," said Ingram. Wherever possible, he helped to find some free time for Muscat's curriculum efforts. As Assistant Principal who most frequently liaised with individual parents over student discipline matters, Colin Bays regularly stepped in and took over other tasks from Muscat "because of the importance of what Bob was doing."

In concert with other teachers, Muscat spent the balance of 1994 researching and evaluating the content and design of various whole-school curricula. Throughout that period Muscat's group regularly fed back progress summaries to Planning Group meetings and staff gatherings. The response from teachers, especially those who did not regularly attend Planning Group meeting, was mixed. Very few teachers indicated outright opposition to the effort to review the school's curriculum. However, as time went on, several regularly questioned the need to dramatically change the status quo, unconvinced that a radically reshaped curriculum would improve student engagement or their knowledge, skill and attitudes.

Perhaps better than Muscat, Ingram realized the project was one that would require enormous patience and tenacity from those who were most keen for such change. Ingram also knew that all of the Heronwood staff would continue to require—and expect—the consistency of support and encouragement from their principal that they had by then been receiving for up to 4 years.

THE FIFTH YEAR – 1995

Not long into the 1995 school year, Ingram conducted an evaluation into the effectiveness of the school's structures and implementation strategies that had been put into place since his arrival at Heronwood. Through a survey, Ingram "essentially asked the community 'Is this what you wanted to happen?' and 'How well have we improved?'" Difficult as it was, technically, to reliably conduct such a study, Ingram nonetheless was pleased that the findings "in '95 were overwhelmingly positive about the things the school was offering." Even though Ingram realized that "most school communities were very happy with their local schools," he nonetheless believed that the survey marked a sign of Heronwood's achievements "being recognized by the town and parents it served."

From the time Ingram took up the principalship at Heronwood, the school had conducted research as a means of informing "both our planning and direction," so, in that sense, the 1995 evaluation process merely built upon earlier initiatives that were designed to identify whether the school was catering to parent, community, student and teacher expectations. Throughout Ingram's first 5 years at Heronwood "two important things repeatedly emerged that the school community valued—apart from being consulted—basic skills and supporting a caring environment for children." The school's regular practice of consulting its community provided the town's leaders, parents, ex-students, students and staff members with ongoing opportunities to shape "the future directions of Heronwood High," he said.

Beyond the key features that the school's community most wanted to distinguish Heronwood High, the survey provided clear evidence of particular expectations. "Kids' critical thinking, their preparedness to work, information technology and staff professional development" remained as issues the school was to attend to. Those more specific priorities, according to Ingram, "pointed to some of the complexity behind the simplicity" attached to the two broad priorities.

During the '90s, Heronwood had been "particularly successful under Andrew's leadership, in building an up-to-date supply of computers for students to use. Andrew also revolutionized the office equipment at Heronwood High. The technological support was terrific, perhaps second to none," claimed Colin Bays, who also considered the overall resources at Heronwood to be "outstanding."

While there was agreement across the staff that the school's computer equipment for students plus the professional support for teachers' technology learning was exceptional, there continued to be less unanimity about student learning, effective teaching strategies and curriculum content. Ingram was, in one sense, unconcerned about those differences of opinion amongst staff. He had been in the education field long enough to know that few contested issues could be resolved without deep and often protracted consideration by those who were directly involved. Rarely had he witnessed single, universal solutions helping the work of teachers. He also believed that critical thinking from staff would, in the end, produce decisions that could have a much greater chance of being effective than anything that was "top-down, imposed on staff."

On the other hand, Ingram continued whenever possible to highlight the work of "exemplary teachers and make them available to staff" in a variety of ways, "in an effort to shift some colleagues' teaching practices."

Although Ingram had made clear his preference for teachers to expand their instructional strategies as well as providing funds for professional development which supported such initiatives, he personally avoided "making strong challenges on the way they were teaching." In the same way that Ingram believed students' behaviour ultimately needed to be supported by their own self discipline, he felt most teachers needed to willingly find individual pathways into "change practice."

As "teachers were increasingly frustrated by student behaviour," said Ingram, the challenge continued to be one of providing support, encouragement, and promoting dialogue.

Paralleling Heronwood's efforts to improve the quality of teaching and learning, were increasingly specific requirements from the Department of Education concerning the student learning outcomes. In general, Ingram embraced initiatives from the Centre which were targeted at improving what students, in particular, experienced at school. He was also grateful that even though he "received circular memorandums every day, the number of times they asked me to do something I was unhappy with, I could count on the fingers of one hand." Ingram suspected that the genuinely supportive and helpful role adopted by the Centre towards schools reflected the state Department of Education's growing recognition "of school personnel as professionals." The net effect of a more generous "official" view of school staff suggested that there was a heightened awareness by the Centre to the extent that if it "wanted stuff implemented, it had to grow from what teachers were doing and what teachers wanted to do," said Ingram.

THE SIXTH YEAR – 1996

When most of the 15 new staff appointed to Heronwood High at the start of 1996 first arrived, they noticed "the staff were friendly," said Andrea Merritt, who had previously been at an inner city school in the capital city of the state. "It was a time of big change, where there was a big staff turnover. But there was the old set of teachers who knew everything and so it didn't take long to find out how my part of the school had to run." New staff were also able to familiarize themselves quickly with the workings of Heronwood High because, Merritt claimed "of a helpful information folder we were all given."

Many of the incoming staff, as with most of those who had just left the school, were "automatically" transferred by the state Department of Education, in keeping with the statewide transfer policy. Nonetheless, several of the outgoing staff as well as those who joined Heronwood High, had chosen to apply for new postings. A few of those who, towards the end of the previous year, opted to leave Heronwood High, had done so because of the challenging nature of the students and the increasingly embedded direction of the school. "They were very happy with what they were doing for many years and didn't see a need for change, didn't see that changing how they worked, how they taught, would improve how kids adapted to high school or how kids got on with each other," claimed May Somerville. She believed that part of the problem related to "some teachers' personalities—a lot of people are very black and white where issues of change are concerned."

Not surprisingly, new staff were largely oblivious to the reasons behind the departures of many Heronwood staff in time for the 1996 school year. In any event, incoming teachers such as Andrea Merritt were focussed on learning as much as possible about Heronwood High and what was required of them for the year. In addition to finding the induction materials valuable, Merritt's impression of her new principal was also favourable. "Andrew seemed so good speaking on his feet and, whenever you went to him, he seemed to know what you were talking about."

By the end of the first term, all the new staff had according to Merritt, "received a note from Andrew, thanking them for what they'd done at the school." As it happened, the notes from Andrew were doubly appreciated by teachers because many were received just prior to the shooting massacre at a well-known tourist destination in another part of the state. The tragedy was deeply distressing to everyone—especially students. As a result, Ingram got together with "the kids who were on Assembly Committee" and organized a special assembly for everyone in the school. "Students on the Assembly Committee did some readings and we listened to some really nice secular music and I spoke to the kids for 10 minutes about what the massacre meant to me." Numerous staff who attended the assembly were "deeply moved by Andrew's address. Students were also very affected by their principal's talk," recalled Catriona Lorimer. For Heronwood High, under Ingram's leadership, the experience of the assembly was a defining moment. Ever conscious of the reactions of others, Ingram too, realized that "the assembly changed the school. There was something different about the school after that assembly."

Veronica Shelley's memory of her first year at the school was also emblazoned with "an impression I got of Andrew on the day set aside to remember those who gave their life for the country in war. He chose to stand up in front of the school— 700 kids and staff—and talked to them really quite emotionally about the meaning of the day. I was quite stunned to see all those sets of eyes that were tightly focussed on him, with no student complaining or being a pain. I considered I was lucky to be teaching at Heronwood."

The cohesiveness of the old staff also struck many of the newcomers although Shelley soon discovered that "there were three pockets of opinion on the matter of discipline. There were those who wanted the discipline policy upheld to the letter. Then there was a group who took the view of 'oh yeah, we'll discipline if we have to' and another group who didn't seem to give a stuff on the issue." Incoming teachers eventually sorted themselves into one of those divisions as the year progressed. The uneven implementation of aspects of the discipline policy by staff led to those teachers who wanted strict adherence to it "often getting very angry," recalled Andrea Merritt.

Because Warren Wallace was new to the school and "took a fair while to adjust," he did not get heavily drawn into debates amongst staff about student discipline. As well, he was "extremely relieved to be at a school which had a pretty supportive staff and really good leadership." The principals at Wallace's last two schools had been "disappointments, because in the first school, there was a lot of fence-sitting from the top, and there wasn't a great deal of respect from kids or teachers toward the principal. In the other school, the situation was worse. The whole community had no time for the principal. He was reluctant to make hard decisions, and certainly didn't have any respect from staff and students."

Against Wallace's negative experiences with principals at his previous schools, Ingram's leadership presence provided an early and sharp contrast. "The big differences were that Andrew was a really strong principal, and there was a vision for where the school was going in the future. In terms of where the school was taking the kids, there was a definite plan, a definite vision. As soon as I walked into the school, I picked that up." The fact, in Wallace's eyes, that "Andrew had excellent interpersonal skills and an excellent relationship with kids, teachers, parents and the community meant Heronwood was a pretty happy school to walk into."

The bleak leadership experiences at Wallace's previous schools had also resulted in him receiving no instructional support from either principal. However, at Heronwood, Wallace sought such assistance from Ingram. "During the first couple of months at the school, I had Andrew come in and run lessons with some kids. He would come in and demonstrate things." Ingram's capacity "to demonstrate good teaching practice and talk generally about teaching as well as offer ideas" proved to be a pivotal point in Wallace's career. The absence of support from his past principals and their inability to provide instructional leadership "had started to take a toll and I became pretty stressed about the situation, which was why I was keen to get out." The instructional leadership provided by Ingram was additionally helpful for Wallace's first year at Heronwood because "I really found it difficult to get a handle on the student-based nature of the school." Wallace had not before experienced a situation where "the principal interacted with the kids in ways to help them become independent learners. Andrew gave the kids a lot of freedom to move about and get on with their learning. It was an example of the way he wanted the school to operate and the outcome was that students were pretty independent learners."

While incoming teachers were adjusting to the school, staff "continued on as usual," recalled Catriona Lorimer. Some longstanding staff members chose to simply tailor courses to suit the particular needs of their classes, rather than make wholesale changes to their teaching or class programs. Others, however, continued to experiment with different ways of engaging their students, in an effort to reach more students and improve the classroom learning cultures.

When teaching and other duties permitted, Bob Muscat continued to spend time on reviewing the school's curriculum, in conjunction with a small group of interested teachers. Abner Mirna, who had been at the school for many years, was deeply sceptical about curriculum reviews, whether they emanated from beyond or within schools. What Muscat's committee had been doing in recent times had not escaped Mirna's attention nor his caution about the worth of what they were doing. Yet, in his own classes, Mirna was teaching in ways that were similar to what

Muscat's group promoted—especially in relation to developing students' critical thinking capacities.

In one of the numerous conversations Muscat had with his principal about curriculum, and in view of their belief about the importance of what Mirna was achieving with his class, it was decided to "try to get Mirna on board," said Warren Wallace. After several separate approaches to Mirna from Ingram and Muscat, Mirna finally agreed to take an active role in the school's curriculum review.

The cooption of Mirna was seen as a "significant step forward in the curriculum process," claimed Wallace. Like many of the school's excellent teachers, Mirna's "organizational memory" was replete with recollections of shallow, poorly developed, or hastily implemented school-based change-initiatives. Too often such efforts had seemingly been harnessed to the specific career aspirations of educators, bureaucrats or politicians, rather than the interests of students. On too many occasions not only had the initiatives subsequently failed but, along the way, they had wasted the time and energies of personnel who were genuinely committed to continuous school improvement. Against such a context and, given Mirna's personal habit of critically weighing up educational issues, his doubts about the Heronwood High curriculum initiatives were predictable. Yet, with the benefit of frank exchanges between himself, Ingram, and Muscat, Mirna resolved to participate in efforts to radically improve the curriculum. Importantly, Mirna had concluded that the change was motivated by colleagues who genuinely had the interests of students at heart. He also realized, from his own teaching experiences, that the anticipated change—if effectively implemented—would provide most Heronwood High students with vastly improved learning opportunities. Those two beliefs explain at least, in part, why Mirna's subsequent involvement in the review resulted not only in him putting forward ideas to the committee but also "becoming one of the most credible advocates for change amongst staff. His classes were engaged, adventurous and achieving, and teachers knew that," said Wallace.

At the same time as the school was grappling with the prospect of redrafting the curriculum, Heronwood High became involved in the Assisted School Self-Review (ASSR), which was to be undertaken by willing public schools throughout the state. The ASSR documentation provided by the state Department of Education—as well as the initiative itself—impressed Ingram. "The materials recognized that school-based personnel had minds of their own. They also provided schools with the opportunity to respond as schools saw fit." On Ingram's part, much of the ASSR process complemented that which the school had been modelling or working toward for nearly 6 years. In that sense, it was unsurprising to Ingram that the staff had agreed to take part in the first "intake" of the rolling process.

That staff had endorsed a process which, invariably, required many of them to commit time to again evidenced their professionalism to Ingram. Yet, as with Ingram, when informed of the process, staff readily identified the likely benefit to the school from gathering a wide range of data and again, canvassing the views of Heronwood's school community.

Whereas by late 1996 most new staff had settled in to their work, Ian Powell was trying to come to grips with "one of the most traumatic years of my life." Despite having transferred by choice to "a school with the reputation of Heronwood" he found the students to "be far more worldly than at my other school." One consequence for Powell was that "it was very difficult getting accepted by the students. I had a few clashes with the kids and found the pressure of dealing with different kids and bigger class sizes than I'd been used to, pretty stressful." That many students in his classes persisted for most of the year "to give me a rough time," resulted in Powell feeling he was "having a battle." In those circumstances, Powell reflected "it was hard to get myself back to where I thought I should be."

Usually the trigger to Powell's most trying moments in classes was misbehaving students. Because Powell had spoken with "the hierarchy" about the student difficulties he experienced "pretty much early on," he found their active support was helpful. "In particular, Pat Hill, who was my AST3, totally supported me, 100% support. If requested, and I had a tough class, he was there—just whipped through and gave me backup." The nature of many students, Powell found, did not accommodate the way he taught. Although Powell believed he had "tried to adapt, from day one," it took almost all of the year before he felt he had achieved a small amount of success in classes.

Even with modest indications of student progress and continued adaptation from Powell, he considered the culture and other features of life in the township of Heronwood made his future chances of "doing what I wanted to do with the students, unlikely."

From Powell's observations, many students would leave Heronwood High and "become lost in their communities." The absence of direction in the lives of many students was in part due to the fact that for them, "there was no employment anymore." What added to the troubles in many students' lives was that "in the town there seemed to be far more social breakdowns of families which affected the kids, the like of which I'd not seen before in 19 years of teaching," said Powell. In that context, Powell realized, "Heronwood was the only stable thing many students knew in their life." With that realization, Powell suggested, "came an extra responsibility on teachers to provide positive role models for students."

As the year progressed, Muscat, Mirna, and other teachers who were keen to change the school's curriculum held a series of evening professional development sessions for staff. According to Mirna, the sessions allowed time "for teachers to talk about the curriculum content we had proposed should be implemented." Although the sessions were always well attended, by the end of the year, many teachers remained unconvinced that the anticipated changes—and their implications for teachers' work and student achievement—would be worth supporting.

THE SEVENTH YEAR – 1997

The start of the 1997 school year at Heronwood High brought with it many new staff, due to the Department of Education's transfer policy. Almost all of the incoming teachers were pleased to have been placed at Heronwood, including those who would—were it not for the transfer policy of moving teachers after 7 years in the one school being enacted—have remained in their previous school. Gus Norman was one of the teachers who, after 16 years in one school, had been "forcibly transferred." Apart from the personal ramifications of being shifted, he found Heronwood High to be a "largely positive place to be in." When Norman was initially posted to his previous school, he believed he was "working in the best school in the state, without any shadow of a doubt." Toward the end of that appointment he considered he was teaching in "the worst school in the state, due to a series of incompetent leaders." Because of that, "it probably wasn't such a bad idea that I was transferred."

Within a relatively short time Norman discovered the staff at Heronwood to be "extremely supportive. If you were having a bad day, you were assisted by someone. The conversations with people in the staffroom were usually relatively frivolous and uplifting and yet, if you wanted to have some serious discussions with somebody, you could always do that." The staff at Heronwood had contributed to Norman "immediately feeling very comfortable at the school."

Ingram's leadership had contrasted sharply with the styles of the principals he had worked with for more than a decade. The favourable contrast restored some of Norman's faith in public education, because at his previous school he had become exasperated with the school's principal. "My last principal couldn't or wouldn't communicate. I wasn't happy there, but the only thing that kept me going was a very solid departmental staff." In Norman's view, his former principal had misplaced priorities and a poor understanding of change processes in schools. "Last winter, in the first week of third term, it was exceptionally cold. Everybody had turned the heaters on in classrooms. In the same week, something had happened in the school that caused some consternation. But rather than deal with that situation, there was a special staff meeting called by the principal to say that the power bill was too high for that week. We were also told that if the staff didn't do something about cutting the power down, the school would be over the top—because the principal's computer analysis of the power meters had shown we'd used too much power. Quite frankly, I didn't give a stuff about that. I wasn't going to have kids in a room so cold that they couldn't do anything."

The vivid and negative nature of Norman's organizational memories were not fuelled by his experiences at Heronwood. Instead, they served as a benchmark of what school leaders should not do. "Whereas the other bloke talked to his computer, Andrew's strength was his ability to talk with staff and kids." Like Norman, Christine Harmon realized early into her first year at the school that the principal and staff "were extremely supportive." After 19 years, she found herself working with "the best boss ever, who gave me scope to do my own thing." As Harmon soon realized, it was a level of support and latitude that she not only appreciated but also needed. "I got such a hard time from the kids. Every day I thought 'how on earth can I go back to that class tomorrow?'"

The "hard time" that Harmon received in classes from students eased over the course of the year. But much about the town's values caused Harmon "to worry because they were evident in the kids." It was not simply that the students' capacity to adapt to newcomers "was the worst I'd come across." The insularity of many students' lives resulted in "poor levels of social skills." From Harmon's conversations with students, she discovered "there were so many kids who had never been to state's capital city, let alone on a plane."

The strength of students' identification with the town in which they lived was also apparent, and concerning, to Norman. "The mind set I found difficult to understand was the one that viewed Heronwood as the be-all and end-all. They were extremely narrow in that sense, which was probably why the local football club had dominated the football league in the area for more than 10 years. The kids only wanted to play football for Heronwood, rather than nearby, for Chaffer, which was part of the statewide league. They preferred to play in a lower league and that pervaded through all their sports—they preferred to play for Heronwood. Chaffer or the next town might only be 15 minutes down the road, but to the people of Heronwood it seems to be almost a chasm."

CURRICULUM REVIEW: SLOW PROGRESS

The culture shock which frequently characterized the experiences of incoming staff in relation to students, added to the arguments which motivated many of the claims by Muscat's curriculum review group. Not only was the need for curriculum change propelled, in Muscat's view, by the need to counter students' limited life experiences through radically different class-based learning opportunities, there was an urgency about the time Heronwood High was taking to make such changes. Regarded across the staff as an outstanding leader, Muscat's verbalized concerns to colleagues about the protracted time curriculum reform was taking nonetheless "fell on many deaf ears," said Warren Wallace. The standing of the assistant principal and other highly skilled teachers who were allied to reshaping the school's curriculum was "only influential in swaying teachers who were open or mildly cautious about the proposals."

Reactions of those teachers who were disinterested in or strongly opposed to dramatically different curriculum being provided by the school remained unchanged by arguments about the process taking too long too implement. What added to Muscat's frustration with the pace of curriculum change—especially given the amount of time the staff had spent in professional development sessions on the issue—was the School District's wish for speedier progress.

Even though Ingram empathized with concerns about the time that curriculum reform had taken, he was undisturbed by the matter. Those, like District Office, who wanted a quicker pace needed to be patient. Ingram believed that proponents of the reforms needed to recognize what they had already achieved. "What they had done was exciting and quite different," said Ingram. It was something "I told the Central Office about, and invited them on several occasions to visit the school." Ingram was disappointed by their lack of follow-through. "What was being done deserved some attention," he said.

Another reason Ingram comfortably accepted that the "transformation of the school's curriculum required even further time to develop" was because he considered lasting change would only be implemented when teachers genuinely believed it was feasible. It was, he claimed, "no good to say 'right, critical thinking—that is where we're going to go to'." To have expected teachers who were not ready or able to work out where critical thinking fitted "in the big scheme of

things would have resulted in it neither being implemented nor effective."
Curriculum reform "was one of those processes" as far as the time required and end
results were concerned, that "was most difficult to predict in schools."

Whereas Muscat and many of the teachers who wished for a quicker rate of
change had "looked at the futures that might be awaiting students," recalled Mirna,
many colleagues had not. The failure of some staff to do so was, according to
Ingram, because of the nature of teachers' work. Irrespective of the rate of change
brought about by economic shifts, the impact of technology and the pace of changes
in society, "teachers in classrooms were actually dealing with values more than
anything else, things which changed slowly in a community, and changed over time
in response to a whole range of pressures." The net result of that for some teachers,
according to Ingram, was that "they had a view that outside the window, there was a
world rushing by, while inside the classroom, they were still dealing with human
behaviour—and values, attitudes and perceptions—that were not going to change
quickly." Although, amongst Heronwood staff there remained several teachers who
wanted little to do with further curriculum change, most accepted that "things would
develop even further," said Melissa Egan.

But by late 1997, staff, according to Egan, "were not at the point of getting
together and working out the hands-on part of actually determining what it would be
that we'd deliver to the children in terms of critical thinking and so on." Egan
figured that teachers "feared the unknown" aspects of the curriculum reform. "The
unknown quantities of whether it could be translated and whether it would take
time," she recalled.

Clara Phineas was at a similar point in her estimation of the curriculum review.
She found it "quite difficult to come to grips with." The upshot for Phineas was that
she "couldn't picture how it was going to work at all." Phineas was appreciative of
"the people who had put forward units of work and ideas which incorporated the
new things," but for them to be meaningful, she "needed to see things working in
practice." Thus, for many teachers who remained unsure about the planned
curriculum change, or their roles within the anticipated arrangement, the substantial
level of support provided to them by Ingram and Muscat's committee proved to be
insufficient. The use of "spaced learning" professional development experiences,
Barrie Bennett's teaching and learning programs, and provision of class programs
for teachers had satisfied the concerns of only some staff members.

Having listened to most of his colleagues express an opinion about the continued
reform of curriculum at Heronwood, Pierce James "thought there were about 50% of
the staff who were sceptical and believed the process had been engineered." James
indicated that teachers who were guarded about further curriculum development
were "comfortable with what they were doing and didn't see why they should have
to change." As a science teacher, James could "see benefits on both sides" but was
not sure whether "the subject was going to be devalued" if the changes progressed.

If the school's curriculum "were to go to the proposed five strands of Maths,
Literacy, Information Technology, Critical Thinking and Social Skills, it would be
doing so without being clear about whether struggling students would be able to
cope with the new programs," James indicated.

Alison Gavin was more accepting of the direction in which the review was headed. She thought "the gist of it was a good idea." She knew the changes would eventually mean "a lot of extra work" for teachers. However, she thought it would be good—"good for us to refocus" and in that was something she expected and was "happy to do because the changes were about the way to teach and the content." Charles Preston counted himself "as one who was supportive of the 5-strand curriculum approach." What had happened at Heronwood "had engendered ownership, by going through an exhaustive process to make sure we owned and saw the need for what would eventuate." The experience "contrasted greatly with my partner's school, where the principal gave ultimatums in order to achieve change— staff had no ownership there." Preston was conscious of concerns about "the implementation phase. But people weren't saying 'this was not right.' They were saying 'this could be difficult, because we're not used to that'. No one was saying it was wrong." The time taken by Heronwood to redevelop curriculum was in Preston's view, "worth the effort. It was not wasted time, it was value time." He was confident the end result would be favourable due to "the capabilities of the leadership and staff."

While the protracted consideration of curriculum change continued, Ingram kept reminding teachers of the enormity and multiplicity of what had been achieved by them. "When I walked around the school and saw what teachers were doing—it was terrific." Compared to when Ingram began at Heronwood, the changes to the school's teaching and learning were dramatic. In more recent years the extent of improvement had heightened, he claimed. "Every teacher had modified, changed and improved their practice, particularly during the previous 3 years."

THE EIGHTH YEAR – 1998

Whereas the 1998 school year was notable because of an influx of new staff, again as a result of the statewide transfer policy, plus the absence of several teachers who had been promoted or chose to leave Heronwood, Ingram's primary efforts were elsewhere. He had become particularly concerned with the behaviours of some students. "The kids," in Ingram's view, were still "fantastic—just fantastic." But he was alarmed at "the bullying and harassment in the school." After nearly a decade of effort by teachers and Ingram in developing a deeply caring ethos toward students, he believed the school was "treading water" on the issue. There was no doubt in the mind of Catriona Lorimer that almost all of the school's 45 teaching personnel had consistently demonstrated an enormous commitment to students" which was symbolized through "the high level of care shown to children." But, like Ingram, she worried about the school's progress in being able to curb the hostility and aggression displayed by some students toward others. "We really haven't shaken from the kids, the teasing stuff."

Ingram was not prepared to accept that bullying and harassment were a normal part of adolescence. Whereas railing against authority—be it parents or teachers was a common part of growing up for many adolescents—bullying was not. "A lot of adolescents go through their youth without having to tease or bully or be teased or be bullied." Amidst Ingram's heightened concern about the extent of aggression displayed by some students toward others in the school grounds and classes, remained a consistent belief about the school: that Heronwood High was one of the few places left, perhaps the only safe environment, for many of the kids.

Even though the school had undertaken "an enormous amount of work" and pursued multiple avenues along the way in an effort to respond to negative student behaviour for nearly a decade, the results were not as good as had been hoped for, according to Bob Muscat.

Although research conducted at the school in recent years had pinpointed some evidence of poor student behaviour, Ingram suspected the data had not fully captured the extent of what was happening, especially in the school grounds during lunch and recess times. Ingram feared the nature and frequency of "bullying and harassment in the school might be above the national average."

A further dimension of the problem to Ingram was an increasing recognition "that there is an underclass of children in school now who are disenfranchised financially, economically and socially." Added to that, "those kids are more and more strident in an institution which seeks to maintain community and family values. They are values those kids have never been exposed to. That's the reason they rail against us." The clash of values was not a case, Ingram claimed of favouring "middle class values. I'm talking about true human values—about the way in which we treat each other and the way we respect each other's person and property plus the way we respect community property."

What added to the issue of dealing with alienated students in school was the comparatively recent arrival in town of "street kids." While some of the street kids had, in years gone by, attended local schools such as Heronwood High, many had shifted to the town from other parts of the State. Whereas some street kids often lived on the streets, many of those in Heronwood simply spent lengthy periods in the streets—congregating at bus shelters, outside coffee shops and near parks. Inevitably, on weekends and after school, some students mixed with the town's street kids. During school hours, and especially at lunch times, several street kids regularly gathered just outside of the school grounds in an effort to talk with, fight or verbally harass particular Heronwood High students. "In the last couple of years it has become a real problem," said Catriona Lorimer. The hostility from some of the street kids toward teachers on yard duty had, on occasion, been "quite considerable, with a few of us fearing for our safety." One of Ingram's responses to the problem involved timetabling either himself or one of the Assistant Principals to yard duty every lunchtime.

"Certainly the vandalism has increased since I've lived in the area," said Clara Phineas. "Destruction of property within the school grounds shows Heronwood High has not escaped being part of that larger problem," said Ingram. Of greater concern than vandalism was what he saw as an increasing volume of psychological aggression being exhibited by many students. Like many teachers who were concerned about the acerbic nature of this hostility, Muscat and Ingram realized the potential of it to threaten school life. Not only did it have the potential to diminish the self-esteem of students who were the brunt of such aggression, but also it had the capacity to reduce the learning culture the school had so assiduously built during the 1990's.

Of particular concern to Muscat was a link that had developed between the families of some students who were in fights of one sort or another at school. Although not widespread, altercations between some students were showing themselves to be related to disputes between families which were taking place out of school hours and beyond the reaches of Heronwood High. Given the importance Ingram gave to a school providing "students with an environment in which they can grow strongly as social individuals—to make decent citizens for the future," he subsequently intensified the time and effort he gave to the issue. "Shaking harassment and bullying has to be our primary focus."

Vital as Ingram indicated the issue was to resolve, he worried that "the usual introduction to the school which new teachers normally received wasn't so good in 1998." As a newcomer to the staff, Ben Stevenson had not formally been provided with an induction. The absence of an induction program had meant he asked questions of colleagues who were "very helpful and either answered my query or told me who I needed to speak to." The experience did not extinguish Stevenson's optimism about Heronwood High. His first impression about the school was "that I'd died and gone to heaven. The hierarchy and the staff were fantastic. The school struck me as being oriented to students rather than staff, which I found to be very different from my old school. But the leadership and staff were very cohesive and very supportive." Terry Smith's entree into Heronwood High left him feeling he was "fortunate to be at the school." His initial lack of knowledge about "how things worked precisely" was, in large part, made up for by the fact that he "knew many of the staff personally or professionally, having worked with a few previously."

The calibre of the school's staff and principal, in particular, were quickly noted by Smith. "The really noticeable thing here was how much Andrew did as principal. Open-door policy, teaching, curriculum and so on. As well as all the other stuff I often saw him out on duty at lunchtime, chasing away outsiders who came into the school. Now, you might say that was a small thing, but it was symbolic of a big thing. Because, by doing that, he was showing all the kids and every teacher in the school that the job was important—so he saw himself in amongst all of that."

One of the first groups Smith became involved with at the school "was Muscat's curriculum committee." As with most of the school's new staff, Smith identified strongly with the need to operate a 5-strand curriculum but soon found that not every teacher agreed with the design. After several conversations with opponents of the change, Smith was unswayed by arguments for "the status quo. Some of those people had been here a fair while and so I was finding a bit of inertia. When all boiled down, it was them coming to grips with personal change and they were resisting that." As Smith discovered, the curriculum change had been years in the making. Although some teachers' opposition to it had not waned during that time, Smith believed "the positive flow-on from the time spent was that the school's curriculum would ultimately produce a deeper change." Many schools which Smith had worked in "had opted for change but ultimately produced superficial change—only structural change where everything went back to the way it was, once someone left."

Richard Montgomery's choice to transfer to Heronwood High had been an outcome of friends at his "other school who said to put Heronwood as my first choice, because Andrew was a top bloke." On that criterion, he was not disappointed. He also found "the staff were impressive." However, the "lack of self-discipline of Heronwood students" shocked Montgomery. "Largely non-existent. Probably for 80% of the Grade 10 kids. It was a difficult thing to come to grips with." That aspect of students' behaviour resulted in Montgomery finding classes "where there are a lot of kids who will not engage in a learning activity at all. They'll sit and look or watch, a really large proportion of students who find it really hard to engage in any activity. Run around and bust yourself for a couple of days trying to organize something, and it flops for no other reason than they really don't want to do it. And that's it, they say 'I'm not going to do this.'" The dispiriting nature of Montgomery's classes was, to some extent, offset by "working with a very gregarious bunch—probably the happiest and most enjoyable staff I've worked with. And it's the whole staff—probably the most easy-going as a group." Yet the absence of Montgomery feeling as if he was effecting considerable student improvement in classes meant "on those days when I've been my best here, I haven't had a strong sense of satisfaction."

Given the nature of many students, and particularly those who were "easily disengaged," Montgomery was a keen supporter of further curriculum reform. Despite his difficulties in classes, he continued to experiment with strategies and teaching practices that were "consistent with what is being proposed." He was cautiously optimistic that more teachers would "come on board. If we can convince those people that what we're doing is better than what we've got at the moment, and there are significant changes in outcomes or changes in students who go into their groups the following year, then we'll have a winner." If positive changes "in those kids or their outcomes" were not then evident, Montgomery anticipated the changes "wouldn't last, or if they did, they wouldn't grow."

Perry Barton, who joined the same department as Montgomery when he started at the school in 1998, also experienced "disastrous classes. I found it extremely difficult, to the stage where it affected my job satisfaction." Students were "suspicious of me—as in suspicious of a stranger. Behaviour was the thing—mainly poor behaviour." The need to improve student behaviour was so vital, according to Barton, that the school needed to "make dramatic changes especially in terms of curriculum. The work that the school has done in the five key learning areas is terrific and should be implemented." To Barton, it was not clear whether, once in place, the 5-strand design would succeed, "because of the tremendous difficulty in actually translating the work that has been done into classroom practice, and due to staff resistance to change."

The 5-strand design needed to be implemented because "the kids will be much more settled and less difficult to manage if things are made far more interesting, accessible and far less regimented than they are now," said Barton. The extent of congeniality amongst staff was on the one hand, "fine," according to Barton. On the other hand, he saw it as a potential "albatross" when any organizational change was mooted "because the cohesion in the staff room manifests itself in an absolute opposition to change."

Yet, at least in part, it was "the tolerance and generosity of staff"—which was underpinned by the cohesion between teachers—that Bob Muscat hoped would finally enable the 5-strand curriculum to be implemented. "It will be a big risk for many teachers, requiring them to take a leap of faith in not only the new program, but themselves as teachers," said Catriona Lorimer. Even with Lorimer's track record and enthusiasm for the change, she claimed it would not be "an easy road ahead. I'm so anxious about not doing well, that I'm always quite terrified inside. But everything has changed and must change. Andrew is aware of that and he won't abandon what is solid. He is never intimidated by either people, change or challenge—and that goes through the whole school, not just staff."

When ultimately implemented, the new curriculum "would be less to do with content and more to do with teaching kids how to think, to build logical thought," said Alison Gavin. By helping "each student to learn how to problem-solve and think—think across it, think out, think in and think back—by learning how to ask questions," she added. Given "the attitudes in this narrow-minded community, Heronwood High is a very forward-looking school even though what we face and do seems to be getting more and more intricate," said Lorimer. The remarkable achievements of Andrew and teachers needed to be kept in mind as the school contended with students, teaching and curriculum. The proposed changes would soon materialize, she predicted, because more than ever before teaching was now "about empowering kids to attack on-going knowledge. Enabling them to feel, when they leave school, that they have the skills to analyse a problem—to ask themselves 'what does this need? What do I know? What do I need to know? Where can I find it? What approaches can I use?'" Teachers' fears, inadequacies, shortages of time and territorial problems would, in the end, be placed second to the "circumstances and futures of kids," claimed Lorimer because "these days that's the only way we can teach."

CHALLENGES

In 1998, most Heronwood staff considered they worked in one of the best high schools in the State. The school was extremely well run by a principal who continually collaborated with staff and used their talents to ensure Heronwood High operated effectively. Not only was their principal easy for teachers to interact with, but also he trusted teachers to do their job. Staff and the material resources at Heronwood High were, in the main, excellent and the school's standing within the local community was very favourable. Almost all Heronwood High teachers knew of friends and former colleagues who worked in schools where circumstances were much less favourable.

Yet, for many staff, the considerable job satisfaction they enjoyed was frequently punctured by the poor behaviour and learning culture of some students. In addition, the anticipated changes to curriculum—which most expected would eventuate—left many teachers concerned about their future capacity to operate effectively in classes. The high esteem in which Ingram was held and the mutuality of respect between teachers and their principal did not provide a sufficient counter to fears about the curriculum shift. Nor did having substantial confidence in the curriculum knowledge and teaching skills of Bob Muscat, Abner Mirna and other leading curriculum and classroom practitioners. The numerous strengths provided by the distributed leadership at Heronwood High, in reality, could offer no guarantees about any successes which would accompany the planned curriculum changes. By contrast, those who were unsure about or unconvinced by the 5-strand curriculum, could draw on their own personal teaching histories—which were largely successful—when evaluating the prospect of curriculum change.

Typically amongst those who doubted the worth of changing the curriculum were teachers who had at least 15 years of school experience. The concrete nature of that experience presented those teachers with a powerful, matter-of-fact basis for not wanting to change and risk an "unknown quantity". Moreover, in their undergraduate years, most teachers were specialist-trained and subsequently identified heavily with as few as two subjects. Against that, the prolific provision and use of professional development at Heronwood High made, at best, negligible in-roads into the subject-based identities of many teachers.

Further, the ongoing efforts of Ingram and Muscat, in particular, to expand teachers' understandings of the ever-changing labour market requirements of school graduates had not been fully grasped by many Heronwood High teachers. Hence, the beliefs which underpinned the proposed changes to curriculum had not convinced those staff. Although the key proponents—and those teachers actively in favour—of such change well understood the urgency of equipping students to be critical and adaptive learners so as to galvanize future job prospects, the imperative was lost on many teachers. While this and related issues continued to be a tension for Ingram, he was aware of the need to maintain a balance between changing structures too quickly and changing teacher's values and practices.

The comprehensive support materials and curriculum documentation provided by Muscat's committee, whilst sufficient for many staff, fell short of what was required by teachers who were most strongly opposed to the change. Instead, they required additional support in the form of being able to witness, first-hand, a series of effective lessons being conducted with their classes. Whilst, in multiple ways, Heronwood High was an exemplary school, the prospects of such support being provided seemed remote, due to the time and resourcing limitations.

What served to limit such an imposing requirement emerging as an essential factor for the cooperation of dissenting teachers was the overriding commitment of most staff to the initiative. Amongst teachers at Heronwood a culture of risk-taking had been developed which, when paired with a way of furthering students' interests, meant that most staff were prepared to implement the 5-strand curriculum. Even to teachers who supported the proposed change, there remained unclear elements— how the new curriculum would unfold would not be apparent until implementation began in earnest. Yet most teachers were prepared to implement the change despite any doubts and uncertainties about what would eventuate.

If ultimately implemented well, the 5-strand curriculum had the potential to better equip students who were undecided about the types of jobs they would eventually seek. At Heronwood High, this cohort amounted to a considerable number of students. In addition, many students had little detailed knowledge of the gamut of careers and jobs that were currently available in workplaces. Indeed, many students came from households where parents had occupied one type of job or a series of jobs which were only in one sector. For example, many parents had held a range of shop assistant positions in various Heronwood shops over a number of years—but essentially they were roles that were confined to the retail sector. For students whose parents had no or limited post school qualifications, it usually meant students could not easily identify with, or did not aspire to obtain, jobs or careers that would ultimately require them to leave Heronwood. While the school had been effective in ensuring an increasing number of Grade 10 students went on to further education, the town's preference for locals to remain local represented a huge and ongoing challenge for Heronwood High to contend with.

Of at least as great a challenge for Heronwood High was the unremitting practice of bullying, especially in the school grounds and, in some instances, after hours in the streets and houses in which students lived. The ever-increasing pressures on family life and children resulted in more and more students harassing and bullying other students. Whereas under Ingram's leadership the school had been effective in stemming the use of physical violence amongst students, as a means of resolving conflict, Heronwood High was, more frequently, having to contend with psychological bullying by students. Because such harassment could often occur without attracting the attention of teachers, it was potentially more difficult for the staff to identify. Although Ingram and Muscat realized the practice of verbal intimidation had begun to take hold amongst "pockets" of students, the underlying triggers to such actions were, in the main, considered by them to lie outside of the school. That is, both Heronwood leaders believed that the home lives of a small but growing number of students were fraught with disputes and, in some instances, aggression.

Although several students may have learned to bully on the basis of what they had observed or more directly experienced—especially out of school—the problem according to the principal required additional responses from the school. Though often subtle, psychological intimidation, as Ingram in particular realized, was potentially pernicious in its effect on those students who were bullied. As well, the upsurge in psychological bullying threatened the inclusive nature of Heronwood High which Ingram and his staff had worked so hard to develop for nearly a decade. The continuing economic and social pressures that the town of Heronwood was experiencing and the resultant family "implosions" were, according to Muscat, expected to continue at least in the medium-term. Given the considerable effort the school continued to expand on promoting the well-being of all children, the interim response of Heronwood High was, Ingram indicated, "to put even more effort into dealing with the issue, because, in the end, schools are about being supportive learning environments for the total well-being of children."

HERONWOOD HIGH SCHOOL CASE STUDY: OUTLINE

Setting the Scene

The Town

regional community where job losses increasing, greater unemployment and casual and part-time work
dominant industries trade, manufacturing and community services
low median incomes
mainly born in the country

Principal (views prior to taking up appointment)

part of local networks
committed to change
strong, long-serving teaching staff
culture of repetition rather than renewal
kids not turned on by their learning

Changing Leaders, Changing Times

Principal (views and actions on taking up appointment in 1991):

trusted teachers and wanted them significantly involved in, and owning, change
promised an open style of leadership characterized by consistency and fairness
flagged his desire to improve the learning culture of students
expected loyalty to the school and colleagues
believed staff needed considerable additional support
discussed a whole range of issues concerning teachers' professional lives
saturated school with professional development
communicated openly
pushed the notion of professionalism
sought to be consistent to teachers and students in good and difficult times
established a Planning Group
sought to involve the school in the community and the community in the school

Teachers (views of their new principal):

different to his predecessor who was shy, arrogant, remote and the assistant
    principal and staff generally ran the school (i.e., empowerment by default)
caution—wanted to see whether his promises would be fulfilled, however, the
    more teachers saw him consistently being a caring, attentive and responsive

leader, the more they continued to consult with him about initiatives they
wanted to pursue
outstanding interpersonal skills
visible in the school and available to teachers at short notice
genuinely interested in what teachers and students were doing
had his finger on the pulse
resource support
no sanctions for risk-taking

The Second Year – 1992

Teachers:

8 new, although grumblings about the resistance and suspicion students
were seen to have towards incoming teachers
grumblings about student discipline with the principal being seen as being
too supportive of students yet principal wanted to affirm students by
being open to their viewpoints
a cohesive group

Principal:

seen to be frank, to have a regular presence in the school grounds and to
teach extraordinarily well
continued to encourage colleagues to take a professional development
opportunities—this investment was starting to have pay-off, e.g., an
increasing effort by teachers to negotiate with students on curriculum
matters and the use of the talents of highly skilled teachers at the
school (e.g., literacy)
sat down and made judgments with the staff or Planning Group about the
suitability of many central initiatives
optimistic and tenacious, prepared for delays in the course of working
towards the greater goal of the whole development of all the children
in the school

The Third Year – 1993

The community continues to decline:

greater numbers of young people encountering unemployment
a growing underclass within the town
frustrations from pressurized home lives show through in the playground
and class

Principal:

convinced that the better the interpersonal relationships between students
and their teacher, the less problematic discipline problems in classes
encouraged teachers to use their initiative and experiment with new
ideas and practices in the classroom—failures seen as part of the price
of school improvement

used humour and engaged in good-natured stirring as a means of
connecting with teachers and encouraging them to put things in
perspective

credibility amongst the kids because they saw him as a teacher

picked up and brought with him every talent of every person with whom he
worked—not a one-man band

Several teachers:

remained unconvinced about the need to change their teaching practices,
especially in respect of ensuring full content coverage

shortage of time was seen as a perennial enemy

different opinions were seen to be sought out and accommodated

The Fourth and Fifth Years – 1994/1995

Context:

most of the dissatisfied teachers left the school

parochialism and small town mindedness increased as the threats from
outside increased

Principal:

conducted an evaluation into the effectiveness of the school's structures and
implementation strategies—part of a continuing strategy to conduct
research as a means of informing both planning and direction

school community valued being consulted, basic skills and supporting a
caring environment for children

continued to be unconcerned about differences of opinion among staff

continued to highlight the work of exemplary teachers and make them
available to staff

saw the Centre as increasingly supportive of school personnel as
professionals

Assistant Principal Muscat:

saw the urgent need, in the context of what was happening in the
community, to be forward and outward looking

saw the home life of many children disappearing

started work, through the Planning Group, staff gatherings and a small
group of interested teachers, to reframe the school's curriculum with a
major aim to better equip students to think critically

coopted a formerly cynical teacher to the curriculum review

Teachers:

being just a teacher, being a new teacher to the school and being female
seemed to result in more resistant student behaviour

disagreements among staff about what should be done about poor
behaviour

continued actions taken included increased number of excursions and
special event activities for students, additional professional
development on student discipline strategies and social skills
curriculum development for teachers, and a refining of the school's
discipline policy

particularly successful was the appointment of counsellors to each grade
level

several teachers regularly question the need to dramatically change the
status quo in respect of the school's curriculum

The Sixth and Seventh Years – 1996/1997

Context:

many new staff appointed, mainly as a result of the Transfer Policy—a
strong induction program

Principal:

good at speaking on his feet and using emotion, e.g., the use of special
assemblies such as when the Special Education kids were being given a
hard time

seen by new staff
as a strong principal with a vision for where the school was going: a
definite plan of how to get there
as having excellent interpersonal schools with kids, teachers, parents
and the community
able to demonstrate good teaching practice and provide instructional
support

involved the school in the first intake into the Department of Education's
Assisted School Self Review process seeing it complementing that
which the school had been modeling or working towards for nearly 6
years. The staff readily identified the likely benefits to the school from
gathering a wide range of data and again, canvassing the views of the
school community.

Teachers:

increasingly see the school as the only stable thing that many students knew
in their life and the responsibility on teachers to provide positive role
models

extremely supportive staff

Curriculum Review:

slow progress

the culture shock which frequently characterized experiences of incoming
staff in relation to students added to the arguments which motivated
many of the claims by the curriculum review group

principal empathized with concerns about the time being taken but was
undisturbed as he considered lasting change would only be

implemented when teachers genuinely believed it was feasible and
owned it. He also kept reminding teachers of the enormity and
multiplicity of what had been achieved by them

a number of teachers needed to see things working in practice before they
would give their commitment to change

most of the school's new staff identified strongly with the need to operate a
five strand curriculum

The Eighth Year – 1998

Context:

arrival in town of "street kids"

Principal:

particularly concerned with, and intensified the time and effort he gave to,
the bullying and harassment behaviours of some students

perceived a growing underclass of children in the school who were
disenfranchised financially, economically and socially. However, the
clash of values wasn't related to middle-class values but true human
values—about the way in which people treat each other and each
other's property.

Teachers:

induction not as good this year as in the past

new staff very enthusiastic about the school, its staff and principal

curriculum change seen as something in the best interests of children and
would last

Challenges

One of the best high schools in the state; yet, despite this, some challenges
persist:

some teachers concerned about student behaviour and the curriculum
change, especially from the more experienced and single subject
teachers

the concept of a need to equip students to be critical adaptive learners so as
to galvanize future job prospects is difficult for some teachers to
understand and act upon.

restrictive parochial community attitude

bullying, especially of a psychological kind

CHAPTER 7

SURVEY DATA

INTRODUCTION

The data presented in this chapter derives from the two case study schools, Altona and Heronwood, and is organized first by teacher views about organizational learning, school management, and principal leadership and second by student views about participation and engagement in school.

All items have been grouped by the factors identified in the LOLSO research project as well as indicating, on an item by item basis, where there are marked differences with the state averages. For example, on item 27, "Most of us think about the future development of the school," Altona High School scored 4.0, the state average was 3.4 and therefore Altona was 0.6 above the state average (on a 5-point scale, with 1 = *strongly disagree* and 5 = *strongly agree*).

ALTONA

ALTONA TEACHER SURVEY RESPONSES

Items on LOLSO Organisational Learning and Leadership Questionnaire where Altona teachers' averages are markedly different from the state averages (i.e., at least +/– 0.4).

ORGANISATIONAL LEARNING (using the four-factor model)

Trusting and Collaborative Climate

1. Most of us think about the future development of the school.
   (Altona 4.0 minus State average 3.4 = 0.6)
2. Discussions among colleagues are honest and candid.
   (4.2 – 3.8 = 0.4)

Other items in this factor where there was no marked difference:

1. There is ongoing professional dialogue among teachers.
2. Colleagues are used as resources.
3. Overall there is mutual support among teachers.
4. Most of us learn from our successes.
5. Most of us actively seek information to improve our work.
6. We are tolerant of each other's opinions.
7. There is a spirit of openness and trust.
8. Problems, errors, and lessons are shared not hidden.

Shared and Monitored Mission

1. Teachers have the opportunity to participate in most significant school-level policy decisions.
   $(4.0 - 3.6 = 0.4)$

Other Items

1. We have a coherent and shared sense of direction.
2. We critically examine current practices.
3. Sensitive issues can be raised for discussion.
4. We actively share information with the parents and community.
5. The effectiveness of the teaching program is regularly monitored.
6. The vision/goals were established collaboratively.
7. The school structures encourage collaboration among staff.
8. The school leaders enunciate clear statements of collaborative expectations.
9. Teachers and administrators work in partnership to learn and solve problems together.
10. The climate is not conducive to cooperative learning.

Taking Initiatives/Risks

1. The school leaders encourage professional risk taking and experimentation.
   $(4.3 - 3.4 = 0.9)$
2. People feel free to experiment and take risks.
   $(4.2 - 3.5 = 0.7)$
3. We value diversity of opinion.
   $(3.9 - 3.5 = 0.4)$
4. School structures support teacher initiative and risk taking.
   $(3.6 - 3.1 = 0.5)$
5. There are rewards for staff who take the initiative.
   $(3.3 - 2.9 = 0.4)$
6. I have a great deal of freedom in how I do my work.
   $(4.8 - 4.3 = 0.5)$

Other Items

1. It is accepted that there is more than one way to accomplish the school's vision/goals.
2. Staff are valued.
3. The administrators empower staff to make decisions.
4. The school leaders protect those who take risks.
5. We acknowledge staff achievements.
6. The administrators model calculated risk taking and experimentation.
7. The school organisation does all it can to encourage staff to develop professionally.
8. The administrators are open to change.
9. The administrators have an explicit procedure to manage the change process.
10. I am satisfied with my job.

Ongoing, Relevant Professional Development

1. We monitor what's happening outside of the school to find out what may impact on the school itself.
   $(3.9 - 3.2 = 0.7)$
2. The climate is stimulating and professionally challenging.
   $(4.1 - 3.2 = 0.9)$

Other Items

1. Staff engage in ongoing professional development.
2. We make use of external advisers e.g., subject associations, project officers, consultants.
3. We learn from other schools.
4. Adequate time is provided for professional development.
5. The administrators facilitate collaboration via release time/resources/skill development programs and the like.
6. We monitor what's happening outside of the school to find out about best practice.
7. We have designed ways to share knowledge.
8. Good use is made of professional readings.
9. Good use is made of membership of teacher professional associations.
10. Groups of staff receive training in how to work and learn in teams.
11. Professional development is closely tied to real school issues.

Other items not falling into the above four-factor model but where there were marked differences:

1. Only a select group are involved in decision making processes.
   $(2.4 - 2.8 = -0.4)$
2. We are left to our own devices in reviewing and improving our work.
   $(3.9 - 3.4 = 0.5)$

3. Only a few of us are concerned with anything beyond the immediate demands of our work.
   (2.0 – 2.8 = –0.8)
4. The potential for negative consequences inhibits risk taking.
   (1.7 – 2.7 = –1.0)
5. Staff engage in new learning opportunities.
   (3.8 – 3.4 = 0.4)
6. On the whole professional development is guided by school rather than individual staff needs.
   (3.0 – 3.5 = –0.5)
7. Staff are engaged in continuous learning for improvement.
   (3.7 – 3.2 = 0.5)
8. I am able to have my professional development needs addressed.
   (3.5 – 3.1 = 0.4)
9. I have been involved in significant professional development in recent years.
   (4.2 – 3.7 = 0.5)

Other Items

None.

PRINCIPAL TRANSFORMATIONAL LEADERSHIP
(using the six-factor model)

Vision and Goals

1. Helps clarify the specific meaning of the school's mission in terms of its practical implications for programs and instruction.
   (3.8 – 3.4 = 0.4)
2. Encourages the development of school culture supporting openness to change.
   (4.5 – 3.7 = 0.8)

Other Items

1. Works toward whole staff consensus in establishing priorities for school goals.
2. Gives us a sense of overall purpose.
3. Helps us understand the relationship between our school's mission and the Department's initiatives and policies.
4. Communicates school mission to staff and students.

Culture

None.

Other Items

1. Shows respect for staff by treating us as professionals.

2. Sets a respectful tone for interaction with students.
3. Models problem-solving techniques that I can readily adapt for work with colleagues and students.
4. Symbolizes success and accomplishment within our profession.
5. Demonstrates a willingness to change his/her own practices in light of new understandings.
6. Promotes an atmosphere of caring and trust among staff.

Structure

1. Provides an appropriate level of autonomy for us in our own decision making.
   $(4.4 - 4.0 = 0.4)$
2. Ensures that we have adequate involvement in decision making related to programs and instructions.
   $(4.0 - 3.6 = 0.4)$

Other Items

1. Delegates leadership for activities critical for achieving school goals.
2. Supports an effective committee structure for decision making.
3. Distributes leadership broadly among the staff representing various viewpoints in leadership positions.
4. Facilitates effective communication among staff.

Intellectual Stimulation

1. Encourages me to try new practices consistent with my own interests.
   $(4.4 - 3.8 = 0.6)$
2. Is a source of new ideas for my professional learning.
   $(3.4 - 3.0 = 0.4)$
3. Encourages me to pursue my own goals for professional learning.
   $(4.2 - 3.6 = 0.6)$
4. Facilitates opportunities for staff to learn from each other.
   $(3.8 - 3.3 = 0.5)$

Other Items

1. Encourages us to develop/review individual professional growth goals consistent with school goals and priorities.
2. Stimulates me to think about what I am doing for my students.
3. Encourages us to evaluate our practices and refine them as needed.

Individualized Support

1. Is aware of my unique needs and expertise.
   $(4.1 - 3.5 = 0.6)$

2. Provides moral support by making me feel appreciated for my contribution to the school.
   (4.1 – 3.6 = 0.5)

Other Items

1. Takes my opinion into consideration when initiating actions that affect my work.
2. Is inclusive, does not show favouritism toward individuals or groups.

Performance Expectations

1. Expects us to be effective innovators.
   (4.4 – 3.6 = 0.8)

Other Items

1. Holds high expectations for students.
2. Has high expectations for us as professionals.

SCHOOL MANAGEMENT

Community Focus

1. Our school administrators are sensitive to the community's aspirations and requests.
   (4.1 – 3.7 = 0.4)
2. Our school administrators attempt to plan and work with community representatives.
   (4.1 – 3.7 = 0.4)
3. Our school administrators seek to incorporate the community characteristics and values in the operation of the school.
   (3.9 – 3.4 = 0.5)
4. Our school administrators have established a productive working relationship with the community.
   (4.1 – 3.5 = 0.6)

Other Items

None.

Distributed Leadership (marked differences at least +/–0.30)

1. Teacher identification of leadership sources in the school and their strength of influence (1 = *minimal*, 2 = *moderate*, 3 = *considerable*, 4 = *very strong*):

   Assistant Principal(s)   (3.5 – 3.2 = 0.3)

Individual Teachers	$(3.1 - 2.7 = 0.4)$
Counsellor(s)	$(2.2 - 1.9 = 0.3)$
Students	$(1.8 - 2.1 = -0.3)$

Other Items

Principal
Department Heads
Teacher Teams
Whole staff
School Council
Union Representatives
Parents/Community Members

Staff Valued

1. The contributions of all staff members, new and established, are valued equally.
   $(3.7 - 3.3 = 0.4)$

Other Items

1. We have an induction process for new staff.
2. Present staff welcome and value new staff members.

School Autonomy

1. Our school administrators have secured a high degree of autonomy for the school.
   $(4.0 - 3.6 = 0.4)$

ALTONA STUDENT SURVEY RESPONSES

> **Items on LOLSO Student Participation and Engagement Questionnaire where Altona students' averages are markedly different from the state averages (i.e., at least +/ − 0.3).**

STUDENT PARTICIPATION AND ENGAGEMENT[1]

Home Educational Environment

1. My parents/guardians make sure I do my homework before having free time.
   (Altona 2.4 minus State average 2.7 = −0.3)

---

[1] For the workshop activities only selected items from the early student questionnaire have been used to represent the variables listed in this section. These lists are samples only of items defining each variable. In Chapter 8, the reader will find a comprehensive set of items for all variables. We encourage you to employ the short form of the LOLSO Project Questionnaires to gather data for your school.

2. My parents/guardians usually go to parent's nights and special school events. (2.9 – 2.4 = 0.4)
3. My parents/guardians are always willing to help me with my schoolwork. (3.6 – 4.0 = –0.4)
4. I have my own workspace at home that is fairly quiet for doing homework and school projects. (3.0 – 3.6 = –0.6)

Other items where there was no marked difference:

1. My parents/guardians encourage me to participate in extracurricular activities and events.
2. My parents/guardians always know whether or not I am at school.
3. I often discuss my schoolwork with my parents/guardians.
4. Study aids at home (e.g., books, an encyclopedia, magazines or computer) help me do better schoolwork.
5. I often have conversations about major world events with my parents/guardians.

Teachers' Work

1. We have the right number of quizzes, tests and exams in my courses. (3.2 – 3.5 = –0.3)
2. I am constantly challenged in class. (3.0 – 3.3 = –0.3)

Other Items

1. I like the way teachers teach in most of my classes.
2. My teachers use a variety of activities in my classes.
3. Most of my classes are well organized.
4. Most of my teachers expect me always to do my best work.

Participation in Extracurricular Activities

1. Participating in school events is a very important part of my life as school. (4.0 – 3.6 = 0.4)
2. I have been an active member of school clubs and/or sports teams throughout school. (3.7 – 3.4 = 0.3)
3. I participate as a spectator at sports events. (2.3 – 1.9 = 0.4)
4. I participate as a spectator at other school events. (2.2 – 1.6 = 0.6)

Other Items

1. I participate in sports events.
2. I participate in school dances/socials, plays/concerts.

3. I participate in one-day special events.
4. Number of activities.

Absenteeism

(At October, 0 = 0 times; 1 = 1-5 times, 2 = 6-10 times, 3 = 10+ times since the beginning of the school year.)

No marked differences.

Other Items

1. Number of times late for school.
2. Skipped class (without permission).
3. Been absent for a whole day.
4. Sent out of class because of misbehaviour.
5. Had a detention.

Engagement

1. I really enjoy school most of the time.
   $(3.5 - 3.2 = 0.3)$
2. I do a lot of extra reading for my own benefit.
   $(2.7 - 3.0 = -0.3)$

Other Items

1. My schoolwork is helping me to prepare for life after I finish school.
2. I really enjoy school most of the time.
3. Most of my teachers are interested in me as a person.
4. I am proud of my school.
5. School spirit is very high in my school.

Academic Self-Concept

1. I am able to understand most of the material covered in my classes.
   $(3.5 - 3.8 = -0.3)$
2. I will graduate from High School.
   $(4.7 - 4.0 = 0.7)$
3. I am satisfied with my marks.
   $(3.3 - 3.9 = -0.6)$

Other Items

1. I feel confident that I will be successful in school.
2. I am learning a lot in school.
3. I believe my marks at the end of this year will be:
   5 = high, 4 = above average, 3 = average, 2 = below average, or *1 = low.*

HERONWOOD

HERONWOOD TEACHER SURVEY RESPONSES

> **Items on LOLSO Organisational Learning and Leadership Questionnaire where Heronwood teachers' averages are markedly different from the state averages (i.e., at least +/– 0.4).**

ORGANISATIONAL LEARNING (using the four-factor model)

Trusting and Collaborative Climate

1. Overall there is mutual support among teachers.
   (Heronwood 4.4 minus State average 4.0 = 0.4)
2. There is a spirit of openness and trust.
   (4.0 – 3.4 = 0.6)

Other items where there was no marked difference:

1. There is ongoing professional dialogue among teachers.
2. Colleagues are used as resources.
3. Most of us think about the future development of the school.
4. Most of us learn from our successes.
5. Discussions among colleagues are honest and candid.
6. Most of us actively seek information to improve our work.
7. We are tolerant of each other's opinions.
8. Problems, errors, and lessons are shared not hidden.

Shared and Monitored Mission

1. We have a coherent and shared sense of direction.
   (4.1 – 3.3 = 0.8)
2. Teachers have the opportunity to participate in most significant school-level policy decisions.
   (4.4 – 3.6 = 0.8)
3. We critically examine current practices.
   (4.0 – 3.4 = 0.6)
4. Sensitive issues can be raised for discussion.
   (4.3 – 3.8 = 0.5)
5. The effectiveness of the teaching program is regularly monitored.
   (3.6 – 3.0 = 0.6)
6. The vision/goals were established collaboratively.
   (4.2 – 3.5 = 0.7)

7. The school leaders enunciate clear statements of collaborative expectations.
   (4.0 – 3.4 = 0.6)
8. Teachers and administrators work in partnership to learn and solve problems together.
   (3.8 – 3.3 = 0.5)
9. The climate is not conducive to cooperative learning.
   (2.1 – 2.6 = –0.5)

Other Items

1. We actively share information with the parents and community.
2. The school structures encourage collaboration among staff.

Taking Initiatives/Risks

1. It is accepted that there is more than one way to accomplish the school's vision/goals.
   (4.1 – 3.6 = 0.5)
2. Staff are valued.
   (4.6 – 3.7 = 0.9)
3. The administrators empower staff to make decisions.
   (3.8 – 3.4 = 0.4)
4. The school leaders protect those who take risks.
   (3.5 – 3.1 = 0.4)
5. School structures support teacher initiative and risk taking.
   (3.5 – 3.1 = 0.4)
6. The administrators model calculated risk taking and experimentation.
   (3.4 – 2.8 = 0.6)
7. The school organisation does all it can to encourage staff to develop professionally.
   (4.0 – 3.4 = 0.6)
8. The administrators are open to change.
   (4.3 – 3.5 = 0.8)
9. The administrators have an explicit procedure to manage the change process.
   (3.7 – 3.0 = 0.7)
10. I am satisfied with my job.
    (3.9 – 3.4 = 0.5)

Other Items

1. The school leaders encourage professional risk taking and experimentation.
2. People feel free to experiment and take risks.
3. We value diversity of opinion.
4. We acknowledge staff achievements.
5. There are rewards for staff who take the initiative.
6. I have a great deal of freedom in how I do my work.

Ongoing, Relevant Professional Development

1. We monitor what's happening outside of the school to find out what may impact on the school itself.
   (3.7 - 3.2 = 0.5)
2. Adequate time is provided for professional development.
   (3.6 – 3.0 = 0.6)
3. The administrators facilitate collaboration via release time/resources/skill development programs and the like.
   (3.6 – 3.0 = 0.6)
4. The climate is stimulating and professionally challenging.
   (4.1 – 3.2 = 0.9)
5. Good use is made of professional readings.
   (2.9 – 2.5 = 0.4)
6. Groups of staff receive training in how to work and learn in teams.
   (3.1 – 2.6 = 0.5)
7. Professional development is closely tied to real school issues.
   (3.8 – 3.3 = 0.5)

Other Items

1. Staff engage in ongoing professional development.
2. We make use of external advisers e.g., subject associations, project officers, consultants.
3. We learn from other schools.
4. We monitor what's happening outside of the school to find out about best practice.
5. We have designed ways to share knowledge.
6. Good use is made of membership of teacher professional associations.

Other items not falling into the above four-factor model but where there were marked differences:

1. Only a select group are involved in decision making processes.
   (2.3 – 2.8 = –0.5)
2. There is a climate of continuous professional improvement.
   (4.1 – 3.6 = 0.5)
3. Curriculum is aligned with our vision/goals.
   (4.0 – 3.4 = 0.6)
4. We are left to our own devices in reviewing and improving our work.
   (2.6 – 3.4 = 0.8)
5. Vision/goals are not a significant feature of this school's functioning.
   (1.6 – 2.4 = –0.8)
6. The school leaders promote inquiry and dialogue.
   (4.1 – 3.4 = 0.7)
7. Staff engage in new learning opportunities.
   (3.8 – 3.4 = 0.4)

8. The reality is that most of us operate on our own.
   (2.6 – 3.3 = –0.7)
9. Staff learning is seen as important.
   (4.5 – 3.7 = 0.8)
10. We regularly monitor progress toward achievement of our vision/goals.
    (3.6 – 3.0 = 0.6)
11. We have effective procedures for making new ideas from outside the school easily accessible for staff.
    (3.1 – 2.7 = 0.4)
12. The administrators establish systems to find and share learning.
    (3.3 – 2.9 = 0.4)
13. Learnings from our reviews are linked to the school's goals/activities.
    (4.1 – 3.3 = 0.8)
14. Staff are engaged in continuous learning for improvement.
    (3.9 – 3.2 = 0.7)
15. The administrators are open to change.
    (4.3 – 3.5 = 0.8)
16. I am able to have my professional development needs addressed.
    (4.0 – 3.1 = 0.9)
17. Systems and structures exist to ensure that important knowledge gained from reviews is made available to those who need and can use it.
    (3.7 – 3.2 = 0.5)

Other Items

1. Most staff are committed to our vision/goals.
2. Only a few of us are concerned with anything beyond the immediate demands of our work.
3. We change our vision/goals as the need arises.
4. People openly assess the results of trying something new.
5. The potential for negative consequences inhibits risk taking.
6. We take time to reflect on and discuss our practice.
7. Most of learn from our mistakes.
8. Looking for new ways to do things is perceived as a sign that you are having difficulty.
9. On the whole, professional development is guided by school rather than individual staff needs.
10. We manage differences of opinion through inquiry and problem solving.
11. There is open discussion of any difficulties identified through reviews.
12. I have been involved in significant professional learning in recent years.

SCHOOL MANAGEMENT

Community Focus

1. Our school administrators attempt to plan and work with community representatives.
   (4.2 – 3.7 = 0.5)
2. Our school administrators have established a productive working relationship with the community.
   (4.0 – 3.5 = 0.5)

Other Items

1. Our school administrators are sensitive to the community's aspirations and requests.
2. Our school administrators seek to incorporate the community characteristics and values in the operation of the school.

Distributed Leadership (marked differences at least +/–0.30)

1. Teacher identification of leadership sources in the school and their strength of influence (1 = *minimal*, 2 = *moderate*, 3 = *considerable*, 4 = *very strong*):

Principal	(4.0 – 3.3 = 0.7)
Individual Teachers	(3.0 – 2.7 = 0.3)
Teacher Teams	(3.0 – 2.7 = 0.3)
Whole staff	(3.1 – 2.8 = 0.3)
Counsellor(s)	(2.7 – 1.9 = 0.8)
School Council	(2.4 – 2.1 = 0.3)

Other Items

   Assistant Principal(s)
   Department Heads
   Students
   Union Representatives
   Parents/Community Members

Staff Valued

1. We have an induction process for new staff.
   (3.4 – 2.9=0.5)
2. The contributions of all staff members, new and established, are valued equally.
   (3.7 – 3.3=0.4)

Other Items

1. Present staff welcome and value new staff members.

School Autonomy

1. Our school administrators have secured a high degree of autonomy for the school.
   (4.3 – 3.6 = 0.7)
2. Satisfaction with total amount of leadership from all sources in the school.
   (3.4 – 2.6 = 0.8)

Other Items

None.

PRINCIPAL TRANSFORMATIONAL LEADERSHIP
(using the six-factor model)

Vision and Goals

1. Works toward whole staff consensus in establishing priorities for school goals.
   (4.5 – 3.7 = 0.8)
2. Gives us a sense of overall purpose.
   (4.7 – 3.6 = 1.1)
3. Helps us understand the relationship between our school's mission and the Department's initiatives and policies.
   (4.6 – 3.8 = 0.8)
4. Communicates school mission to staff and students.
   (4.7 – 3.7 = 1.0)
5. Helps clarify the specific meaning of the school's mission in terms of its practical implications for programs and instruction.
   (4.5 – 3.4 = 1.1)
6. Encourages the development of school culture supporting openness to change.
   (4.5 – 3.7 = 0.8)

Other Items

None.

Culture

1. Shows respect for staff by treating us as professionals.
   (4.7 – 4.1 = 0.6)
2. Sets a respectful tone for interaction with students.
   (4.7 – 4.0 = 0.7)
3. Models problem-solving techniques that I can readily adapt for work with colleagues and students.
   (3.9 – 3.0 = 0.9)
4. Symbolizes success and accomplishment within our profession.
   (4.7 – 3.7 = 1.0)

5. Demonstrates a willingness to change his/her own practices in light of new understandings.
   (4.4 – 3.6 = 0.8)
6. Promotes an atmosphere of caring and trust among staff.
   (4.7 – 3.7 = 1.0)

Other Items

None.

Structure

1. Provides an appropriate level of autonomy for us in our own decision making.
   (4.4 – 4.0 = 0.6)
2. Delegates leadership for activities critical for achieving school goals.
   (4.6 – 4.0 = 0.6)
3. Supports an effective committee structure for decision making.
   (4.6 – 3.8 = 0.8)
4. Distributes leadership broadly among the staff representing various viewpoints in leadership positions.
   (4.5 – 3.7 = 0.8)
5. Ensures that we have adequate involvement in decision making related to programs and instructions.
   (4.4 – 3.6 = 0.8)
6. Facilitates effective communication among staff.
   (4.4 – 3.5 = 0.9)

Other Items

None.

Intellectual Stimulation

1. Encourages me to try new practices consistent with my own interests.
   (4.4 – 3.8 = 0.6)
2 Is a source of new ideas for my professional learning.
   (3.9 – 3.0 = 0.9)
3. Encourages me to pursue my own goals for professional learning.
   (4.3 – 3.6 = 0.7)
4. Encourages us to develop/review individual professional growth goals consistent with school goals and priorities.
   (4.4 – 3.6 = 0.8)
5. Facilitates opportunities for staff to learn from each other.
   (4.0 – 3.3 = 0.7)
6. Stimulates me to think about what I am doing for my students.
   (4.0 – 3.1 = 0.9)
7. Encourages us to evaluate our practices and refine them as needed.
   (4.0 – 3.5 = 0.5)

Other Items

None.

Individualized Support

1. Takes my opinion into consideration when initiating actions that affect my work.
   (4.4 − 3.8 = 0.6)
2. Is inclusive, does not show favouritism toward individuals or groups.
   (4.0 − 3.6 = 0.4)
3. Is aware of my unique needs and expertise.
   (4.1 − 3.5 = 0.6)
4. Provides moral support by making me feel appreciated for my contribution to the school.
   (4.3 − 3.6 = 0.7)

Other Items

None.

Performance Expectations

1. Holds high expectations for students.
   (4.6 − 4.0 = 0.6)
2. Expects us to be effective innovators.
   (4.1 − 3.6 = 0.5)
3. Has high expectations for us as professionals.
   (4.6 − 4.1 = 0.5)

Other Items

None.

HERONWOOD STUDENT SURVEY RESPONSES

Items on LOLSO Student Participation and Engagement Questionnaire where Heronwood students' averages are markedly different from the state averages (i.e., at least +/ − 0.3).

STUDENT PARTICIPATION AND ENGAGEMENT[2]

Home Educational Environment

1. My parents/guardians always know whether or not I am at school.
   $(3.8 - 4.1 = -0.3)$

Other items where there was no marked difference:

1. My parents/guardians make sure I do my homework before having free time.
2. My parents/guardians encourage me to participate in extracurricular activities and events.
3. My parents/guardians usually go to parent's nights and special school events.
4. I often discuss my schoolwork with my parents/guardians.
5. Study aids at home (e.g., books, an encyclopedia, magazines or computer) help me do better schoolwork.
6. My parents/guardians are always willing to help me with my schoolwork.
7. I often have conversations about major world events with my parents/guardians.
8. I have my own workspace at home that is fairly quiet for doing homework and school projects.

Teachers' Work

No marked differences.

Other Items

1. I am constantly challenged in class.
2. We have the right number of quizzes, tests and exams in my courses.
3. I like the way teachers teach in most of my classes.
4. My teachers use a variety of activities in my classes.
5. Most of my classes are well organized.
6. Most of my teachers expect me always to do my best work.

Participation in Extracurricular Activities

1. I have been an active member of school clubs and/or sports teams throughout school.
   $(3.1 - 3.4 = -0.3)$
2. I participate as a spectator at other school events.
   $(1.2 - 1.6 = -0.4)$
3. I participate in other school events.
   $(0.9 - 1.5 = -0.6)$

---

[2] For the workshop activities only selected items from the early student questionnaire have been used to represent the variables listed in this section. These lists are samples only of items defining each variable. In Chapter 8, the reader will find a comprehensive set of items for all variables. We encourage you to employ the short form of the LOLSO Project Questionnaires to gather data for your school.

4. I participate in school dances/socials.
(2.5 − 2.2 = 0.3)

Other Items

1. Participating in school events is a very important part of my life at school.
2. I participate as a spectator at sports events.
3. I participate in sports events.
4. I participate in one-day special events.
5. Number of activities.

Absenteeism
(At October, 0 = 0 times; 1 = 1-5 times, 2 = 6-10 times, 3 = 10+ times since the beginning of the school year.)

No marked differences.

Other Items

1. Number of times been late for school.
2. Skipped class (without permission).
3. Been absent for a whole day.
4. Sent out of class because of misbehaviour.
5. Had a detention.

Engagement

1. I am proud of my school.
(3.5 − 3.1 = 0.4)
2. School spirit is very high in my school.
(3.4 − 3.0 = 0.4)

Other Items

1. I really enjoy school most of the time.
2. I do a lot of extra reading for my own benefit.
3. My schoolwork is helping me to prepare for life after I finish school.
4. I really enjoy school most of the time.
5. Most of my teachers are interested in me as a person.

Academic Self-Concept

1. I will graduate from High School.
(4.6 − 4.0 = 0.6)
2. I am satisfied with my marks.
(3.6 − 3.9 = −0.3)
3. I believe my marks at the end of this year will be:
5 = *high*, 4 = *above average*, 3 = *average*, 2 = *below average*, or 1 = *low*.
(3.6 − 3.3 = 0.3)

Other Items

1. I feel confident that I will be successful in school.
2. I am learning a lot in school.
3. I am able to understand most of the material covered in my classes.

Table 2. Other data on Altona.

1. Percentage distribution of Altona and all State Government school Year 7 students in 1998

	Numeracy			Literacy		
Level	Altona	All	Difference	Altona	All	Difference
1 (*High*)	1	4	−3	5	3	2
2	7	4	3	2	1	1
3	57	37	20	6	5	1
4	34	50	−16	34	26	8
5	1	5	−4	34	47	−13
6 (*Low*)				18	19	−1

2. Percentage comparison of Altona staff and student absences and staff transfer applications

	1994	1998	Difference
Student absences Term 2	11	8	−3
Staff absences Term 2	10	8	−2
Staff transfer applications	36	7	−29

3. Percentage of Altona Year 10 by destination

Destination	1996	1997	1998	1999
Year 11/12College	63	65	81	68
Technical College	2	5	5	5
Apprentice Training	9	0	0	6
Employed	15	14	13	17
Unplaced	11	15	1	0
Interstate	0	2	1	2
Uncontactable	0	0	0	1

4. Percentage comparisons of Altona student's perceptions of positive aspects of the school

Response	1994	1998	Difference
the new subjects	55	64	9
specific teachers	30	39	9
meeting new friends	10	29	19
the friendly people	0	17	17
boy/girlfriends	17	4	−13

(continued)

Table 2 — continued

4. Percentage comparisons of Altona student's perceptions of positive aspects of the school			
Response	1994	1998	Difference
recess and lunch	18	10	−8
the canteen	34	10	−24
the range of teachers	30	6	−24
the way the place is set up	0	13	13

5. Percentage comparisons of Altona student's descriptions of the school			
Response	1994	1998	Difference
positive comments	55	90	35
negative comments	17	8	−9

Table 3. Other data on Heronwood.

6. Percentage of Heronwood Year 10 by Destination		
Destination	1996	1997
Year 11/12 College	63	74
Technical College	4	6
Apprentice Training		
Employed	11	14
Unplaced	2	6
Interstate		
Uncontactable	20	

Table 4. Other data on Altona and Heronwood.

7. SCHOOL GOVERNANCE AND EDUCATIONAL OUTCOMES PROJECT (Mulford et al., 2001)
Student survey responses at Altona and Heronwood, 1996

Variable	Altona (N = 96)	Heronwood (N = 160)	Scale
Level of Education			
Mother	5.09	5.18	1 = Primary/4 = Secondary/7 = University
Father	5.57	5.40	
Student Ratings of Teachers			
establish a good working atmosphere	1.47	1.86	1 = Excellent/5 = Very Poor
communicate well with students	1.92	1.73	
manage discipline well	1.59	1.66	
explain things clearly	2.21	1.98	
maintain student interest	1.43	1.49	
well prepared and organized	1.84	2.15	
respect students as young adults	0.59	0.83	
know their subject matter	2.22	2.01	

(continued)

Table 4 — continued

Variable	Altona	Heronwood	Scale
Student Ratings of School	2.39	2.62	4 = Excellent/1 = Poor
Student Ratings of own Academic Ability	3.40	3.56	1 = Well Above Average/ 5 = Well Below Average
Tertiary Certificate of Education (TCE) Scores			TCE weighted for level of difficulty
Weighted Maths Score	4.06	5.74	1 = *higher/best score*; 10 = *lowest score*
Weighted English Score	4.85	5.27	

SECTION 4:

A CHALLENGE

CHAPTER 8

THE SURVEY INSTRUMENTS AND A CHALLENGE
TO USE THEM IN YOUR OWN SCHOOL

INTRODUCTION

You are encouraged to ask your staff and students to complete the following shortened version of the LOLSO Project questionnaires. It would be helpful to get responses from at least 15 teachers and 25 Grade 10 students.

You are then encouraged to collate the responses and enter the data on the scoring sheets provided. The comparative data on these sheets are based on responses gathered in Australia in 1997 from 2,503 high school teachers and 3,508 Year 10 students.

In examining the difference in scores between your school and the national figures, you may wish to ask the following questions:

- Which teacher and student items more closely relate to your school's current goals and directions?
- Of these items, which have means falling 0.4 or more below the national figures and above the national figures?
- Which teacher and student items can be placed in a table indicating categories of school success and those the school needs to improve?
- What are the priorities for your school to address given your current goals and directions?

You may wish to network or get together with others who have participated in a workshop based on this book and who have collected data from their schools to:

- compare results and differences and possible reasons for them;
- examine lessons from Chapter 1 and the Leithwood and Louis' (1998) book for how to move your school forward;
- categorize the items with marked differences to get a profile for your school of what teachers and students identify as going well and what falls short;
- compare your school's profile with other school profiles obtained using the short form by others in your group;

- develop strategies based on your experience in the group for moving your school forward.

VALIDITY AND RELIABILITY

How do we know they will provide you with a useful evidence base for school improvement? These are questions about validity and reliability.

All research requires some form of observation. When we develop a questionnaire we are constructing a device to help us gather information about our environment that will provide us with a greater understanding of the nature and characteristics of the things we are observing. When we want to measure constructs such as organizational learning, transformational leadership or student engagement with school, we construct questionnaire items that represent observed characteristics of these constructs. Responses to related items can be grouped to provide scales that measure various aspects of the same construct. The items included in any questionnaire are a small sample of the universe of items associated with a particular construct that could have been selected. How good we are at both choosing the sample of items that best represent the population of observations that can be made and constructing scales from related items for our questionnaires indicates the validity of our instrument. We need to be confident that the scores we obtain from the selected items and the constructed scales are meaningful, strong and generalizable. This means that the measures used must be reliable and valid to allow a range of inferences to be made from them (Cronbach, Gleser, Nanda, & Rajaratnam, 1972).

We have taken a number of steps in constructing our questionnaires and in analysing item responses to provide valid and reliable measures of the constructs we have used in the LOLSO research.

First, we conducted extensive literature reviews to identify what was known about characteristics of the constructs we were investigating—leadership and organizational learning. For instance, we identified seven categories of characteristics that we hypothesized could be associated with conceptualising schools as learning organisations. These were schools that:

> employed processes of **environmental scanning***;*
> developed **shared goals**;
> established **collaborative teaching** and **learning environments**;
> encouraged **initiatives** and **risk taking**;
> **regularly reviewed** all aspects related to and influencing the work of the school;
> **recognized** and **reinforced** good work; and,
> provided **opportunities** for **continuing professional development**.

This specification of characteristics provided the seven constructs representing organizational learning items incorporated in one of the questionnaires. Subsequently, the questionnaire was piloted, revised, and then administered to teachers and principals in the project who responded to each item on a self-report 5-point Likert scale ranging from 1 (*strongly disagree*) to 5 (*strongly agree*). This procedure was employed for all sections of both questionnaires used in the LOLSO Project.

As it is difficult to analyse results from hundreds of questionnaire items, several data reduction procedures were employed. These data reduction procedures included: rating scale analysis from the Quest program (Adams & Khoo, 1993) to reduce the number of questionnaire items to be analysed to those that fitted the Rasch scale and to establish uni-dimensionality for each section of the two questionnaires; exploratory factor analysis with principal component extraction and varimax rotation to help develop scales underlying the constructs to be used in further analysis; and, principal component extraction to confirm the structure of the scales. The factor solutions of the major constructs, organizational learning and transformational leadership were then tested using a further confirmatory procedure employing the structural equation modelling software, LISREL 8 (e.g., Jöreskog & Sörbom, 1993). This resulted in a four-factor correlated nested model for organizational learning being the best fit for the observed data, and a six-factor correlated nested model as the best fit for leadership. These procedures strengthened the construct validity of the measures used to operationalize the constructs employed so that judgments could be made about their meaning with some confidence and inferential methods could be used to draw conclusions and make judgments about the population they represented.

Reliability estimates for each scale from both questionnaires were calculated using Cronbach's alpha (α). All scales indicated an adequate reliability in the range of $\alpha = .74 - .92$.

The LOLSO Project relied on statistical procedures such as Latent Variable Path Analysis with Partial Least Squares (PLSPATH; Sellin, 1990). This procedure allows the testing of models in which variables have been selected on the basis of theory and logical argument in order to predict and explain the effects of variables on one or more criteria (Sellin & Keeves, 1997). The main aims of developing a path model are: (a) to test the construction of the latent variables from observed or manifest variables, (b) to examine causal relationships between the constructs of the model, and (c) to estimate the magnitudes of the hypothesized relationships. A path model represents the concepts and their interrelations as an attempt to bring them into a structured and meaningful order. Model building forces clarification of the ideas and theoretical assumptions involved enhancing further the validity and reliability of the measures employed. The theoretical model thus developed is accepted as adequate or rejected using empirical data and considered methods of measurement and analysis appropriate to the context of the phenomena being examined. Developments in model building using structural equation modelling have provided the opportunity for examining interrelationships among variables not as simple bivariate relationships but as multivariate relationships that more closely represent the complexity of the real world (Keeves, 1986).

The variances of outcomes explained for all models constructed and tested with LOLSO Project data using PLSPATH have resulted in final models where R^2 (the variance explained for the final model) has ranged between .80 to .90. The large amount of variance explained has always been associated with a high Q^2 (indicates well defined and stable models). The strong loadings of the observed variables on the latent variables or constructs and the high variances explained in the models tested are themselves measures of the strength and validity of the items and scales used. Since these have been high in all models tested, the scales and items are serving a meaningful purpose in these models and we can have confidence in their validity and reliability (Kaplan, 1997).

Finally, Kaplan (1964) has argued that the ultimate test of the reliability of instruments used in inquiry methods is their usefulness in providing meaningful data that move us forward in understanding our world. All schools that participated in the LOLSO Project were provided with feedback on the perceptions of teachers and students about their school as measured by the LOLSO constructs employed in the questionnaires. Many of the principals and staff of the cooperating schools used this feedback successfully to enhance the processes and structures in their schools to promote leadership for organizational learning and improved student outcomes.

THE SHORT FORM OF THE LOLSO PROJECT QUESTIONNAIRES

THE SHORT FORM OF THE LOLSO PROJECT QUESTIONNAIRES

- We are interested in the extent to which you agree or disagree with the following statements for your school.
- Base your responses on your personal perceptions and impressions. Avoid dwelling on items—we want your first responses or best guess.
- Use the "N/A" (Not Applicable) response as a last resort if the item does not apply or you don't know.

Please circle only ONE response for each item.

TEACHER QUESTIONNAIRE

To what extent do you agree that the principal:

	Strongly Disagree				Strongly Agree	

PRINCIPAL TRANSFORMATIONAL LEADERSHIP

Vision and Goals

	Strongly Disagree				Strongly Agree	
Gives us a sense of overall purpose.	1	2	3	4	5	N/A
Helps clarify the specific meaning of the school's mission in terms of its practical implications for programs and instruction.	1	2	3	4	5	N/A
Communicates school mission to staff and students.	1	2	3	4	5	N/A
Works toward whole staff consensus in establishing priorities for school goals.	1	2	3	4	5	N/A

Culture

Shows respect for staff by treating us as professionals.	1	2	3	4	5	N/A
Sets a respectful tone for interaction with students.	1	2	3	4	5	N/A
Demonstrates a willingness to change his/her own practices in light of new understandings.	1	2	3	4	5	N/A
Promotes an atmosphere of caring and trust among staff.	1	2	3	4	5	N/A

Structure

Delegates leadership for activities critical for achieving goals.	1	2	3	4	5	N/A
Distributes leadership broadly among the staff representing various viewpoints in leadership positions.	1	2	3	4	5	N/A
Ensures that we have adequate involvement in decision making related to programs and instructions.	1	2	3	4	5	N/A
Supports an effective committee structure for decision making.	1	2	3	4	5	N/A

	Strongly Disagree				Strongly Agree	
Facilitates effective communication among staff.	1	2	3	4	5	N/A

Intellectual Stimulation

Is a source of new ideas for my professional learning.	1	2	3	4	5	N/A
Stimulates me to think about what I am doing for my students.	1	2	3	4	5	N/A
Encourages me to pursue my own goals for professional learning.	1	2	3	4	5	N/A
Encourages us to develop/review individual professional growth goals consistent with school goals and priorities.	1	2	3	4	5	N/A
Encourages us to evaluate our practices and refine them as needed.	1	2	3	4	5	N/A

Individual Support

Takes my opinion into consideration when initiating actions that affect my work.	1	2	3	4	5	N/A
Is aware of my unique needs and expertise.	1	2	3	4	5	N/A
Is inclusive, does not show favouritism toward individuals or groups.	1	2	3	4	5	N/A

Performance Expectations

Has high expectations for us as professionals.	1	2	3	4	5	N/A
Holds high expectations for students.	1	2	3	4	5	N/A
Expects us to be effective innovators.	1	2	3	4	5	N/A

In our school:

Staff Valued

The contributions of all staff members are valued equally.	1	2	3	4	5	N/A

School Autonomy

Our school administrators have secured a high degree of autonomy for the school.	1	2	3	4	5	N/A

	Strongly Disagree			Strongly Agree		

Community Focus

Our school administrators have established a productive working relationship with the community.	1	2	3	4	5	N/A

What is the amount of influence the following have on activities within your school:

	Minimal			Very High	

Distributed Leadership

Teacher committees and/or teams.	1	2	3	4	N/A
The whole staff working together.	1	2	3	4	N/A

In our school:

	Strongly Disagree			Strongly Agree	

ORGANISATIONAL LEARNING

Trusting and Collaborative Climate

Discussions among colleagues are honest and candid.	1	2	3	4	5	N/A
Overall there is mutual support among teachers.	1	2	3	4	5	N/A
Most of us actively seek information to improve our work.	1	2	3	4	5	N/A
We are tolerant of each other's opinions.	1	2	3	4	5	N/A
Colleagues are used as resources.	1	2	3	4	5	N/A
There is ongoing professional dialogue among teachers.	1	2	3	4	5	N/A

Shared and Monitored Mission

Teachers have the opportunity to participate in most significant school-level policy decisions.	1	2	3	4	5	N/A

	Strongly Disagree				Strongly Agree	
We have a coherent and shared sense of direction.	1	2	3	4	5	N/A
We critically examine current practices.	1	2	3	4	5	N/A
Teachers and administrators work in partnership to learn and solve problems together.	1	2	3	4	5	N/A
We actively share information with the parents and community.	1	2	3	4	5	N/A
The effectiveness of the teaching program is regularly monitored.	1	2	3	4	5	N/A

Taking Initiatives/Risks

The school leaders protect those who take risks.	1	2	3	4	5	N/A
The administrators are open to change.	1	2	3	4	5	N/A
School structures support teacher initiatives and risk taking.	1	2	3	4	5	N/A
The administrators empower staff to make decisions.	1	2	3	4	5	N/A
There are rewards for staff who take the initiative.	1	2	3	4	5	N/A
People feel free to experiment and take risks.	1	2	3	4	5	N/A
Staff are valued.	1	2	3	4	5	N/A

Ongoing, Relevant Professional Development

We monitor what's happening outside of the school to find out about best practice.	1	2	3	4	5	N/A
Good use is made of professional readings	1	2	3	4	5	N/A
Groups of staff receive training in how to work and learn in teams.	1	2	3	4	5	N/A
Good use is made of membership of teacher professional associations.	1	2	3	4	5	N/A
We make use of external advisers, e.g., subject associations, project officers, consultants.	1	2	3	4	5	N/A
Adequate time is provided for professional development.	1	2	3	4	5	N/A
Staff engage in ongoing professional development.	1	2	3	4	5	N/A

STUDENT QUESTIONNAIRE

	Strongly Disagree				Strongly Agree	

Home Background

My parents/guardians encourage me to participate in extracurricular activities and events.	1	2	3	4	5	N/A
I often discuss my schoolwork with my parents/guardians.	1	2	3	4	5	N/A
Study aids at home (e.g., books, an encyclopaedia, magazines or computer) help me do better schoolwork.	1	2	3	4	5	N/A
My parents/guardians are always willing to help me with my schoolwork.	1	2	3	4	5	N/A
I often have conversations about world events with my parents/guardians.	1	2	3	4	5	N/A
I have my own workspace at home that is fairly quiet for doing homework and school projects.	1	2	3	4	5	N/A

Teachers' Work

I like the way teachers teach in most of my classes.	1	2	3	4	5	N/A
My teachers use a variety of activities in my classes.	1	2	3	4	5	N/A
My teachers frequently discuss my work with me.	1	2	3	4	5	N/A
Most of my classes are well organized.	1	2	3	4	5	N/A
Most of my teachers expect me always to do my best work.	1	2	3	4	5	N/A
I am constantly challenged in class.	1	2	3	4	5	N/A

PARTICIPATION

Absenteeism

	O	1-5	6-10	+10
Number of times late for school.	1	2	3	4
Number of times skipped class without permission.	1	2	3	4
Number of times absent for whole days.	1	2	3	4

Involved in Classwork

I respond whenever I am asked questions during class.	1	2	3	4	5	N/A
I enjoy giving my opinion during class discussions.	1	2	3	4	5	N/A

Own Goalsetting

Making my own decisions about what to study helps make my schoolwork worthwhile.	1	2	3	4	5	N/A
In my classes, students help decide what we will do for projects and assignments.	1	2	3	4	5	N/A
As a student, I have helped to decide what the rules will be for our school.	1	2	3	4	5	N/A

Extracurricular Activities

	Never	Rarely	S/times	Frequ	Always
I participate in sports events.	1	2	3	4	5
I participate in other school events like plays, concerts etc.	1	2	3	4	5
I participate in one-day events like casual days.	1	2	3	4	5

To what extent do you agree or disagree with the following statements:						
	Strongly Disagree				**Strongly Agree**	

Academic Self-Concept

I am able to understand most of the material covered in my classes.	1	2	3	4	5	N/A
I feel confident that I will be successful in school.	1	2	3	4	5	N/A
I am learning a lot at school.	1	2	3	4	5	N/A
I will graduate from high school.	1	2	3	4	5	N/A
I am satisfied with my marks.	1	2	3	4	5	N/A

ENGAGEMENT

Student-Teacher Relationship

Most of my teachers go out of their way to help students.	1	2	3	4	5	N/A
Most of my teachers are interested in me as a person.	1	2	3	4	5	N/A
Most of my teachers are willing to spend extra time with me.	1	2	3	4	5	N/A
Most of my teachers make me feel comfortable in class.	1	2	3	4	5	N/A
My teachers spend time just talking with me.	1	2	3	4	5	N/A
Most of my teachers seem to understand me.	1	2	3	4	5	N/A
I get along with most of my teachers.	1	2	3	4	5	N/A

Peers

I have got to know other students in our school really well.	1	2	3	4	5	N/A
I get along with most other students I meet in my school.	1	2	3	4	5	N/A

	Strongly Disagree				Strongly Agree	

Utility

My schoolwork is helping me to prepare for life after I finish school.	1	2	3	4	5	N/A
The things I learn in school are useful in my life outside school.	1	2	3	4	5	N/A

Identification With School

School spirit is very high in my school.	1	2	3	4	5	N/A
I feel that I "belong" at this school.	1	2	3	4	5	N/A
I am proud of my school.	1	2	3	4	5	N/A
I really enjoy school most of the time.	1	2	3	4	5	N/A

SCORING SHEETS: TEACHER QUESTIONNAIRE

	Your School Mean	National Mean	Difference

PRINCIPAL TRANSFORMATIONAL LEADERSHIP

Vision and Goals

	Your School Mean	National Mean		Difference
Gives us a sense of overall purpose.	_____	−3.54	=	_____
Helps clarify the specific meaning of the school's mission in terms of its practical implications for programs and instruction.	_____	−3.42	=	_____
Communicates school mission to staff and students.	_____	−3.64	=	_____
Works toward whole staff consensus in establishing priorities for school goals.	_____	−3.50	=	_____

Culture

Shows respect for staff by treating us as professionals.	_____	−3.98	=	_____
Sets a respectful tone for interaction with students.	_____	−4.04	=	_____
Demonstrates a willingness to change his/her own practices in light of new understandings.	_____	−3.49	=	_____
Promotes an atmosphere of caring and trust among staff.	_____	−3.58	=	_____

Structure

Delegates leadership for activities critical for achieving goals.	_____	−3.89	=	_____
Distributes leadership broadly among the staff representing various viewpoints in leadership positions.	_____	−3.66	=	_____
Ensures that we have adequate involvement in decision making related to programs and instructions.	_____	−3.47	=	_____
Supports an effective committee structure for decision making.	_____	−3.77	=	_____
Facilitates effective communication among staff.	_____	−3.39	=	_____

	Your School Mean	National Mean		Difference

Intellectual Stimulation

	Your School Mean	National Mean		Difference
Is a source of new ideas for my professional learning.	_____	−2.92	=	_____
Stimulates me to think about what I am doing for my students.	_____	−3.03	=	_____
Encourages me to pursue my own goals for professional learning.	_____	−3.56	=	_____
Encourages us to develop/review individual professional growth goals consistent with school goals and priorities.	_____	−3.52	=	_____
Encourages us to evaluate our practices and refine them as needed.	_____	−3.44	=	_____

Individual Support

Takes my opinion into consideration when initiating actions that affect my work.	_____	−3.62	=	_____
Is aware of my unique needs and expertise.	_____	−3.32	=	_____
Is inclusive, does not show favouritism toward individuals or groups.	_____	−3.50	=	_____

Performance Expectations

Has high expectations for us as professionals.	_____	−4.08	=	_____
Holds high expectations for students.	_____	−3.98	=	_____
Expects us to be effective innovators.	_____	−3.63	=	_____

Staff Valued

The contributions of all staff members are valued equally.	_____	−3.53	=	_____

School Autonomy

Our school administrators have secured a high degree of autonomy for the school.	_____	−3.50	=	_____

Community Focus

Our school administrators have established a productive working relationship with the community.	_____	−3.58	=	_____

	Your School Mean	National Mean	Difference

Distributed Leadership

Teacher committees and/or teams.	_____	−2.57	= _____
The whole staff working together.	_____	−2.62	= _____

ORGANISATIONAL LEARNING

Trusting and Collaborative Climate

Discussions among colleagues are honest and candid.	_____	−3.65	= _____
Overall there is mutual support among teachers.	_____	−3.90	= _____
Most of us actively seek information to improve our work.	_____	−3.70	= _____
We are tolerant of each other's opinions.	_____	−3.49	= _____
Colleagues are used as resources.	_____	−3.92	= _____
There is ongoing professional dialogue among teachers.	_____	−3.59	= _____

Shared and Monitored Mission

Teachers have the opportunity to participate in most significant school-level policy decisions.	_____	−3.50	= _____
We have a coherent and shared sense of direction.	_____	−3.18	= _____
We critically examine current practices.	_____	−3.30	= _____
Teachers and administrators work in partnership to learn and solve problems together.	_____	−3.23	= _____
We actively share information with the parents and community.	_____	−3.85	= _____
The effectiveness of the teaching program is regularly monitored.	_____	−2.98	= _____

Taking Initiatives/Risks

The school leaders protect those who take risks.	_____	−3.01	= _____
The administrators are open to change.	_____	−3.33	= _____
School structures support teacher initiatives and risk taking.	_____	−3.03	= _____

	Your School Mean	National Mean		Difference
The administrators empower staff to make decisions.	_____	−3.18	=	_____
There are rewards for staff who take the initiative.	_____	−2.85	=	_____
People feel free to experiment and take risks.	_____	−3.29	=	_____
Staff are valued.	_____	−3.53	=	_____

Ongoing, Relevant Professional Development

We monitor what's happening outside of the school to find out about best practice.	_____	−3.16	=	_____
Good use is made of professional readings.	_____	−2.49	=	_____
Groups of staff receive training in how to work and learn in teams.	_____	−2.59	=	_____
Good use is made of membership of teacher professional associations.	_____	−2.86	=	_____
We make use of external advisers, e.g., subject associations, project officers, consultants.	_____	−3.18	=	_____
Adequate time is provided for professional development.	_____	−2.85	=	_____
Staff engage in ongoing professional development.	_____	−3.97	=	_____

SCORING SHEETS: STUDENT QUESTIONNAIRE

	Your School Mean	National Mean	Difference

Home Background

	Your School Mean	National Mean		Difference
My parents/guardians encourage me to participate in extracurricular activities and events.	_____	−3.26	=	_____
I often discuss my schoolwork with my parents/guardians.	_____	−3.28	=	_____
Study aids at home (e.g., books, an encyclopaedia, magazines or computer) help me do better schoolwork.	_____	−3.82	=	_____
My parents/guardians are always willing to help me with my schoolwork.	_____	−3.97	=	_____
I often have conversations about world events with my parents/guardians.	_____	−3.08	=	_____
I have my own workspace at home that is fairly quiet for doing homework and school projects.	_____	−3.62	=	_____

Teachers' Work

	Your School Mean	National Mean		Difference
I like the way teachers teach in most of my classes.	_____	−3.02	=	_____
My teachers use a variety of activities in my classes.	_____	−3.14	=	_____
My teachers frequently discuss my work with me.	_____	−3.19	=	_____
Most of my classes are well organized.	_____	−3.36	=	_____
Most of my teachers expect me always to do my best work.	_____	−4.08	=	_____
I am constantly challenged in class.	_____	−3.18	=	_____

PARTICIPATION

Absenteeism

	Your School Mean	National Mean		Difference
Number of times late for school.	_____	−0.95	=	_____
Number of times skipped class without permission.	_____	−0.50	=	_____
Number of times absent for whole days.	_____	−1.44	=	_____

	Your School Mean	National Mean		Difference

Involved in Classwork

	Your School Mean	National Mean		Difference
I respond whenever I am asked questions during class.	_____	−4.01	=	_____
I enjoy giving my opinion during class discussions.	_____	−3.44	=	_____

Own Goalsetting

Making my own decisions about what to study helps make my schoolwork worthwhile.	_____	−4.04	=	_____
In my classes, students help decide what we will do for projects and assignments.	_____	−2.60	=	_____
As a student, I have helped to decide what the rules will be for our school.	_____	−1.99	=	_____

Extracurricular Activities

I participate in sports events.	_____	−2.10	=	_____
I participate in other school events like plays, concerts etc.	_____	−1.27	=	_____
I participate in one-day events like casual days.	_____	−1.44	=	_____

Academic Self-Concept

I am able to understand most of the material covered in my classes.	_____	−3.76	=	_____
I feel confident that I will be successful in school.	_____	−3.74	=	_____
I am learning a lot at school.	_____	−3.66	=	_____
I will graduate from high school.	_____	−4.21	=	_____
I am satisfied with my marks.	_____	−3.56	=	_____

ENGAGEMENT

Student-Teacher Relationship

Most of my teachers go out of their way to help students.	_____	−3.27	=	_____
Most of my teachers are interested in me as a person.	_____	−2.99	=	_____

	Your School Mean	National Mean		Difference
Most of my teachers are willing to spend extra time with me.	_____	−3.12	=	_____
Most of my teachers make me feel comfortable in class.	_____	−3.45	=	_____
My teachers spend time just talking with me.	_____	−2.82	=	_____
Most of my teachers seem to understand me.	_____	−3.07	=	_____
I get along with most of my teachers.	_____	−3.56	=	_____

Peers

	Your School Mean	National Mean		Difference
I have got to know other students in our school really well.	_____	−4.20	=	_____
I get along with most other students I meet in my school.	_____	−4.01	=	_____

Utility

	Your School Mean	National Mean		Difference
My schoolwork is helping me to prepare for life after I finish school.	_____	−3.90	=	_____
The things I learn in school are useful in my life outside school.	_____	−3.34	=	_____

Identification With School

	Your School Mean	National Mean		Difference
School spirit is very high in my school.	_____	−2.81	=	_____
I feel that I "belong" at this school.	_____	−3.20	=	_____
I am proud of my school.	_____	−3.00	=	_____
I really enjoy school most of the time.	_____	−3.10	=	_____

APPENDIXES

APPENDIX 1

CONDITIONS FOSTERING ORGANIZATIONAL LEARNING IN SCHOOLS[3]

Kenneth Leithwood
Ontario Institute for Studies In Education, University of Toronto
252 Bloor St. West, Toronto, Ontario, M5S 1V6

Laurie Leonard
Louisiana Tech University
Ruston, Louisiana 91272

Lyn Sharratt
Superintendent of Schools, York Region Board of Education
Newmarket, Ontario

This article reports the results of synthesizing evidence from three independent studies of conditions that foster organizational learning in schools carried out in different contexts but with comparable methods. Its purpose was to identify such conditions from state, district, and school sources and to assess the context sensitivity of each of the conditions. Qualitative data were provided by a total sample of 111 teachers in 14 schools. Results identified a large number of conditions that fostered organizational learning in all schools. Among the most important of these conditions was transformational forms of principal leadership.

The persistence of calls for school reform, along with the ambitious yet uncertain nature of that reform, has prompted growing support for the importance of OL in schools (e.g., Chapman, 1996; Fullan, 1991; Louis, 1994). Such support gives voice to widespread disenchantment with the results of what Louis (1994) calls "managed" change, along with new levels of respect for "local capacity" in successful school improvement efforts. The report of the National Commission on Teaching and America's Future provides a recent case in point. In her summary of this report,

---

[3] Leithwood, K., Leonard, L., and Sharratt, *Educational Administration Quarterly*, *34*(2), 243-276, copyright (c) 1998 by Corwin Press. Reprinted by permission of Corwin Press, Inc.

187

Darling-Hammond (1996) offers a hard-hitting critique of the current status of teacher preparation in the United States. According to Darling-Hammond, the commission concludes that

> Children can reap the benefits of current knowledge about teaching and learning only if schools and schools of education are dramatically redesigned. . . . It is now clear that most schools and teachers cannot produce the kind of learning demanded by the new reforms – not because they do not want to, but because they do not know how, and the systems they work in do not support their efforts to do so. (p. 194)

The commission argues that schools are presently structured for failure: They bear little resemblance to the flatter, more complex organizational designs associated with high performance (e.g., Banner & Gagne, 1995; Lawler, 1986). Schools need to be redesigned, recommends the commission, "to become genuine learning organizations for both students and teachers" (Darling-Hammond, 1996, p. 198).

The commission makes a strong plea for the redesign of schools as learning organizations. Motivated, as they might be, to heed the call of the commission, however, those responsible for school redesign have little more than a handful of recent empirical studies in which to draw for authoritative knowledge about the characteristics of schools that foster OL (e.g., Louis & Kruse, 1995; Mitchell, 1994).

This article synthesizes the results of three studies (Leithwood, Jantzi, & Steinbach, 1995; Leonard, 1996; Sharratt, 1996), each of which inquired about leadership and other conditions that foster or inhibit OL in schools. Each study was guided by the same theoretical framework, collected qualitative, multicase study data, and analyzed these data in comparable ways. However, each study was conducted in quite different contexts. These contextual differences, in combination with similarities in the studies' purposes, guiding conceptual frames and methods, provide unique opportunities to explore questions about the similarity of OL conditions under different organizational contexts. Given different stimuli for learning, and different organizational contexts, to what extent are there similarities and differences in the conditions that foster or inhibit such learning? Which conditions seem most robust across stimuli and contexts? Which conditions seem to vary by stimuli and context? These are the central questions explored in this article.

FRAMEWORK

An extensive literature on OL in non-school organizations (reviewed in Cousins, 1996; Leithwood & Aitken, 1995) was used to develop the framework for the three studies providing the data for the study described in this article. This framework includes a perspective on the nature of OL processes, causes and consequences of such processes, and forms of school leadership likely to foster such conditions and processes. Although school leadership is reasonably conceptualized among the causes and/or consequences of OL, it was of special interest to us and, therefore, was treated separately in the framework.

OL Processes

Collective learning is not just the sum of individual learning even though individual learning is a necessary part of collective learning. Nevertheless, most accounts of collective learning assume that it is either literally or metaphorically very similar to individual learning. In these accounts, cognitive explanations of individual learning are used to represent the nature of OL processes (e.g., Cohen, 1996; Cohen & Bacdayan, 1996; Gioia, 1986; Hedberg, 1981).

The metaphorical use of individual cognitive processes to explain OL has added considerably to our understanding of collective learning. An obvious example of such use is Morgan's (1986) image of organizations as brains; a more subtle use is Cohen and Bacdayan's (1996) analysis of organizational routines as if they were individual procedural memories. Such evidence notwithstanding, it is important to be clear on the limitations of this approach. As Cook and Yanow (1996) inquire, why should two things so different in other ways as individuals and organizations be expected to carry out the same processes in order to learn? Additionally, cognitive conceptions of individual learning are very much under development and, in many respects, are contested. Although they have contributed a good deal to an appreciation of how learning occurs among individuals, they cannot be adopted uncritically, even as metaphors, for insights about OL.

For the concept of OL to be viable, it is useful to have a concept of a collective mind that is doing the learning even if such mind is not the seat of cognitive activity. Wegner (1987) suggests,

> [Collective] mind may take the form of cognitive interdependence focused around memory processes. . . . People in close relationships enact a single transactive memory system, complete with differentiated responsibility for remembering different portions of common experience. People know locations rather than the details of common events and rely on one another to contribute missing details that cue their own retrieval. (Cited in Weick & Roberts, 1996, p. 332)

According to this explanation, only individuals can contribute to a collective mind and only the mind of individuals can be conceptualized as a set of internalized processes controlled by a brain. Collective mind must be an external representation, mind as activity rather than mind as entity. The collective mind, then, is to be found in patterns of behavior that range from *intelligent* to *stupid*. This view of collective learning has similarities with connectionist explanations of the individual mind. From this perspective, mind can be knowledgeable without containing knowledge.

> The new metaphor suggested by connectionism is mind as pattern recognizer. . . . The idea is that the mind acquires abilities and dispositions to recognize and respond in various ways to various patterns, but the patterns are not in the mind. We can say that the patterns are in the environment or, more cautiously, that the patterns are a way for us as observers to describe relations between the mind and the environment. (Bereiter & Scardamalia, in press)

Collective learning develops from the actions of individuals as those individuals begin to act in ways heedful of the "imagined requirements of joint action" (Weick & Roberts, 1996, p. 338). These requirements might be implied in the organization's culture (Cook & Yanow, 1996). But they could also include more immediate and explicit demands on joint action. March (1991), Hutchins (1991), and Schoenfeld (1989) describe the type of learning in which individual members of groups engage in "mutual adaptation" an essentially connectionist view of individual learning applied to the collective.

Mutual adaptation can be of two sorts. One sort is largely unreflective. For example, in the case of Hutchin's (1991) navigation team, when individual team members confronted a change in what they believed was required of the whole team, each of the members adapted their usual contribution to the team as best they could, hoping that other members would be able to do whatever else was required. This was implicit negotiation of the division of labor. When it seemed not to be sufficient as a response to the team's new challenge, individual members then attempted to recruit others to take on part of what was assumed to be her part of the team's job, a second form of mutual adaptation.

In the case of Schoenfeld's (1989) research team, the task was to construct a coherent explanation for a set of data about a student's mathematical learning processes.   Individual members or subgroups of the whole team typically constructed their own explanations of the data set first. Then, they shared these explanations and engaged in some form of interaction that often produced a shared explanation significantly different than any of the individual member's or subgroup's explanations. Schoenfeld describes the process as follows:

Let the subgroups be A and B, the idea [original explanation] in its old form X1, and in its improved form X2. The schema [process] goes as follows:

- A either ignores or rejects X1 (so X1 would remain as it is);
- B considers X1 important (but is unlikely to produce X2);
- In group interactions, B convinces A to seriously consider X1; A suggests the change from X1 to X2, which the group ratifies; Hence the group produces the change from X1 to X2, while neither subgroup A or B would have done so by itself. (p. 74)

In both the Hutchins (1991) and Schoenfeld (1989) examples, an imagined new challenge for the team serves as the stimulus for individual team members to adapt their contributions to the team's actions. In this way, the individual is contributing to the learning of the team. As other team members adapt their contributions not only in response to their sense of the team's new challenge but also in response to the responses of other members, each team member learns about the adequacy of her initial response and perhaps the need to adapt further. This is the way in which the individual learns from the team. And, as Schoenfeld explains, "the result of the group interactions extended significantly beyond the 'natural' sum of the contributions that could have been made individually by the people involved" (p. 76).

This theoretical account of OL processes is provided as important conceptual background for understanding the main focus of the article, the conditions influencing such OL processes. Empirical evidence concerning the nature of these processes, while collected in each of the three separate studies, is beyond the scope of this article.

Causes and Consequences of OL Processes

Our explanation of the causes and consequences of OL processes is framed by five sets of variables, and the relationships among them, identified in two extensive literature reviews described in detail elsewhere (Cousins, 1996; Leithwood & Aitken, 1995). The five sets of variables include the following: the stimulus for OL, out-of-school conditions influencing OL, in-school conditions influencing OL, leadership, and, the outcomes of OL. Relationships among these variables are complex. Whereas the stimulus for OL is considered to have a direct effect on OL processes, the nature of these processes, in response, is mediated by leadership, out-of-school, and in-school conditions. Relationships among these variables are themselves reciprocal. Only OL processes influence OL outcomes.

Stimulus for Learning

OL is assumed to be prompted by some felt need (e.g., to respond to the call for implementing a new policy) or perception of a problem prompted from inside or outside the school that leads to a collective search for a solution. Watkins and Marsick (1993) suggest that relatively dramatic events (a labor strike, for example) are needed to stimulate OL. As in the case of OL processes, although this variable is part of our framework, no empirical evidence concerning it is reported in this article.

Out-of-School Conditions

Included within the meaning of out-of-school conditions are initiatives taken by those outside the school (e.g., Ministry or state personnel, district staff), or conditions that exist outside the school (e.g., economic health of the community) that influence conditions and initiatives inside the school. Our studies focused only on those out-of-school conditions created by the Ministry of Education, the local school community, and the school district. We asked, What sorts of conditions outside of schools have a bearing on OL in schools? What is it about school districts, local school communities and the Ministry of Education that fosters or inhibits OL in schools? What would be the characteristics of such an "external environment" that unambiguously nourished the development of schools as learning organizations?

School Conditions

These are initiatives taken by those in the school, or conditions prevailing in the school, that either foster or inhibit OL. Starting from Fiol and Lyles (1985) and Watkins and Marsick (1993) suggestions, our studies associated such conditions with the school's mission and vision, culture, decision-making structures, strategies used for change, and the nature of policies along with the availability and distribution of resources. Our studies asked, What do schools look like when they are behaving like learning organizations? Specifically, what is it about a school's vision, culture, structure, strategies, decision processes, and policies and resources that gives rise to or detracts from OL?

School Leadership

Defining our meaning of school leadership were practices of those in formal administrative roles, usually principals, that help determine the direction of improvements in the school and that influence the nature and extent of efforts by school members to learn how to bring about these improvements. Research on OL in nonschool organizations suggests that leadership by those in formal leadership roles is an especially powerful influence on OL, both directly and indirectly (Kofman & Senge, 1995). Mohrman and Mohrman (1995) assert that such leadership

> entails being a continual catalyst for the change process by formulating and updating a compelling change agenda, helping the organization envision the future, unleashing the energy and resources to fuel the change process and helping the organization experience change as success rather than failure. (p. 101)

Senge (1990) views such processes as the outcome of leaders acting as stewards, designers, and teachers. Through enacting such roles, they help build organizations "where people expand their capabilities to understand complexity, clarify vision, and improve shared mental models" (p. 340).

These views resonate closely with a model of transformational school leadership developed in some of our previous work (e.g., Leithwood, 1994; Leithwood & Jantzi, 1990; Leithwood & Steinbach, 1993) and for which there was preliminary evidence of effects on OL. As a consequence, the starting point for our perspective on leadership in the three studies was the eight dimensions of leadership practice associated with this model. These dimensions include practices aimed at identifying and articulating a vision, fostering the acceptance of group goals, and providing individualized support for staff members. Transformational leadership practices also aim to stimulate organizational members to think reflectively and critically about their own practices, and to provide appropriate models of the practices and values considered central to the organization. Holding high performance expectations, building shared norms and beliefs (culture), and structuring the organization to permit broad participation in decision making also can have important consequences for OL.

With this initial view of transformational school leadership, our studies asked: What sorts of leadership practices on the part of school administrators contribute significantly to OL and to the conditions which foster OL? Are these practices consistent with our initial model of transformational leadership or should this model be revised or abandoned?

Outcomes

To be worth continuing attention, OL must result in something consequential for schools. These are likely to be individual and collective understandings, skills, commitments, and overt practices resulting from OL in schools. Such outcomes are assumed to mediate the effects of the school's learning on student growth.

METHODS

Research Design

A qualitative, multicase study design was adopted for the three individual studies providing the data for this study. The most frequent assumption made about theory in the methodological literature concerning such a design is that it will be developed from the case study data using grounded techniques (e.g., Strauss & Corbin, 1994). In contrast with this assumption, the research design for our studies is best characterized as framework guided. This approach was used for several reasons. The essential reason (Merriam, 1988; Miles & Huberman, 1984) is that a considerable body of relevant research literature was already available. Although much of that research was not specifically developed in school contexts, it identified "gaps in understanding, . . . [provided one means] to interpret findings, . . . [and helped] to delineate important variables for study and suggest relationships among them" (Strauss & Corbin, 1994, p. 49). Second, each of the three studies was carried out in multiple sites: the three studies combined having been conducted in a total of 14 school sites. A prior framework increased the likelihood of being able to make useful comparisons across sites (Miles & Huberman, 1984). Third, limited resources for each study precluded unfocused data collection and analysis of the large volumes of data often associated with more grounded approaches. These second and third reasons, of course, are only legitimate if the first essential reason or condition is met.

The three individual studies, as well as this cross-study analysis, are multicase to increase the external validity of the results. Indeed, external validity is one of the main questions for this study (To what extent are the variables influencing OL processes context-sensitive?). Such generalizability is not often the concern of those using case study methods (Merriam, 1988). But, as Miles and Huberman (1984) argue, there is no theoretical reason that such methods cannot be used for this purpose. This is especially so, as in our work, when the purpose of the research lies at a midpoint between exploration of a poorly understood phenomenon and confirmation of a well-developed theory.

Sample

The bases on which the three samples of schools were chosen did not guarantee that these schools would be exemplary learning organizations. Nor was this important for purposes of the study. Informed by Watkins and Marsick's (1993) evidence, we assumed that OL is a necessary activity within virtually all schools but the nature, direction, speed, use, and the like, vary widely across schools. Two issues were important in selecting the schools. First, there needed to be sufficient demand for learning in the selected schools that it would be detectable with the research methods available to us. Participation in an external reform initiative seemed to provide such a demand. Second, school conditions needed to vary significantly to discriminate among those that fostered, inhibited, or had no effect on OL. We assumed that typically, this would be the case across schools without manipulation of the selection process beyond ensuring variation in school size and level (elementary, secondary). A total of 14 schools and 111 teachers were included in the three studies: 6 schools and 72 teachers in Study 1; 5 schools and 24 teachers in Study 3; and 3 schools and 15 teachers in Study 2.

Study 1 schools were selected as promising sites of OL from two sources of evidence. One of these sources was the data available about the school as a result of its participation in one or more earlier phases of our research (Leithwood, Jantzi, & Steinbach, 1995): This was the case for 4 schools. Another source was a school's reputation, among two or more district staff, as making substantial progress toward restructuring (2 schools), something akin to Rosenholtz's (1989) "moving schools." The cases also were selected to represent the full K-12 spectrum of school levels : 1 primary, 1 elementary, 1 junior secondary, 2 secondary, and 1 senior secondary. Principals in each school were asked to nominate up to 12 teachers who would be willing to be interviewed. Nominees were to be broadly representative of the staff with differences in curricular areas taught, years of experience, and gender reflecting the variety of experience and expertise within the school.

Selection of schools and teachers for Studies 2 and 3 was constrained by the special nature of the challenges with which they were dealing. Only 9 schools in total were part of the Newfoundland school council pilot study. In addition to their participation in the pilot study, the three schools chosen for Study 2 together covered the full K-12 spectrum of grades, were not under the jurisdiction of only one school district, and were located in the same general geographic region of the province for ease of data collection. Principals were asked by the researcher to select teachers who were broadly representative of the staff: At least 1 teacher selected had to be a member of the school council. All schools and teachers with access to the necessary computer hardware and software volunteered to participate in Study 3.

Data Collection and Analysis

Interview data were collected from teachers in Study 1 using an instrument which consisted of 28 questions about all components in the conceptual framework. This instrument served as the basis for interviews in Studies 2 and 3 supplemented to accommodate the special nature of the contexts in which the schools were working (school council implementation in Study 2 and electronic access to curriculum resources in Study 3). Principals also were interviewed with a similar instrument in Studies 1 and 2. Teacher interviews averaged about 50 minutes in length, principal interviews about 90 minutes. All interviews were tape recorded and transcribed, producing approximately 1,500 pages of double-spaced text.

The first stage of transcript analysis consisted of identifying idea units corresponding to subcategories (described more fully below) within each of the five categories included in the framework section of this article (stimulus, out-of-school conditions, school conditions, leadership, and OL outcomes). To help ensure the internal validity or dependability (Lincoln & Guba, 1985) of our results, all three studies used triangulation (multiple coders), and left very explicit "audit trails" (Merriam, 1988). All data were analyzed by a team of at least two researchers (three in the case of Study 1). The Study 1 team jointly coded 1 entire transcript to help in developing the list of preliminary codes. After the coding list was compiled, three researchers, none of whom were the interviewers (to maintain objectivity) worked together on 12 transcripts to arrive at a common understanding of how each statement should be coded; this entailed not only allocating preliminary codes to statements but also adding new codes and revising some of the preliminary codes. To determine reliability, three researchers subsequently coded five additional transcripts independently. Agreement ranged from 71% to 83%, with a mean score of 75%; discrepancies in judgement were resolved through discussion. Finally, three researchers independently coded the remaining transcripts, consulting each other frequently to resolve dilemmas.

Studies 2 and 3 used variations on the coding scheme developed in Study 1. Each member of the two-person teams coded all transcripts and differences in coding were resolved through discussion, sometimes with the participation of a third researcher.

A second stage of analysis of the interview data in all the three studies entailed recording explicit links or associations made by teachers among two or more individual codes. Links or associations were segments of transcribed text in which teachers talked about a relationship between two or more variables related to OL. For example, "Most of us in the history department began to use some cooperative learning strategies in our classrooms after spending a number of meetings, organized by our new head, discussing Amelia's experiences with this method." The associations being made by this teacher are among OL outcomes (use of cooperative learning strategies), leadership (the head's initiative), and a school condition that would be coded as "structure" (the meetings which allowed for learning from Amelia's experience).

Such excerpts were pulled from the transcripts using one of two software programs for qualitative analysis (HyperQual 2, NUD*IST). Summaries were then developed of the number of teachers who had made associations between the major sets of variables being studied and the number of different connections that were made within each school. Because the number of teachers varied among the schools, an average number of association per teacher was calculated to allow comparison of schools.

The total number of associations coded was 1,241 in the case of Study 1, 1,111 in Study 2, and 1,491 in Study 3. These numbers may underestimate the actual linkages made between variables within the schools. Because this was a new method of analysis for us, coders tended to be conservative in making assumptions about associations if teachers' responses were not unquestionably explicit. If associations were underreported, such would be the case across all schools; no individual school would have been treated differently.

This quantification of verbal associations has both advantages and disadvantages. We chose to do it because one of our goals was to discover the importance of the many relationships explicit in our framework: Were some of these relationships more prevalent in teachers' experience than others?   Counting associations accomplishes this purpose. On the other hand, reducing the links between variables made by teachers to frequency counts eliminates the possibility of better understanding the nature of the relationship and the reasons why teachers perceived such relationships to be significant. Subsequent efforts to analyze verbal data about associations, both qualitatively and quantitatively, would be useful.

Context

Both geographical location and educational context were quite different across the three studies. Study 1 was carried out in British Columbia. At the time of the study, schools in that province were about 4 years into their responses to the province's comprehensive Year 2000 school restructuring policy (Ministry of Education, 1989). Although these schools had their own local priorities, it would have been difficult for them not to feel acutely aware of the need to make some response to the provincial initiative, and each was making such a response.

The province of Newfoundland was the location of Study 2. Schools included in this study were part of a pilot project initiated by the province in relation to its new policy creating local school councils on which was strong parent and other community representation, although in an advisory capacity (Newfoundland, 1992). The aim of the pilot project was to generate knowledge that could be used by other schools in the province, beginning in 1997-1998, when all were required to have such councils. An important early task facing the pilot schools was to negotiate a "protocol agreement" with their districts that set out precisely their relationship with their districts.

Schools in Study 3 were located in one large school district in south-central Ontario and were part of an experiment in technology integration. A provincial professional association had developed a set of curriculum resources for teachers of Grades 7 through 9 and had made it available to teachers throughout the province in hard copy. In addition, an electronic data base including the same resources had been provided to teachers in Study 3 schools, along with the computer hardware and training required to access the resource in electronic form.

RESULTS

This comparison of results across studies is reported in three parts. First, relationships among the categories of variables in our framework are examined for the purpose of identifying those that exercise the greatest influence on OL processes and the extent to which their influence is context dependent. Second, specific characteristics of each variable, identified in the first section as an especially strong influence on OL processes, are described except for leadership practices which foster OL; they are described in the third and final part.

Variables Influencing OL Processes

This section is concerned with two questions: Which variables have the strongest overall influence on OL processes? and To what extent is the influence of these variables context dependent? Figure 1 and Tables 1, 2, and 3 provide the information available from the three studies to answer these questions. Figure 1 summarizes the framework which guided the three studies. This figure also indicates the relative influence on OL processes of 9 individual variables within each of three categories of variables. Three variables are classified as out-of-school (district, community, and Ministry); 5 variables are classified as in-school (vision, culture, structure, strategy, and policy and resources). School leadership is treated as a single, independent variable.

The arrows in the three rectangles in Figure 1 are intended to show either direct or indirect relationships between out-of-school conditions, in-school conditions, school leadership, and OL processes. Arrows pointing to the left signify a direct association or relationship with OL processes. Arrows pointing to the right indicate a relationship with OL processes mediated by some other variable or set of variables: For example, some teachers indicated that the community influenced OL processes through its influence on such aspects of the school as its culture, structure, and the like.

The relative influence on OL processes of these variables is indicated by numbers representing a rank. Data in Tables 1, 2, and 3 are the basis for these ranks. Table 1 compares the frequency with which teachers interviewed in all three studies made explicit, direct associations in their own words between the 9 variables and OL processes (e.g., expressed the opinion that frequent opportunities to collaborate with their colleagues, which we coded as a feature of their school's structure, stimulated several of them to read and discuss, an OL process, how to do authentic student assessment). For each study, the number of explicit associations made by teachers between each variable and OL processes is reported as a percentage of the total sum of all explicit associations made (see columns headed "%"), including those associations made with other components of the framework. Based on these percentages, each variable is ranked in relation to all other variables in each study (see columns headed "Rank"). For instance, numerous associations were made between stimuli and OL processes as well as between OL processes and OL outcomes. These data, though undoubtedly important to our further understanding of OL in schools, are beyond the scope of this article. The two columns at the far right of Table 1 report mean percentages across the three studies for each of the 9 variables as well as the overall rank of each variable based on the mean percentage.

These overall ranks appear in Figure 1 on the small arrows pointing directly (left) to OL processes.

Table 2, following the same format as Table 1, is the basis for ranking the indirect influence on OL processes of out-of-school and leadership variables. In both cases, as Figure 1 indicates, this indirect influence is exercised through in-school conditions (e.g., a teacher states that provision of substitute teachers to the school by the district allows for the school to pay for the substitutes needed to engage in the frequent meetings of colleagues which directly foster OL processes). Table 3 combines the results reported in Tables 1 and 2 reporting the combined direct and indirect effects of the three sets of variables influencing OL processes.

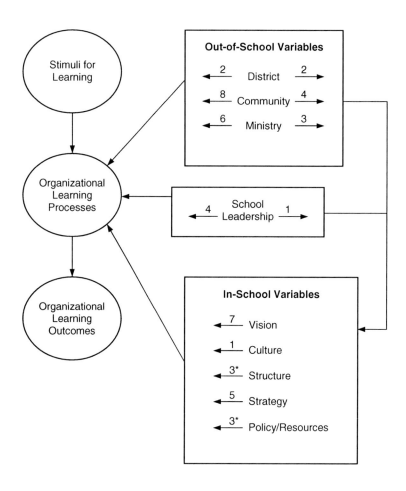

Figure 1. A Summary of influences on organizational learning processes.

Note. Numbers denote relative "strength of influence" based on the frequency with which teachers associated the variable with organizational learning (OL) processes. Arrows pointing left denote direct influence on OL processes. Arrows pointing right denote indirect influence on OL processes through in-school variables.
*Tied in importance.

Table 1. Direct Effects on Organizational Learning Processes

	Study 1 (British Columbia)	Study 2 (Newfoundland)	Study 3 (Ontario)	Mean (all studies)
	Rank (%)	Rank (%)	Rank (%)	Rank (%)
Out-of-school variable				
District	2(5.4)	2(10.7)	1(8.3)	2(8.1)
Ministry	7(1.9)	4(5.8)	5(1.7)	6(3.1)
Community	9(0.2)	8(3.4)	6(1.1)	8(1.6)
Total	(7.5)	(19.9)	(11.1)	(12.8)
In-school variable				
Vision	8(0.7)	6(4.5)	7(0.6)	7(1.9)
Culture	1(7.0)	1(11.4)	2(6.6)	1(8.3)
Structure	3(3.9)	7(4.1)	3(6.1)	3(4.7)
Strategy	4(3.8)	6(4.5)	5(1.7)	5(3.3)
Policy and resources	5(3.0)	5(5.6)	4(5.5)	3(4.7)
Total	(18.4)	(30.1)	(20.5)	(22.9)
Leadership	6(2.9)	3(5.9)	5(1.7)	4(3.5)

Note. This table summarizes the relative importance of each of the 9 identified variables in terms of direct associations teachers made with OL processes in their schools. Due to the variation in the numbers of teachers interviewed in the schools and in the studies, raw frequencies were converted to percentages and, subsequently, to rankings for the individual case studies as well as for the overall means.

Variables Most Strongly Influencing OL Processes

In terms of estimating overall influence, the mean percentages across all three studies reported in Table 3 (far right column) is most useful. As the percentages of total direct and indirect associations with OL processes reported in this column indicate, the district (13.8%), school leadership (11.4%), and school culture (8.3%) were cited as influential much more frequently that the remaining 6 variables.

When only overall direct associations with OL processes are considered (Table 1, far right column), both district (8.1%) and school culture (8.3%) retain their preeminent influence. In addition, school structures (4.7%) and policies/resources (4.7%) emerge as moderately influential. The direct effects of school leadership were mentioned next in frequency (3.5%) but not much more often than the school's strategies for change (3.3%), and the Ministry (3.1%). As Table 2 indicates (far right column), school leadership, and the district were mentioned considerably more frequently by teachers (7.9% and 5.7%, respectively), as indirect influences on OL processes, than were either the community or the Ministry (2.7% and 1%).

Based on the teacher interview evidence from our three studies, in sum, the 5 key variables that appeared to account for teachers' individual and collective learning were (especially) the district, school leadership, school culture, and (less critical but still influential) school structure and policies and resources. The specific characteristics of these 5 variables are outlined in the second part of this section.

Effects of Context on Variables Influencing OL Processes

Our estimate of the extent to which context affects the variables influencing OL processes is based on the degree of consistency found across the three studies in the frequency of associations made by teachers between the 9 variables in our framework and OL processes. As Tables 1, 2, and 3 illustrate, if proportions of total associations are used to estimate consistency, context seems to make an enormous difference. In Table 1, for example, differences in the highest and lowest percentages across the three studies for each of the 9 variables range from a low of 37% (structure) to a high of 95% (community), with a mean difference of approximately 60%. Similar ranges also are evident in Tables 2 and 3.

Using rankings rather than percentages to estimate consistency across studies in the influence of variables on OL processes tells a very different story, however. Evidence concerning direct effects on OL processes (see Table 1) indicates that across the three studies, there were differences of:

- only one rank position for the variables district, culture, and policy and resources;
- only two rank positions for vision and strategy;
- more than two rank positions for the remaining 4 variables (structure was ranked identically in two of the three studies, however).

Table 2. *Indirect Effects on Organizational Learning Processes.*

	Study 1 (British Columbia)	Study 2 (Newfoundland)	Study 3 (Ontario)	Mean (all studies)
	Rank (%)	Rank (%)	Rank (%)	Rank (%)
Out-of-school variable				
District	2(4.2)	3(2.0)	2(11.0)	2(5.7)
Ministry	4(1.5)	4(0.3)	4(1.1)	4(1.0)
Community	3(3.5)	2(2.4)	3(2.2)	3(2.7)
Total	(9.2)	(4.7)	(14.3)	(9.4)
Leadership	1(7.1)	1(4.5)	1(12.2)	1(7.9)

Note. This table summarizes the relative importance of each of the 9 identified variables in terms of indirect associations teachers made with OL processes in their schools. Due to the variation in the numbers of teachers interviewed in the schools and in the studies, raw frequencies were converted to percentages and, subsequently, to rankings for the individual case studies as well as for the overall means.

Evidence concerning combined direct and indirect effects indicates that across the three studies there were differences of

- only one rank position for the variables district, culture, vision, and community;
- only two rank positions for the variable leadership;
- more than two rank positions for the remaining 4 variables, although one of these (structure) was ranked identically in two of the three studies.

Table 2, concerned with indirect effects and only 4 variables, reported identical rankings for 2 variables and a difference of only 1 rank position for the others.

Evidence of consistency across contexts based on rankings seems quite convincing. This is especially the case for district and culture, 2 of the 5 variables most frequently associated by teachers with their OL processes. Of the remaining 3 variables associated most frequently with OL processes,

- Leadership was the first ranked variable across all three studies in terms of indirect effects, and seemed also to be a highly ranked, combined, direct and indirect influence on OL processes with teachers in Studies 1 and 3, and slightly lower in Study 2.
- Structure was ranked identically (third) as a direct influence by teachers in Studies 1 and 3, but quite differently (seventh) by teachers in Study 2.
- Policy and resources was ranked almost identically (fourth and fifth) as a direct influence by teachers in all three studies.

In sum, at least the evidence concerning consistency of rankings offers reasonably compelling support for the claim that those variables most frequently cited by teachers as contributing to their individual and collective learning were similar across the different contexts of the three studies.

Specific Characteristics of Variables Strongly Influencing OL

District

Teachers in the three studies identified five categories of district features, and a total of three dozen specific features within these categories, associated with their OL processes. Little distinction was evident in the data between district conditions which affected individual as distinct from collective learning.

The "missions and visions" of school districts were potentially fruitful sources of learning for school staffs. But to realize this potential, such visions had to be clear, well understood, and meaningful. To foster OL in schools, district visions and missions also had to engender a sense of commitment on the part of school staffs. When these conditions were met, and when district visions acknowledged the need for continuous professional growth, teachers and administrators used the visions as starting points and frameworks for envisioning more specific futures for their own

Table 3. Combined Direct and Indirect Effects on Organizational Learning Processes.

	Study 1 (British Columbia)	Study 2 (Newfoundland)	Study 3 (Ontario)	Mean (all studies)
	Rank (%)	Rank (%)	Rank (%)	Rank (%)
Out-of-school variable				
District	2(9.6)	1(12.7)	1(19.3)	1(13.8)
Ministry	7(3.4)	4(6.1)	7(2.8)	6(4.1)
Community	6(3.7)	5(5.8)	6(3.3)	5(4.3)
Total				(22.8)
In-school variable				
Vision	9(0.7)	8(4.5)	9(0.6)	8(1.9)
Culture	3(7.0)	2(11.4)	3(6.6)	3(8.3)
Structure	4(3.9)	9(4.1)	4(6.1)	4(4.7)
Strategy	5(3.8)	7(4.5)	8(1.7)	7(3.3)
Policy and resources	8(3.0)	6(5.6)	5(5.5)	5(4.7)
Total				(22.9)
Leadership	1(10.0)	3(10.4)	2(13.9)	2(11.4)

Note. This table summarizes the relative importance of each of the 9 identified variables in terms of the combined (i.e., direct and indirect) associations teachers made with OL processes in their schools. Due to the variation in the numbers of teachers interviewed in the schools and in the studies, raw frequencies were converted to percentages and, subsequently, to rankings for the individual case studies as well as for the overall means. Percentages do not total 100, as only those associations made between organizational learning processes and the 9 identified variables were included for the purposes of this report.

schools. In the process, staff also were establishing the long-term goals for their own professional learning. Widely shared district missions and visions, furthermore, sometimes provided filters for screening and evaluating the salience of external demands for change. Also, they served as nonprescriptive clues about which initiatives, taken by schools, would be valued and supported by district personnel. As one principal said, in the context of implementing school councils,

> Most of the initiatives, for instance, on the pilot projects that we are involved in our school, they have all been district originated; so for that reason I think they have a vision towards school improvement and accountability for our school.

"Collaborative and harmonious" captures much of what was considered to be important about district cultures when they contributed to OL. Rather than a we-they attitude, perceived to promote hostility and resistance toward district initiatives, learning appears to have been fostered by a shared sense of district community. This sense of community was more likely when there was interaction with other schools (e.g., feeder schools), something noticed when it did not happen. As one teacher in our studies complained,

> They don't get together here. . . . It wouldn't be hard for two or three schools to get together and have a little science fair and involve everybody. I don't see many of that kind of thing happening very often.

Sense of community also was more likely with clear communication, with support for district initiatives (training, professional development), and when disagreements in the district were settled in ways perceived to be professional. District cultures fostered OL also when the need for continuous change was accepted, and when new initiatives clearly built on previous work.

District structures fostered OL when they provided ample opportunity for school-based staff to participate in shaping both district and school-level decisions. As one teacher in our studies explained,

> The committees get the job done because committees consist of people who are experiencing the difficulties and the questions and the problems, or the goods and the strengths of the program, and bring it back and that's what gets shared.

Participation in district decisions also taught those involved about the wider issues faced by the district and those influences not readily evident in schools that were, nevertheless, germane to district decisions. Considerable delegation of decision making to schools (possibly through site-based management) enhanced opportunities for improving the collective problem-solving capacities of staff. Such decision making also permitted staff to create solutions that were sensitive to important aspects of the school's context. Multiple forums for participation in district decision making were helpful, as was (in the case of Study 3) the electronic networking of schools.

To foster learning, it was perceived to be useful for districts to use many different strategies for reaching out to schools—through newsletters, workshops, informal and electronic forms of communication and the like. Especially influential were workshops and mentoring programs, and specific change initiatives designed to assist in achieving district goals and priorities. Strategies that buffered schools from excessive turbulence or pressure from the community were identified as helpful for learning as well.

District policies and resources, identified as promoting learning, included the provision of release time for common planning and for professional development, especially when these resources could be used in flexible ways. Access to special expertise or "technical assistance" in the form of consultants, lead teachers, and classroom visitations, for example, also was claimed to foster learning; although teachers reported that such resources were, by now, quite scarce ("in the past," they had been quite useful). One means identified for creating a critical mass of expertise about a focus within the school from which others could learn was to ensure that more than one participant from a school attended the same in-service event. In districts that had professional development libraries or central resource centres, teachers cited them as significant aids to their professional learning.

Among district conditions, policies and resources, especially professional development resources, were most often cited as important by teachers in their learning. As one teacher explained approvingly, "This summer the school board offered a lot of courses: day courses, week-long courses—open and available to any teacher who chose to take advantage of them." There was, however, considerable variation among schools within the same district in the conditions which fostered their learning.

School Culture

Teachers in all three studies frequently identified specific features of their school's cultures that fostered OL processes. Such cultures were described as collaborative and collegial. Norms of mutual support among teachers, respect for colleagues' ideas, and a willingness to take risks in attempting new practices were also aspects of culture that teachers associated with their own learning. Some teachers indicated that receiving honest, candid feedback from their colleagues was an important factor in their learning. Teachers' commitments to their own learning appeared to be reinforced by shared celebrations of successes by staff and a strong focus on the needs and achievements of all students. Collaborative and collegial cultures resulted in informal sharing of ideas and materials among teachers that fostered OL, especially when continuous professional growth was a widely shared norm among staff. One teacher in our studies explained, for example,

> I think at grade levels we keep in very close contact. . . . We make sure that . . . we run ideas by each other. We may not be doing exactly the same thing at the same time, but it's more or less a team approach.

School Structure

For the most part, school structures believed to support OL were those that allowed for greater participation in decision making by teachers. Such structures included brief weekly planning meetings, frequent and often informal problem-solving sessions, flexible and creative time-tabling, regularly scheduled professional development time in school, and common preparation periods for teachers who needed to work together. Other structures also associated with OL were the cross-department appointment of teachers, integrated curriculum teams, and team teaching. When decisions were made by staff through consensus, something easier to do in smaller schools, more learning was believed to occur. The physical space of schools had some bearing on teachers' learning, when it either encouraged or discouraged closer physical proximity of staff.

Policies and Resources

Teachers reported that current and sufficient resources to support essential professional development in aid of school initiatives were a decided boost to their learning. Within their own schools, teachers used colleagues as professional development resources, along with professional libraries and any professional readings that were circulated among staff. Access to relevant curriculum resources and to computer hardware and software aided teachers' learning, in their view, as did access to technical and program assistance (e.g., consultants, technology site administrators) for implementing new practices. Teachers also noted that access to some community facilities helped them to learn.

Leadership

There are good theoretical reasons, discussed earlier in the article, to expect that transformational leadership practices foster OL, and empirical evidence from the three studies supported this expectation. All specific leadership practices associated by teachers, in the three studies, with their individual and collective learning were readily coded in relation to the dimensions of transformational leadership.

Identifies and articulates a vision. This dimension encompasses leadership practices aimed at identifying new opportunities for the school and developing (often collaboratively), articulating, and inspiring others with a vision of the future. Of the total number of associations teachers made with the principals' vision building, more than half were associated with school conditions. For example, although a relatively rare occurrence, some principals' visions were reported to have a powerful impact on the culture of the school. And, a modest number of teachers described how the principal's vision directly influenced their collective learning.

Fosters the acceptance of group goals. This leadership dimension includes practices aimed at promoting cooperation among staff and assisting them to work together toward common goals. Although there was at least one teacher comment from most schools affirming their principals' role in goal development, most of the comments simply indicated that the principal initiated the process, was a member of the goal setting committee, or asked for input. For example, the principal of one school was reported to be actively involved in building a consensus about goals.

That same principal was also the only one who was viewed (by three teachers) as helping staff develop individual growth plans. During goal setting, the principal in another school was perceived to foster OL by encouraging staff to systematically reflect on the activities of the past year.

Conveys high performance expectations.   Included as part of this leadership dimension are practices that convey expectations for excellence, quality, and/or high performance on the part of staff. The interviews provided relatively little evidence that principals in the 14 schools, as a group, held high performance expectations for their staffs, at least that their staffs could detect. But those principals who were viewed as conveying such expectations demanded high professionalism, and held high expectations for professional growth.

Encouraging teachers to be creative and to try new strategies were indicators of high expectations to teachers. For example, one teacher said that her principal's commitment to fulfilling provincial mandates and keeping the school on the cutting edge of changes in education encouraged the staff's commitment to the same vision. Another teacher in the same school said that her principal's expectation that staff will try new teaching strategies influenced her to learn about them. In another school, professional growth was a "taken-for-granted" expectation.

Provides appropriate models.   This dimension of leadership encompasses practices that set examples for staff to follow and that are consistent with the values espoused by those exercising leadership. Many teachers across the 14 schools believed that their principal was a good role model and that this fostered their collective learning. These principals set an example by working hard, having lots of energy, being genuine in their beliefs, modeling openness, having good people skills, and showing evidence of learning by growing and changing themselves. Being involved in all aspects of the school and showing respect for and interest in the students also was considered to exemplify the modeling of excellence.   One principal modeled good instructional strategies in the classroom.

Provides individualized support. This dimension of leadership includes practices that indicate respect for individual members of staff and concern about their personal feelings and needs. Most teachers in all case study schools indicated that their principal provided support for their professional learning. Typically, this meant providing resources to aid professional learning in the form of money, books, furniture, or materials. Teachers in several schools considered their principal to be particularly adept at procuring funds to assist with their professional development. Some teachers reported that their principals even used their own administrative professional development funds for things that teachers needed. Other kinds of tangible support for professional learning included providing release time or other scheduling help, sharing information or finding speakers, and encouraging participation in decision making by collecting and distributing information.

Providing moral support was mentioned by many teachers in almost all schools. There was the sense that these principals "are always there for us," do whatever they can to get staff what they need, and generally support what teachers do. Sometimes, this support was shown by an eagerness to listen and be accessible, fair, open, and sympathetic. Sometimes, support was shown by offering positive reinforcement that made staff feel appreciated, and it encouraged further learning. Support was also shown in the form of encouragement to take risks. And leaders' signs of appreciation were reported to build a collaborative culture.

Provides intellectual stimulation. This dimension of leadership includes practices that challenge staff to reexamine some of the assumptions about their work and to rethink how it can be performed. About a third of all teachers interviewed claimed that their principals provided such challenges. Intellectual stimulation also meant passing on information from journals or other sources, bringing new ideas into the school, and providing professional development at staff meetings. Yet, other forms of intellectual stimulation included organizing and chairing professional development sessions, finding out what staff needed to learn, encouraging staff to put on workshops or to lead staff meetings, and discussing individual teachers' progress in achieving personal growth goals.

Builds a productive school culture. This category of practices encompasses behavior which encourages collaboration among staff and assists in creating a widely shared set of norms, values, and beliefs consistent with continuous improvement of services for students. Many teachers did not consider their principals to have much influence on school culture. But, the majority of principals were perceived by at least some of their teaching colleagues as being fundamental to that culture. Inspiring respect, being kind, thoughtful, sincere, honest, and hard working were attributes that contributed to this perception. Demonstrating an interest in the students and clearly setting their needs as a priority was considered to be an important influence in half the schools.

A strong belief in the value of honest and open communication, collegiality, and a willingness and ability to be flexible were considered to be characteristics conducive to a collaborative culture in which collective learning was fostered. Teachers also valued principals who showed them respect, treated them as professionals, and who were an integral part of the staff. Being seen as working more for the school than for the school district was mentioned by one teacher as being important. Hiring staff who share the same philosophy (e.g., a commitment to the use of technology) or who can work well with existing staff was mentioned by some teachers as a way that their principals contributed to a collaborative culture. Principals also influenced culture by encouraging parental involvement in the school. Teachers in two of the British Columbia schools credited their principals' philosophy with fostering their child-centered culture. One teacher said her principal set that tone by "putting student needs above timetable needs," for example. Another teacher claimed that respect among staff for students was engendered by the administrator's actions. A third teacher in the same school said the principal's actions demonstrated clearly the importance of being understanding of people from many nationalities and backgrounds. In one school , the principal's strong belief in collaborative decision making fostered a collegial culture, according to some teachers.

Helps structure the school to enhance participation in decisions. Included in this dimension of leadership are practices that create opportunities for all stakeholder groups to participate effectively in school decision making. More teachers talked about leadership influences on this aspect of school structure than on any other school condition. In spite of the high degree of collaboration that was exhibited in these schools, several teachers noted that their principals could make unilateral decisions when appropriate or for efficiency. Principals were seen to encourage participation on committees and to support the committee structure by being actively involved and by organizing or spearheading activities. Many teachers applauded the autonomy their principals gave them to make their own decisions in certain areas. About a third of the principals shared power and responsibility by asking teachers to give workshops, lead staff meetings, and help manage the budget, and by delegating many duties to the vice principals.

To facilitate collaboration, some teachers said their principals altered working conditions by making changes to the physical plant (e.g., creating convenient meeting rooms), restructuring the timetable (e.g., creating large blocks of time for language arts), and by arranging for leadership positions specifically designed to foster their learning.

In sum, evidence indicates that all dimensions of transformational leadership contributed significantly to school conditions fostering OL processes as well as to OL processes directly. There were almost twice as many associations made by teachers between leadership and school conditions as between leadership and OL. This lends support to the assertion that the effects of school leadership are most often indirect (Hallinger & Heck, 1996).

DISCUSSION AND CONCLUSION

If it has not already, the term *restructuring* is in imminent danger of becoming simply a catch-all phrase for a host of complex and often largely untested changes hotly advocated for schools in developed countries around the world. Such changes create for schools those postmodern conditions of uncertainty, lack of stability, and impermanence faced by most organizations approaching the end of the millennium. These conditions severely challenge virtually all organizational designs that rely on centralized planning, control, and direction. As organizational theorists have begun to acknowledge (e.g., Morgan, 1986), productive designs in the face of such conditions must have the capacity for self-organization: the complexity of this postmodern environment demands full use of the intellectual and emotional resources of organizational members. As Mitchell, Sackney, and Walker (1996) argue, "The postmodern era suggests a conception of organizations as processes and relationships rather than as structures and rules" (p. 52), with conversation as the central medium for both the creation of individual meaning and organizational change. From this perspective, conceiving of schools as learning organizations seems like a promising organizational design response to the continuing demands for restructuring. And beginning to identify those specific conditions that foster OL is an urgent research goal for educational researchers.

Weick and Westley (1996), however, recently have claimed, "There appear to be more reviews of OL than there is substance to review. Most reviews now available are competent summaries of a common body of work" (p. 440). This is a comment on the state of the art of empirical research on OL across all organization types. A review of empirical research on OL in schools alone would make a very quick read indeed (Leithwood & Louis, in press). So, although there are compelling reasons to view schools from an OL perspective, and some powerful theoretical tools to shape such a perspective, empirical evidence is thin, to say the least.

The three studies of OL in schools described in this article add to this meager knowledge base. Evidence from the studies was synthesized to identify conditions within and outside the school that foster the individual and collective professional learning of school staff and to inquire about the generalizability of these conditions across organizational and reform contexts. Data for the study were provided through interviews with a total of 111 teachers in 14 elementary and secondary schools. These schools were involved in one of three significant restructuring initiatives including changes in teaching and learning processes (British Columbia), school-based management (Newfoundland), and increased use of computer technology for curriculum development (Ontario). Although many conditions were identified as influencing individual and collective learning, teachers interviewed in these studies gave greatest weight to five conditions—the district (including its mission, culture, structure, policies and resources, and strategies for change), school culture, school structure, school policies and resources, and school leadership. The relative frequency with which teachers associated these five sets of conditions with OL was similar across the three contexts of our studies.

District Conditions

Most often mentioned by teachers as directly and indirectly associated with their learning were several different sets of district conditions. Studies of district effects are relatively small in number, but evidence does suggest that district-level organizations make important contributions to the work of schools. For example, the results of our three studies concerning district effects on teachers' learning have been essentially duplicated by Coffin (1997) in respect to principals' learning. In addition, for example: district culture may be important in the work lives of teachers (McLaughlin, 1990), district size (part of district structure) may explain a significant proportion of the variation in student achievement (Walberg & Fowler, 1987), and district policies intended to control curriculum and instruction may standardize the content of instruction taught by teachers (Archbald, 1997).

In general, these results appear to warrant more research energy focused on district effects and the mechanisms through which these effects are felt. From an OL perspective, such research ought to inquire with greater precision than we have been able to, so far, about the nature of those district-school relationships that foster learning at the school level, and those conditions that give rise to collective learning at the district level. This research should include the development of robust theoretical explanations for the effects of both district and school conditions fostering OL.

Evidence of potentially powerful district effects also has significant policy implications. This is especially so during a period, as now, in which district organizations seem to be every policy maker's favorite scapegoat and school-based management their restructuring instrument of choice. In New Zealand, district organizations have been eliminated, and in the United Kingdom, they have been severely downsized and refocused. Canadian provincial governments are in the midst of either reducing the number of districts as in British Columbia, Ontario, and Nova Scotia, or eliminating them entirely, as in New Brunswick. Yet, school personnel are being asked to learn many new practices and attitudes as schools transform their ways of doing business. So, eliminating a central source of such learning seems misguided, at least until other sources of such learning are created.

From a broader perspective, it is not clear whose interests such policy directions serve. Empirical studies of school-based management effects quite clearly indicate that it is not students' interests (Leithwood & Menzies, in press). Parents have little or no access to central provincial and state decision-making bodies, although they do have potentially greater influence in their local schools. That seems to leave politicians, who can claim to be doing something in the name of restructuring, and taxpayers, whose wins and losses through weakening or eliminating district-level organizations are by no means clear (Swanson & King, in press). In sum, rather than eroding or eliminating the functioning of district-level educational organizations, a more defensible policy goal would be to alter the nature of their relationships with schools and to improve their capacities to support professional learning in schools.

School Conditions

Culture, structures, and policies and resources were the three school-level conditions which teachers in our studies associated most frequently with their professional learning. Although these sets of conditions readily can be distinguished from one another conceptually, their effects on OL seem likely to depend on high levels of interdependence or coherence: This also is the case for district cultures, structures, and policies and resources. Shared norms, values and beliefs about, for example, professional responsibilities, the nature of teaching, and the value of colleagues' expertise, influence the level of individual and collective motivation to learn. Collaborative decision-making structures have the potential to create the environment in which such learning can occur And, policies and resources in support of professional growth, for example, may influence the extent to which teachers are able to find the time to participate in that environment. This interdependent view of what we have identified as three different sets of school conditions reflects Cook and Yanow's (1995) definition of organizational culture: "A set of values, beliefs, and feelings, together with the artifacts of their expression and transmission . . . . that are created, inherited, shared, and transmitted within one group of people and that, in part, distinguish that group from others" (p. 440).

Two types of challenges seem especially important to address in subsequent research aimed at developing a more refined understanding of school conditions influencing OL. These are challenges suggested, for example, by Argyris' (1978) distinction between single- and double loop learning and the closely related distinction by March (1996) and others between exploration and exploitation learning. Although all these forms of learning are important for an organization, the conditions fostering each seem likely to be quite different. Preliminary evidence suggests that under most circumstances, however, schools engage exclusively in single loop or exploitative learning (Scott, 1996). Should such results be confirmed by further research, this means that even the modest knowledge base developed to date is only (or mostly) about the conditions influencing single-loop or exploitative forms of OL. Future research about the conditions fostering OL needs to acknowledge these different forms of OL and to inquire about differences in the conditions giving rise to each.

Although most of what is known about conditions fostering OL may be limited to single-loop or exploitative learning, this is still a little explored area. Although certainly not the only alternative, an especially promising framework for further developing knowledge in this area is the cognitive heuristics that have been found to introduce bias into learning and decision making under conditions of uncertainty (see Tenbrunsel, Galvin, Neale, & Bazerman, 1996, for a review). Research in nonschool contexts suggests that some of the biases that shape individual's learning and decision making (e.g., overconfidence, insensitivity to base rates) are also evident in the learning and decision making of groups (Sniezek & Henry, 1989). As well, groups exhibit unique biases: For example, we examined the learning of secondary school teams through Janis and Mann's (1977) conception of biases leading to groupthink, with promising results (Leithwood, Jantzi, Steinbach, & Ryan, 1997). Guided by frameworks such as these, future research about conditions fostering single-loop learning in schools ought to focus on such questions as: What biases are evident in the learning and decision making of school teams and the school, acting as a whole? What accounts for such biases? and, Under what conditions are such biases minimized?

As discussed earlier, a fundamental purpose for OL is to enhance the school's capacity for self-organization or self-design (Morgan, 1986; Weick & Westley, 1996), processes that seem likely to depend on double-loop and exploratory learning. Self-organization entails organizational members working together to restructure, reculture, and otherwise reorient themselves in response to new challenges without the need for external intervention.

Several theoretical attempts have been made to identify the conditions required for self-organization. For example, Morgan (1986) proposes four such conditions: minimal critical specification (providing people freedom from restrictive policies and the like, enabling them to use their intelligence on behalf of the organization), redundancy of function (the avoidance of compartmentalized specialization adding the flexibility of organizational responses), learning to learn (getting better at problem solving), and requisite variety (many different initiatives underway at the same time as a means of expanding the alternative solutions eventually available to the organization).

As another example, Weick and Westley (1996) contend,

> In a self-designing organization, routine interaction with the task environment should generate information about ways to improve performance. . . . [Such] continuous updating results from a combination of continuous redesign, underspecified structures, reduced information filtering, intentional imbalance, and cultivation of doubt. (p. 443)

Self-organization and OL seems to be an optimal response by schools to an ever-changing and uncertain organizational environment, and our studies may have touched on important sources of conditions fostering self-organization. But, the differences between the theoretical speculations of Morgan (1986) and Weick and Westley (1996), for example, and the empirical results of our studies suggest that a more comprehensive theory of self-organizing conditions in schools, along with empirical exploration of such a theory, is an important goal for subsequent research. Until such evidence begins to accumulate, the call for self-organization on the part of organizational theorists has no clear value for school practitioners.

School Leadership

Results of the three studies confirmed our initial expectations about the contribution of transformational leadership practices to OL and provided information about the specific leadership practices that teachers associated with OL. These data add to evidence that has accumulated over the past half dozen years (e.g., Hipp & Bredeson, 1995; Leithwood, 1996; Silins, 1992) in support of the general claim that transformational conceptions of leadership are well matched to the context of a school restructuring agenda, one that demands considerable new learning on the part of teachers and administrators. But, such a conception of leadership, focused on building the commitments and capacities of organizational members, appears to compete with models of instructional leadership for dominance as an ideal form, especially for those in administrative leadership positions.

Early versions of contemporary instructional leadership models had their genesis in the U.S. effective schools movement. They were highly control oriented and narrowly focused on the core technology of curriculum and instruction. But, efforts to generalize the application of this model of leadership to different organizational levels (Kleine-Kracht, 1993; Murphy, Peterson, & Hallinger, 1986) has considerably broadened its focus and produced a more participative view of how it should be exercised. For example, 6 of the 10 dimensions of instructional leadership specified in Hallinger's model (Hallinger & Murphy, 1985), are concerned with something other than curriculum and instruction directly.

This observation gives rise to one major implication with which we conclude. There may be fewer differences than appear on the surface between current specifications of instructional and transformational leadership. An explicit comparison of the specific practices associated with each, and the identification of those practices from both models that have received empirical support could lead to a new synthesis of school leadership. For example, Sheppard (1996) reports that most of the variation in three different organizational outcomes included in his study was explained by fewer than half of the full set of practices included in Hallingers' (Hallinger & Murphy, 1985) version of instructional leadership. Similarly, a much reduced set of practices associated with Leithwood's (1994) model of transformational leadership also explains most of the variation in the handful of organizational outcomes included in his studies. This suggests the possibility of relying much less than we have to date on a priori theorizing about effective forms of school leadership and much more on model building based, first, on "what works," letting the development of a theoretical explanation for what works come second.

Clearly, much remains to be understood about the nature, causes, and consequences of OL in schools. But, as we have tried to point out in this concluding section, the task of building such understanding is an exciting one. Questions in need of most attention focus on the core of school organizations' functioning and effectiveness, promising a refreshingly new and productive agenda for research in educational administration.

REFERENCES

Archbald, D. (1997). Curriculum control policies and curriculum standardization: Teachers' reports of policy effects. *International Journal of Educational Reform, 6*(2), 155-173.

Argyris, C. (1978). *Organizational learning.* Reading, MA: Addison-Wesley.

Banner, D. K., & Gagne, T. E. (1995). *Designing effective organizations.* Thousand Oaks, CA: Sage.

Bereiter, C., & Scardamalia, M. (in press). Rethinking learning. In D. R. Olson & N. Torrence (Eds.), *Handbook of education and human development: New models of learning, teaching, and schooling.* Cambridge, MA: Basil Blackwell.

British Columbia Ministry of Education (1989). *Year 2000: A framework for learning.* Victoria: Queen's Printer for British Columbia.

Chapman, J. (1996). A new agenda for a new society. In K. Leithwood, J. Chapman, D. Carson, P. Hallinger, & A. Hart (Eds.), *International handbook of educational leadership and administration* (pp. 27-59). Dordrecht, the Netherlands: Kluwer Academic.

Coffin, G. (1997). The impact of district conditions on principals' experientially acquired learning. Unpublished doctoral dissertation, University of Toronto.

Cohen, M. D. (1996). Individual learning and organizational routine: Emerging connections. In M. D. Cohen & L. G. Sproull (Eds.), *Organizational learning* (pp. 188-194). Thousand Oaks, CA: Sage.

Cohen, M. D., & Bacdayan, P. (1996). Organizational routines are stored as procedural memory: Evidence from a laboratory study. In M. D. Cohen & L. G. Sproull (Eds.), *Organizational learning* (pp. 403-429). Thousand Oaks, CA: Sage.

Cook, S. D. N., & Yanow, D. (1995). Culture and organizational learning. In M. D. Cohen & L. G. Sproull (Eds.), *Organizational learning* (pp. 430-459). Thousand Oaks, CA: Sage.

Cousins, B. (1996). Understanding organizational learning for school leadership and educational reform. In K. Leithwood, J. Chapman, D. Carson, P. Hallinger, & A. Hart (Eds.), *International handbook of educational leadership and administration* (pp. 589-652). Dordrecht, the Netherlands: Kluwer Academic.

Darling-Hammond, L. (1996). What matters most: A competent teacher for every child. *Phi Delta Kappan, 78*(3), 193-200.

Fiol, C. M., & Lyles, M. A. (1985). Organizational learning. *Academy of Management Review, 10,* 803-813.

Fullan, M. (1991). *The new meaning of educational change.* New York: Teachers College Press.

Gioia, D. A. (1986). Conclusion: The state of the art in organizational social cognition. In H. P. Sims, Jr., D. A. Gioia & associates (Eds.), *The thinking organization* (pp. 336-356). San Francisco: Jossey-Bass.

Government of Newfoundland and Labrador. (1992). *Our children, our future*. The report of the Royal Commission of Inquiry into Programs and Services in Primary, Elementary, and Secondary Education. St. John's, Newfoundland: Author.

Hallinger, P., & Heck, R. H. (1996). Reassessing the principal's role in school effectiveness: A review of empirical research, 1980-1995. *Educational Administration Quarterly, 32*, 5-44.

Hallinger, P., & Murphy, J. (1985). Assessing the instructional management behavior of principals. *Elementary School Journal, 86*(2), 217-247.

Hedberg, B. (1981). How organizations learn and unlearn. In P. C. Nystrom & W. H. Starbuck (Eds.), *Handbook of organizational design: Vol. 1. Adapting organizations to their environments*. New York: Oxford University Press.

Hipp, K. A., & Bredeson, P. V. (1995). Exploring connections between teacher efficacy and principals' leadership behaviors. *Journal of School Leadership, 5*(2), 136-150.

Hutchins, E. (1991). Organizing work by adaptation. *Organization Science, 2*(1), 14-39.

Janis, I. L., & Mann, L. (1977). *Decision making*. New York: Free Press.

Kleine-Kracht, P. (1993). Indirect instructional leadership: An administrators' choice. *Educational Administration Quarterly, 18*(4), 1-29.

Kofman, F., & Senge, P. (1995). Communities of commitment: The heart of learning organizations. *Organizational Dynamics*, 5-22.

Lawler, E. E., III. (1986). *High-involvement management*. San Francisco: Jossey-Bass.

Leithwood, K. (1994). Leadership for school restructuring. *Educational Administration Quarterly, 30*, 498-518.

Leithwood, K. (1996). School restructuring, transformational leadership, and the amelioration of teacher burnout. *Anxiety, Stress, and Coping, 9*, 199-215.

Leithwood, K., & Aitken, R. (1995). *Making schools smarter*. Thousand Oaks, CA: Corwin.

Leithwood, K., & Jantzi, D. (1990). Transformational leadership: How principals can help reform school cultures. *School Effectiveness and School Improvement, 1*(4), 249-280.

Leithwood, K., Jantzi, D., & Steinbach, R. (1995). An organizational learning perspective on school responses to central policy initiatives. *School Organization, 15*(3), 229-252.

Leithwood, K., Jantzi, D., Steinbach, R., & Ryan, S. (1997). *Distributed leadership in secondary schools*. Paper presented at the annual meeting of the American Educational Research Association, Chicago.

Leithwood, K., & Louis, K. (in press). *Organizational learning in schools*. Dordrecht, the Netherlands: Swets & Zeitlinger.

Leithwood, K., & Menzies, T. (in press). Forms and effects of school-based management: A review. *Educational Policy*.

Leithwood, K., & Steinbach, R. (1993). Total quality leadership: Expert thinking plus transformational practice. *Journal of Personnel Evaluation in Education, 7*(4), 311-338.

Leonard, L.J. (1996). *Organizational learning and the initiation of school councils*. Unpublished doctoral dissertation, University of Toronto.

Lincoln, Y., & Guba, E. (1985). *Naturalistic inquiry*. Beverly Hills, CA: Sage.

Louis, K. S. (1994). Beyond "managed change": Rethinking how schools improve. *School Effectiveness and School Improvement, 5*(1), 2-24.

Louis, K. S., & Kruse, S. D. (1995). *Professionalism and community*. Thousand Oaks, CA: Corwin.

March, J. G. (1991). Exploration and exploitation in organizational learning. *Organization Science, 2*(1), 71-87.

March, J. G. (1996). Exploration and exploitation in organizational learning. In M. D. Cohen & L. S. Sproull (Eds.), *Organizational learning* (pp. 101-123). Thousand Oaks, CA: Sage.

McLaughlin, M. W. (1990, April). *District contexts for teachers and teaching*. Paper prepared for the annual meeting of the American Educational Research Foundation, Boston.

Merriam, S. B. (1988). Case study research in education: A qualitative approach. San Francisco: Jossey-Bass.

Miles, M. B., & Huberman, A. M. (1984). *Qualitative data analysis*. Beverly Hills, CA: Sage.

Mitchell, C. (1994). Organizational learning and educational reform: Learning to do things differently. *The Canadian Administrator, 33*(5), 1-9.

Mitchell, C., Sackney, L., & Walker, K. (1996). The postmodern phenomenon: Implications for school organizations and educational leadership. *Journal of Educational Administration and Foundations, 11*(1), 38-67.

Mohrman, S. A., & Mohrman, A. M. (1995). *Designing team-based organizations: New forms for knowledge work*. San Francisco: Jossey-Bass.

Morgan, G. (1986). *Images of organization*. Newbury Park, CA: Sage.

Murphy, J., Peterson, K., & Hallinger, P. (1986). The administrative control of principals in effective schools: The supervision and evaluation functions. *Urban Review, 18*(3), 149-175.

Rosenholtz, S. J. (1989). *Teachers' workplace*. New York: Longman.

Schoenfeld, A. H. (1989). Ideas in the air: Speculations on small group learning, environmental and cultural influences on cognition, and epistemology. *International Journal of Educational Research, 13*(1), 71-88.

Scott, A. (1996). *Towards a theory of school administrative team learning*. Unpublished doctoral dissertation, University of Toronto.

Senge, P. M. (1990). *The fifth discipline*. New York: Doubleday.

Sharratt, L. (1996). The influence of electronically available information on the stimulation of knowledge use and organizational learning in schools. Unpublished doctoral dissertation, University of Toronto.

Sheppard, B. (1996). Exploring the transformational nature of instructional leadership. *Alberta Journal of Educational Research, 42*(4), 325-344.

Silins, H. (1992). Effective leadership for school reform. *Alberta Journal of Educational Research, 38*(4), 317-334.

Sniezek, J. A., & Henry, R. A. (1989). Accuracy and confidences in group judgement. *Organizational Behavior and Human Decision Processes, 43*, 1-28.

Strauss, A., & Corbin, J. (1994). Grounded theory methodology: An overview. In N. K. Denzin & Y. S. Lincoln (Eds.), *Handbook of qualitative research* (pp 273-285). Thousand Oaks, CA: Sage.

Swanson, A. & King, R. (in press). *School finance: Its economics and politics* (2nd ed.). New York: Longman.

Tenbrunsel, A. E., Galvin, T. L., Neale, M. A., & Bazerman, M. H. (1996). Cognitions in organizations. In S. R. Clegg, C. Hardy, & W. R. Nord (Eds.), *Handbook of organization studies* (pp. 313-337). Thousand Oaks, CA: Sage.

Walberg, H. J., & Fowler, W. J. (1987). Expenditure and size effectiveness of public school districts. *Educational Researcher, 16*(7), 5-13.

Watkins, K E., & Marsick, V. J. (1993). *Sculpting the learning organization*. San Francisco: Jossey-Bass.

Wegner, D. M. (1987). Transactive memory: A contemporary analysis of the group mind. In B. Mullen & G. Goethels (Eds.), *Theories of group behavior* (pp. 185-208). New York: Springer-Verlag.

Weick, K. E., & Roberts, K. H. (1996). Collective mind in organizations: Heedful interrelating on flight decks. In M. D. Cohen & L. G. Sproull (Eds.), *Organizational learning* (pp. 330-358). Thousand Oaks, CA: Sage Publications.

Weick, K. E., & Westley, F. (1996). Organizational learning: Affirming an oxymoron. In S. R.Clegg, C. Hardy, & W. R. Nord (Eds.), *Handbook of organization studies* (pp. 440-458). Thousand Oaks, CA: Sage.

APPENDIX 2

LEADERSHIP FOR ORGANIZATIONAL LEARNING IN AUSTRALIAN SECONDARY SCHOOLS[4]

Halia Silins

Bill Mulford

Silia Zarins

Pamela Bishop

INTRODUCTION

Too often educational reforms have been thwarted by the robust nature of established school practices (Bishop & Mulford, 1999; McLaughlin, 1998; Sarason, 1998). Some forms of school restructuring, however, are proving to be more beneficial than others. Schools moving from competitive, top-down forms of power to more collective and facilitative forms (Mulford, 1994) are finding greater success, as are those attempting to make not only first-order changes (i.e., in curriculum and instruction) but also those second-order changes (i.e., culture and structure) which support efforts to implement first-order changes. Louden and Wallace's (1994) research on the Australian National Schools Network concludes that reforms, no matter how well conceptualized or powerfully sponsored, are likely to fail in the face of cultural resistance from teachers.

Resistance to change is likely given that certain forms of restructuring challenge some existing teacher paradigms. Smylie, Lazarus and Brownlee-Conyers (1996) have shown, for example, that the greater the participative nature of decision-making, the greater the increase in perceived accountability, the more organisational learning opportunities for teachers. The greater the increases in accountability and the more learning opportunities available, the greater are the reports of instructional

---

[4] Reprinted from *Understanding Schools as Intelligent Systems*, K. Leithwood (Ed.)., Pages 267-291, Copyright (2000), with permission from Elsevier.

improvement. The greater the reports of instructional improvement, the more positive are the teacher-reported student outcomes, and the more are likely improvements in reading and mathematics achievement test scores. However, at each stage of this sequence, teachers also reported a decline in perceived individual autonomy. The change in paradigm seems to be away from the individual teacher in his or her own classroom to the development of learning communities which value differences, support critical reflection and encourage members to question, challenge and debate teaching and learning issues (Peters, Dobbins, & Johnson, 1996). How to promote this change is far from clear, but we believe the area of organizational learning (OL) offers valuable clues.

The indications are that the successful restructuring agenda depends on teams of leaders, whole staffs and school personnel, working together in collaboration with community members. The challenges these groups face require significant development of their collective, as well as their individual, capacities. While such OL has long been the object of study in non-school organisations (e.g., Watkins & Marsick, 1993), until recent times little attention has been given to its nature or the conditions which foster it, including leadership practices, in schools (Mulford, 1998).

This chapter seeks to redress this situation by first examining some of the research on leadership and OL in school reform and then reporting in detail on the first phase of a major Australian research project, the Leadership for Organisational Learning and Student Outcomes (LOLSO) Project. This project is focussing on the nature of leadership contributions to the stimulation of OL in secondary schools and the effects of both leadership and OL on desired student outcomes.

LEADERSHIP AND ORGANIZATIONAL LEARNING RESEARCH

Leadership

The contributions of school leadership to past and current reform efforts have been found to be undeniably significant. Extensive research by Leithwood and his collaborators has identified those leadership practices that facilitate school restructuring in general (Leithwood, 1992, 1993, 1994; Silins, 1992, 1994a, 1994b). Most of the practices identified by this research are encompassed by a transformational model of leadership (Leithwood, Jantzi, & Steinbach, 1999). Research describing productive forms of leadership has referred to aspects of this transformational model of leadership, for example, leadership which is empowering (Reitzug, 1994), sensitive to local community aspirations (Limerick & Nielsen, 1995), supportive of followers (Blase, 1993), builds collaborative school cultures (Deal & Peterson, 1994); and emphasizes the importance of developing a shared vision (Mulford, 1994). The transformational conception of leadership includes: developing a vision for the school and maintaining its relevance for all concerned; developing and maintaining a school culture supportive of the school's vision and the work required to achieve that vision; and nurturing the capacity and commitment of staff (Duke & Leithwood, 1994). This view of leadership also includes:

structuring the school to facilitate the achievement of its vision and goals; ensuring the continuous improvement of programs and instruction; building and maintaining high levels of support for the school among parents and the wider community; and providing administrative support for the achievement of the school's vision and goals (Leithwood & Duke, 1999).

Leithwood, Jantzi, and Steinbach's (1999) study of six Canadian schools that were considered promising sites of organizational learning, including four secondary schools, sought to link leadership and other conditions which fostered organisational learning. They found that school leadership practices had among the strongest direct and indirect influences on OL. Those practices included identifying and articulating a vision, fostering the acceptance of group goals, structuring the school to enhance participation in decisions, providing intellectual stimulation, and conveying high expectations. In other words, practices associated with the transformational conception of leadership made uniformly positive contributions to OL.

Organizational Learning

While the literature on OL in non-school situations continues to expand, unconstrained by criticism, such as the charge of a lack of a common language (Gheradi, 1999), there is also growing support for the importance of OL in schools (Chapman, 1997; Leithwood, Leonard & Sharratt, 1998; Leithwood & Louis, 1998; Louis, 1994; Mulford, Hogan, & Lamb, 1997). However, as Leithwood and Louis (1998, p. 7) point out, while the logical case for OL is compelling, "empirical support for the claim that increases in such learning will contribute to organizational effectiveness or productivity is embarrassingly slim." These authors conclude that "a review of empirical research on organizational learning in schools alone would make a very quick read indeed" (p. 7).

A review of the empirical work that is available from countries as wide apart as the Netherlands, Canada, Britain, the United States, and Australia (Berends Heilbrunn, McKelvey, & Sullivan, 1998; Bishop & Mulford, 1999; Bodilly, 1998; Brown, Boyle, & Boyle, 1999; Glennan, 1998; Hannay & Ross, 1999; Louis & Marks, 1998; Sheppard & Brown, 1999; Van Den Berg & Sleegers, 1996), while not always specifically addressing OL, does suggest that common themes are emerging about secondary schools which are successfully restructuring for change. These themes include a school's commitment to, and ownership of, transparent, inclusive, collaborative efforts that include greater use of distributed leadership, taking the initiative rather than always reacting, focussing on the learning needs of all students, and recognizing and acting on the need for all staff to be continuously learning.

Five studies are illustrative of these themes. Van Den Berg and Sleegers (1996), for example, selected Dutch secondary schools as highly innovative or lowly innovative on the basis of how early they began with the preparation for a core curriculum initiated by the government as well as their tradition of quickly and frequently implementing innovations. Schools of high, as opposed to low, innovative capacity were found to have greater team involvement, more people working for a harmonious atmosphere, fewer barriers to discussing professional matters including alternative opinions about an innovation, more delegation and distributed leadership, and more teachers feeling the need to continually develop themselves. Those findings have recently been confirmed by the authors in Dutch primary schools (Geijsel, Van Den Berg, & Sleegers, 1999).

Case studies of two Canadian high schools recognized as outstanding in dealing with multiple changes resulted in Sheppard and Brown (1999) identifying key factors in a successful change process. Those factors included taking ownership of and formalizing their collaborative efforts, focusing directly on the learning of all students, recognizing the need for all staff to be continuous learners and taking action through professional development activities, and establishing partnerships with outside groups. Also in Canada, Hannay and Ross (1999) explored the reform efforts of nine secondary schools over a 3-year period. The reform efforts were triggered when an Ontario school district empowered their secondary schools to develop site-specific organizational structures which deviated from the traditional subject departmental structure. While the mandated mantra that "the status quo was not acceptable" began the process, it was only when participants examined the contextual needs of their students that deeper cultural beliefs were challenged. In order to identify and act on these needs, members of each school staff had to engage in dialogue about what was important for their schools. Collaboration was found to be the first reculturing outcome to emerge followed by an acceptance of change and a whole school focus. Staff collectively developed a common direction and functioned in an interactive and reflective manner. Continual stress was placed by participants in the study on the importance of transparency of process, that is, of openness, communication, and dialogue. The leadership role in the school was also found to be broadened beyond line authority positions.

A study of 21 secondary schools in northwest England and Wales (Brown et al., 1999) examined interview evidence of alternative models of management of decision making as perceived by principals and heads of department. Vast differences were found between what they categorized as "type A" and "type C" schools. Type A schools were completely committed to, and put formal structures in place for, team management and sharing of expertise. As well, staff felt actively involved and consulted in whole school policy and decision making, and good communication and systems of information-sharing were in place. Words such as dialogue, collaboration, problem solving, enabling, valued, open, empowered, respect, and trust were commonly used in type A schools. In contrast, type C schools had little collaboration, sharing, or consultation. Static, hierarchal management structures that focussed on being reactive to external pressures were common. The result of those differences was evident, for example, when heads of departments in type A schools expressed a real sense of job enjoyment, satisfaction, and motivation whereas those in type C schools did not.

Finally, Louis and Marks (1998) examined teachers' work and student experiences in U.S. public schools which had made substantial progress in organizational restructuring. The sample included eight primary, eight middle, and eight secondary schools. It was found that the organization of teachers' work in ways that promoted professional community had a positive relationship with the organization of classrooms for learning and the academic performance of students.

While middle and secondary schools were more organizationally complex, had less respect from the community, less participation in decision making, and were less open to innovation than primary schools, on other factors that contributed to professional community, there was no significant difference by level of school. Those factors included a supportive principal, feedback from parents and colleagues, and focussed professional development. The authors argued that the significance of professional community for what happens in classrooms demands attention to school work-place relationships that promote openness, trust, genuine reflection, and collaboration focused on student learning.

Partnerships with other groups, especially the central office, are also an emerging theme in secondary schools that are successfully restructuring for change. For example, in a recent in-depth case study of a secondary school in Australia, Bishop and Mulford (1999) reported that teachers employed strategies of resistance in response to externally imposed edicts. Teacher resistance emerged when principals required staff to implement an externally imposed curriculum. Teachers' perceptions of this curriculum change as being unnecessary and of the principal being co-opted by the central authority (and thus changing from an educational leader who was "one of them" to being "the doer of the centre's bidding") contributed to feelings of personal alienation and disempowerment, which underpinned teachers' strategies of resistance. Of particular concern, were the negative effects on the trust relationship between teachers and their principal. For example, critical comment, which may have benefited the school, was often a casualty when teachers perceived they could not be sure of the consequences of frank dialogue with their principal.

In 1991, in the United States, a multi-million dollar New American Schools initiative was begun to fund the development of designs aimed at transforming entire schools for improved student performance and then scaling up the designs to form a critical mass of schools within partnering districts. RAND Education's (e.g., Berends et al., 1998; Bodilly, 1998; Glennan, 1998) large-scale monitoring of this initiative indicated that schools were likely to make more implementation progress if, among other factors, they did not have leadership turnover and were involved with design teams that emphasized curriculum and instruction and supported implementation with whole school training. As well, implementation progress was greater where schools had districts with stable, supportive leadership, a culture of trust between the central office and schools that provided some school-level autonomy, and resources for professional development and planning. Leithwood, Jantzi, and Steinbach's (1999) research also pointed to the important role played by central, or in their case, district office. The crucial elements in this relationship were district professional development policies and resources that facilitated the social processing of new ideas.

As we have pointed out previously (Mulford, 1998), and despite the continuing paucity of educational OL research, what is available suggests some consistency of definition and similar lists of identifying characteristics are emerging. In addition, some of the interrelationships among these characteristics are becoming clearer. For example, the identifying characteristics tend to describe OL as a journey rather than a destination, and to group themselves sequentially and developmentally. The first stage of OL largely focuses on developing common understandings, honesty and trust through dialogue, sharing and distributed leadership, plus managing the inevitable risk and conflict involved. These learning processes are then employed to make links to the outside, to examine current practice critically, to develop shared values as well as a vision for the school. The processes, the content (or identified changes), and shared values are employed in actually making the changes that have been identified and include a commitment and ability to repeat the stages, that is, to continuously learn and improve. These organizational and leadership characteristics are set within more or less powerful external parameters such as central office policies, especially toward professional development.

However, while the promise of the OL vision for restructured schools would appear to be significant, insufficient empirical evidence remains concerning the specific characteristics of schools able to operate as learning organizations and the contribution leadership makes to these characteristics. One of the aims of the Australian LOLSO Project is to provide such evidence.

THE LOLSO PROJECT

LOLSO is a collaborative research project funded for 3 years (1997-1999) by the Australian Research Council. The partners in this project are Flinders University of South Australia, the University of Tasmania, the South Australian Department of Education, Training and Employment, the Tasmanian Department of Education, and the Centre for Leadership Development, University of Toronto.

The LOLSO Project addresses the need to extend present understandings of school restructuring initiatives that aim to change school practices with the intention of supporting enhanced student learning and development of students. The LOLSO Project is unique in Australia in a number of ways, including its: large sample; longitudinal nature; attempt to operationalize the concept of organizational learning; examination of the relationships among leadership processes, organizational learning, and student outcomes; use of a measure of student outcomes that is wider than standardized testing; international comparisons; and use of findings to develop professional development for educational leaders.

In brief, the LOLSO Project aims to extend present understandings of the nature of effective leadership in the context of school restructuring in Australian public schools. It focuses on investigating the nature of leadership contributions to the stimulation of OL and inquires about the effects of both leadership and OL on desired secondary school student outcomes. This chapter focuses on the first of these relationships. What school and leadership characteristics and processes are associated with secondary schools identified as learning organizations?

Research Design

The research design of the LOLSO Project required three phases of data collection conducted over 3 years. In Phase 1, surveys of Year 10 students, their teachers and principals were conducted during 1997 in 96 secondary schools from two Australian States, South Australia and Tasmania. South Australian Year 12 students, teachers, and principals in those schools are being resurveyed in 1999. In the second phase of the study (1998), cross-sectional and longitudinal case study data were collected from schools selected from the sample to triangulate and enrich the information generated by the survey data. The third phase in 1999 also saw the results from the quantitative and qualitative data gathering used to develop and trial professional development interventions for school leaders. Thus the project design allowed for iterative cycles of theory development and testing, using multiple forms of evidence.

Towards the end of the project, comparisons will be made with similar data collected from three Canadian provinces by Professor Kenneth Leithwood, Centre for Leadership Development, University of Toronto, Canada.

The LOLSO Project is addressing the following specific research questions:

1. How is the concept of organisational learning defined in Australian secondary schools?
2. What conditions inside and outside Australian high schools account for variations in organizational learning? That is, why are some schools seen as learning organizations and others are not?
3. Does the level of organizational learning in secondary schools contribute to the extent of students' participation in and engagement with school?
4. What proportion of organizational learning is accounted for by school leadership?
5. What leadership practices promote organizational learning in schools?
6. What leadership training experiences can develop such practices and capacities in leaders?

The results reported in this chapter of the analysis of data obtained from the first phase of the data collection provide the findings that address aspects of research questions 1, 2, 4, and 5.

Teacher and Principal Questionnaire

From an extensive review of the mainly nonschool literature, we defined learning organizations as schools that: employed processes of environmental scanning; developed shared goals; established collaborative teaching and learning environments; encouraged initiatives and risk taking; regularly reviewed all aspects related to and influencing the work of the school; recognized and reinforced good work; and, provided opportunities for continuing professional development. This definition provided the constructs representing organizational learning items incorporated in the questionnaire. Subsequently, the questionnaire was piloted, revised, and then administered to teachers and principals in our study.

School management variables were also included in the questionnaire. These were drawn from items developed by Leithwood and Jantzi, Centre for Leadership Development, University of Toronto. Examples of the variables used were: processes employed for effective staffing, instructional support available for teachers, proximity of administrators to the core work of the school (i.e., teaching), the level of community focus in the school, and, teachers' perceptions of the degree of school autonomy secured by the administrators.

The sources of leadership in the school and the principal's leadership practices were identified. The questionnaire items were informed by the transformational model of leadership (Duke & Leithwood, 1994). In relation to the principal, the following categories of items were included: setting the tone of the school; the nature of the decision-making structures; the level of individualized support and intellectual stimulation provided; and, establishment of school direction, goals, and performance expectations.

Sample

The teacher and principal survey yielded a total of 2,503 responses. A random sample, stratified by size, of 50 schools was drawn in South Australia. This represented just over half of the public secondary schools in South Australia. The Tasmanian sample consisted of 46 schools representing the full population of secondary schools. The analysis of the data from a total of 96 schools has proceeded in three stages.

Stages of Analysis

Stage 1 involved the exploration and identification of the nature of the teacher, principal, and student information for South Australia and Tasmania. Version 6.0.3 SPSS statistical software package was used to develop working files containing the data from teacher and student questionnaires for each state. Several data reduction procedures were employed including: rating scale analysis from the Quest program (Adams & Khoo, 1993) to reduce the number of questionnaire items to be analyzed to those that fitted the Rasch scale and to establish unidimensionality for each section of the two questionnaires; exploratory factor analysis with principal component extraction and varimax rotation to help develop scales underlying the constructs to be used in further analysis; and principal component extraction to confirm scales. Reliability estimates for each scale were calculated using Cronbach's alpha. All scales indicated a high reliability in the range of alpha = .74 – .92.

Stage 2 involved an empirical investigation of the dimensions of the hypothesized variables. The structure of the Leader construct was confirmed and defined in terms of a six-factor nested model. The six factors are operationally defined and presented in Table 1. Also, the development of the OL construct was confirmed as a four-factor nested model. The four factors are operationally defined and presented in Table 2. Empirical investigations of the dimensions of these two hypothesized variables were carried out using confirmatory factor analyses and analysis of covariance structures employing the maximum likelihood estimation process with the LISREL 8 program (see, e.g., Jöreskog & Sörbom, 1993). The procedures and results of this process have been reported elsewhere (Mulford & Silins, 1998; Silins, Zarins, & Mulford, 1998).

Table 1. Conceptual and operational definitions of the six factor model for Leader.

Construct	Description
Vision and Goals	Works toward whole staff consensus in establishing school priorities and communicates these priorities and goals to students and staff giving a sense of overall purpose. Ex. The principal helps clarify the specific meaning of the school's mission in terms of its practical implications for programs and instruction.
Culture	Promotes an atmosphere of caring and trust among staff, sets a respectful tone for interaction with students and demonstrates a willingness to change his or her practices in the light of new understandings. Ex. The principal shows respect for staff by treating us as professionals.
Structure	Supports a school structure that promotes participative decision making, delegating and distributing leadership to encourage teacher autonomy for making decisions. Ex. The principal distributes leadership broadly among the staff representing various viewpoints in leadership positions.
Intellectual Stimulation	Encourages staff to reflect on what they are trying to achieve with students and how they are doing it; facilitates opportunities for staff to learn from each other and models continual learning in his or her own practice. Ex. The principal is a source of new ideas for my professional learning.
Individual Support	Provides moral support, shows appreciation for the work of individual staff and takes their opinion into account when making decisions. Ex. The principal provides moral support by making me feel appreciated for my contribution to the school.
Performance Expectation	Has high expectations for teachers and for students and expects staff to be effective and innovative. Ex. The principal has high expectations for us as professionals.

Stage 3 involved the development of a Path Model. This development included the formulation of hypothesized models to test the nature and strength of the relationships between the variables included in the study and to understand the interactive nature of leadership and OL. A hypothesized model, Model 1, was developed using path analysis with latent variables to investigate the nature and strength of all the relationships in the model and to address aspects of the research

Table 2*. Conceptual and operational definitions of the four-factor model for Organizational Learning

Construct	Description
Collaborative Climate	Schools where collaboration is the norm and discussions amongst colleagues are open and candid; staff seek information to improve their work and use colleagues as resources. Ex. There is ongoing professional dialogue among teachers.
Taking Initiatives and Risks	Schools where staff are empowered to make decisions and school structures support staff initiatives; school administrators are open to change and reward staff for taking the initiative. Ex. People feel free to experiment and take risks.
Shared and Monitored Mission	School staff participate in school-level policy decisions and have a shared sense of direction; current practices are reviewed and problems are solved by teachers and administrators working together; information is shared with parents and the community; the climate promotes cooperative learning. Ex. Effectiveness of the teaching program is regularly monitored.
Professional Development	Staff are encouraged to develop professionally; other schools, external advisers and professional reading are sources of learning; developing skills of working in teams and sharing knowledge is seen as important. Ex. Adequate time is provided for professional development.

Note. *The Organizational Learning and Leadership questionnaire has been developed to provide information on the school as a learning organization, the nature and source of the leadership in the school and the principal's leadership practices. The full questionnaire is available from the first author. Email: halia.silins@flinders.edu.au

questions of the project. In summary, the main aims of developing a path model were:

- To test the construction of the latent variables from the observed or manifest variables (provided by the strength of the estimated loadings of the observed measures on the constructed variables),
- To examine causal relationships between the constructs or latent variables of the model (provided by the strength of the path coefficients between the variables in the model),
- To estimate the magnitudes of the hypothesized relationships (provided by the estimates of variance explained for each variable).

In Model 1, 11 latent variables (described in Table 3) were constructed from the manifest variables, based on questionnaire items, and used to examine the influence of school, leader, and teacher variables on OL as an outcome measure. The selection of variables for the study was made taking into account the review of the leadership and educational restructuring literature and the preliminary correlation analysis. OL was defined by four factors (Collaborative Climate, Taking Initiatives and Risks, Shared and Monitored Mission, and Professional Development).

A combination of contextual external and internal influences on the organization and functioning of schools as learning organizations was selected from the teacher data base. External predictors were school profile (size in 1997, area [metropolitan or country], and principal's gender) and teacher profile (years in education, years at their school, age, and gender). The internal organization predictors were based on teacher responses and included: resources (perceived availability of resources to improve staff effectiveness); leader (principal's transformational practices); community focus (the extent to which the school is working with the community); distributed leadership (a profile of the identified sources of leadership in the school); staffing policies (the extent to which staff are placed in areas of competence and consulted); active involvement (evidence of administrators' interest in student progress and extent of positive presence in the school); staff valued (the extent to which new staff are welcomed and all staff contributions valued equally); and, school autonomy (extent of teacher satisfaction with leadership and the level of autonomy secured for the school by the principal).

Path Analysis

The path model was tested using a latent variables partial least squares path analysis (PLSPATH) procedure at the school level of analysis with 96 schools (Sellin & Keeves, 1997). The initial design of the model was fully recursive wherein each variable was positioned as it was predicted to influence the succeeding variables in the model. Along with the contextual factors in Model 1 (school profile and teacher profile), resources, leader factors, and the internal school organization factors depicted as community focus, distributed leadership, staffing policies, active involvement, staff valued, and school autonomy were hypothesized to influence OL. Resources, leader, community focus, distributed leadership, staffing policies, active involvement, staff valued, and school autonomy were depicted as mediating variables by their placement between the antecedent external variables and the criterion variable, OL.

Analysis proceeded in two stages. First, the outer model was refined by successively deleting the manifest (direct measure) variables that did not contribute to explaining the latent variable (construct). All measures that had a loading (in the same sense as a principal components analysis) of at least twice their standard error were retained. Once the outer model was stable, the inner model was refined. Again, all paths were deleted where the path coefficient (similar to regression coefficient) was less than twice its standard error.

The final model, Figure 1, illustrates the variables that exerted an effect on both the outcome variable and the other latent variables. Table 4 reports the direct, indirect, and total effects along with the jackknife standard errors and correlations.

The School as the Unit of Analysis

The LOLSO Project's research focus is on school level factors associated with leadership, OL, and student outcomes. School characteristics such as size of school, school area (metropolitan or country), and gender of the principal as well as teacher profiles consisting of years of educational experience, years at their school, age, and gender were included in this study. The SES and Home Background variables were taken from the student data that were then aggregated to the school level. The school is a well-defined and logical unit of analysis for addressing the research questions in this study.

Research in the field is often associated with constraints, which have to be accommodated if the research is to proceed. At the time of this study, teachers in South Australia were involved in industrial action and they were particularly reluctant to be identified on the questionnaires. Schools were more likely to participate if students and teachers remained anonymous. Analysis of the data was restricted at the outset to the school level, since information that would allow complete nesting of the student data within teachers, and teachers within schools, was not obtainable.

School level models have been presented to indicate the way in which teachers, students and principals work and think in the school. Aggregation to the school level has an inherent meaning in this study since the teachers and leader are providing information about the same leader and his or her operation in the school. Aggregation bias will inflate the intensity of the same level relationships in the model, although the relative strengths of the variables included in the model will probably be preserved.

In order to counteract the effects of aggregation bias that are present, a parallel individual-level teacher model was developed and compared with the school-level teacher model. An examination of the nature and strength of the relationships in this teacher-level data model indicated a picture not inconsistent with the relationships in the school-level model. Therefore, the school-level models were accepted as valid representations of what goes on in Australian secondary schools.

Profile of Secondary Schools as Learning Organizations – Model 1

Table 3 reports the significant estimation loadings of the observed variables for each construct in Model 1. The strength of the loadings indicates which of the manifest variables predominated in the definition of their construct. In these results for the final Model 1, school profile was defined as the size of the school in 1997 and the school area. The gender of the principal was not significant in this model. The strength and positive sign of the loadings indicate that the larger, metropolitan schools predominated. Similarly for teacher profile, the genders of the teachers and

Table 3. *Description of variables in the model of factors influencing*
Organizational Learning – Model 1.

Variables description and coding	Mean	SD	PLS Estimation Loading*
SCHOOL PROFILE [outward mode]			
Area (country or metropolitan)	0.56	.50	0.86
Size in 1997	632	283	0.90
Principal's Gender (deleted)	—	—	—
TEACHER PROFILE [outward mode]			
Years in Education	4.60	.65	0.98
Years at their School (deleted)	—	—	—
Age	3.04	.49	0.97
Teacher's Gender (deleted)			
RESOURCES [unity mode]			
Resource to improve staff effectiveness	3.26	.36	1.00

LEADER [outward mode]
Teacher level of agreement on six aspects of principal's leadership practices in the school.
1 = strongly disagree; 2 = mostly disagree; 3 = in between; 4 = mostly agree; 5 = strongly
agree.

Goal	3.57	.44	0.98
Culture	3.63	.54	0.96
Structure	3.68	.40	0.95
Intellectual Stimulation	3.34	.43	0.95
Individualized Support	3.50	.50	0.94
Performance Expectation	3.89	.36	0.88

COMMUNITY FOCUS [outward mode]
Teacher level of agreement on four aspects of working with the school community.
1 = strongly disagree; 2 = mostly disagree; 3 = in between; 4 = mostly agree; 5 = strongly
agree.

Administrators sensitive to community (Ld5)	3.73	.37	0.95
Administrators work with community reps. (Ld8)	3.67	.40	0.95
Administrators incorporate community values (Ld18)	3.44	.41	0.95
Productive working relations with community (Ld20)	3.47	.44	0.95

(continued)

Table 3 — continued

Variables description and coding	Mean	SD	PLS Estimation Loading
DISTRIBUTED LEADERSHIP [outward mode]			
Teacher identification of the leadership sources in the school and their strength of influence.			
1 = *minimal*; 2 = *moderate*; 3 = *considerable*; 4 = *very strong.*			
Principal	3.30	.46	0.31
Deputy principal	3.04	.44	0.46
Department heads/coordinators	2.84	.27	0.52
Individual teachers	2.68	.26	0.61
Teacher committees/teams	2.57	.28	0.76
Whole staff working together	2.64	.41	0.79
School counsellors	2.17	.46	0.52
Students	2.08	.27	0.65
School Council	2.20	.34	0.59
Union representative(s)	2.03	.43	0.34
Parents/other community members	2.08	.30	0.69
STAFFING POLICIES [outward mode]			
Teacher level of agreement on three aspects of staffing.			
1 = *strongly disagree*; 2 = *mostly disagree*; 3 = *in between*; 4 = *mostly agree*; 5 = *strongly agree.*			
Staff placed in areas of competence (Ld6)	3.40	.46	0.91
Staffing is fair and equitable (Ld10)	3.20	.46	0.87
Staff consulted on staffing requirements (Ld13)	3.05	.56	0.87
ACTIVE INVOLVEMENT [outward mode]			
Teacher level of agreement on eight aspects of administrative involvement in the school's activities.			
1 = *strongly disagree*; 2 = *mostly disagree*; 3 = *in between*; 4 = *mostly agree*; 5 = *strongly agree.*			
Administrators have positive presence (Ld2)	3.64	.58	0.94
Administrators visible (Ld7)	3.75	.57	0.93
Administrators easily accessible (Ld12)	3.92	.47	0.93
Administrators interested (Ld16)	3.50	.50	0.96
Administrators observe or inquire (Ld14)	2.71	.52	0.89
Administrators work with teachers (Ld17)	3.00	.44	0.93
Administrators discuss educational issues (Ld22)	3.86	.33	0.89
Administrators review student progress (Ld21)	3.54	.42	0.86

(continued)

Table 3 — continued

Variables description and coding	Mean	SD	PLS Estimation Loading
STAFF VALUED [outward mode]			
Teacher level of agreement on three aspects of staff being valued.			
1 = strongly disagree; 2 = mostly disagree; 3 = in between; 4 = mostly agree; 5 = strongly agree.			
Induction process for new staff (Ld3)	3.28	.68	0.54
New staff valued and welcomed (Ld15)	3.78	.39	0.91
Staff contributions valued (Ld19)	3.23	.46	0.91
SCHOOL AUTONOMY [outward mode]			
Teacher level of agreement on perceived school autonomy and satisfaction with school leadership.			
1 = strongly disagree; 2 = mostly disagree; 3 = in between; 4 = mostly agree; 5 = strongly agree.			
Secured high degree autonomy	3.50	.40	0.94
Teacher satisfaction with leadership	2.56	.39	0.96
ORGANIZATIONAL LEARNING [outward mode]			
Teacher level of agreement on four outcomes related to organizational learning.			
1 = strongly disagree; 2 = mostly disagree; 3 = in between; 4 = mostly agree; 5 = strongly agree.			
Collaborative climate	3.62	.32	0.88
Taking initiatives and risks	3.20	.33	0.94
Shared and monitored mission	3.41	.35	0.95
Professional development	3.22	.22	0.90

* PLS Path Estimation reported as factor loadings.

the years at their school were dropped from the model because they did not satisfy the criterion for inclusion. The significant characteristics of the teachers in this model are their years of experience and their age. For all the other constructs in the model, the observed variables contributed significantly.

Table 4 reports the nature and strength of the relationships between the 11 latent variables in Model 1. Five variables emerged as direct predictors of OL: School Autonomy ($p = .35$)[5], Staff Valued ($p = .32$), Leader ($p = .16$), Distributed Leadership ($p = .15$) and School Profile ($p = -.12$). Resources ($t = .65$)[6] and Leader ($t = .63$) emerged as the two dominant factors in terms of their total effect on Organizational Learning. However, Active Involvement ($t = .44$), School Profile ($t = .37$), School Autonomy ($t = .35$), Distributed Leadership ($t = 0.34$) and Staff Valued ($t = .32$) contributed strongly. Community Focus ($t = .22$) had a moderate and indirect effect whereas Staffing Policies had the smallest, significant total ($t = .11$) and indirect effect on OL. Teacher Profile had no influence on OL.

---

[5] p = Direct Effects path coefficient, see Table 4.
[6] t = Total Effects, see Table 4.

The hypothesized initial model was tested and resulted in Model 1 (Figure 1). The combined effect of variables in this model explains 87% of the variance in OL, with a $Q^2 = .86$ indicating a very stable outcome measure and stable model. It is acknowledged that the estimates in analyses are inflated because of aggregation bias. However, the parallel individual level model explained 70% of the variance in OL which was associated with a high $Q^2 = .70$ indicating stability of the outcome measure and model. These measures indicate that the school level model results can be interpreted with some confidence and Model 1 can be accepted as a well-defined model.

Model 1 illustrates the nature and strength of the significant relationships between the variables in this study. It offers a snapshot of Australian secondary schools conceptualized as learning organizations and presents a profile of secondary schools summarizing the significant characteristics and processes, and their inter-relationships, that promote OL.

A closer examination of this profile reveals negative paths associated with the external predictor, School Profile. This indicates that the smaller schools (less than 900 students) rather than the larger schools (above 900 students) are more likely to be identified as achieving OL outcomes. Staff of these smaller secondary schools perceive their schools as having sufficient resources to improve staff effectiveness. This perception is a strong, indirect predictor of OL and operates through its strongest association with the principal's leadership style. These perceptions seem contrary to the reality of resourcing schools since it would be more likely that the larger schools attract more government funding. Perceptions of adequate resourcing are also associated with staffing policies that are consultative and that take account of teachers' competencies.

Principals who practise transformational leadership emerge as strong promoters of OL outcomes. Furthermore, when transformational leaders establish a community focus within their school then these factors (i.e., smaller schools, adequate resources, transformational leadership, and community focus) result in a greater distribution of leadership responsibilities throughout the school community (including students and parents). This distributed leadership promotes OL outcomes directly as well as through helping staff feel valued, having staff perceive the principal as securing a high degree of autonomy for the school and engendering an overall satisfaction with the leadership in the school.

This profile represents a secondary school that is successful at promoting OL. Elements of this profile are referred to in the model which is used to address the research questions in more detail.

Table 4. Direct, total and indirect effects and correlations of latent variables influencing Organizational Learning – Model 1.

Variable	Direct Effects p	JknStd Error	Total Effects t	Indirect Effects i	Correlation r
TEACHER PROFILE	$R^2 = .33$	$(d = .83)$	$Q^2 = .28$		
School Profile	.55	.07	.55	—	.55
RESOURCES	$R^2 = .10$	$(d = .94)$	$Q^2 = .06$		
School Profile	−.32	.08	−.32	—	−.32
LEADER	$R^2 = .53$	$(d = .68)$	$Q^2 = .51$		
School Profile	—	—	−.23	−.23	−.25
Resources	.73	.06	.73	—	.73
COMMUNITY FOCUS	$R^2 = .61$	$(d = .62)$	$Q^2 = 60$		
School Profile	—	—	−.18	−.18	−.11
Resources	—	—	.57	.57	.63
Leader	.78	.03	.78	—	.78
DISTRIBUTED LEADERSHIP	$R^2 = .62$	$(d = .62)$	$Q^2 = .58$		
School Profile	−.16	.07	−.34	−.18	−.31
Resources	.25	.09	.57	.32	.65
Leader	—	—	.43	.43	.69
Community Focus	.55	.07	.55	–	.73
STAFFING POLICIES	$R^2 = .69$	$(d = .56)$	$Q^2 = .66$		
School Profile	—	—	−.16	−.16	−.19
Teacher Profile	.12	.06	.12	—	.06
Resources	.31	.09	.71	.40	.71
Leader	.29	.11	.55	.26	.76
Community Focus	.33	.09	.33	—	.75
ACTIVE INVOLVEMENT	$R^2 = .87$	$(d = .36)$	$Q^2 = .85$		
School Profile	—	—	−.23	−.23	−.29
Teacher Profile	—	—	.03	.03	−.10
Resources	.16	.06	.77	.61	.77
Leader	.60	.07	.73	.13	.90
Community Focus	—	—	.08	.01	.80
Staffing Policies	.24	.06	.24	—	.81

(continued)

Table 4 — continued

Variable	Direct Effects p	JknStd Error	Total Effects t	Indirect Effects i	Correlation r
STAFF VALUED	$R^2 = .69$	$(d = .56)$	$Q^2 = .67$		
School Profile	—	—	−.24	−.24	−.20
Teacher Profile	—	—	.02	.02	−.03
Resources	—	—	.62	.62	.71
Leader	—	—	.55	.55	.75
Community Focus	—	—	.23	.23	.70
Distributed Leadership	.34	.08	.34	—	.73
Staffing Policies	—	—	.13	.13	.74
Active Involvement	.56	.09	.56	—	.80
SCHOOL AUTONOMY	$R^2 = .83$	$(d = .41)$	$Q^2 = .82$		
School Profile	—	—	−.24	−.24	−.19
Teacher Profile	—	—	.02	.02	−.09
Resources	—	—	.70	.70	.73
Leader	—	—	.64	.64	.85
Community Focus	—	—	.18	.18	.80
Distributed Leadership	.22	.07	.22	—	.75
Staffing Policies	—	—	.18	.18	.78
Active Involvement	.74	.06	.74	—	.90
ORGANIZATIONAL LEARNING	$R^2 = .87$	$(d = .36)$	$Q^2 = .86$		
School Profile	−.12	.04	−.37	−.25	−.33
Teacher Profile	—	—	.01	.01	−.20
Resources	—	—	.65	.65	.77
Leader	.16	.07	.63	.47	.84
Community Focus	—	—	.22	.22	.75
Distributed Leadership	.15	.06	.34	.19	.80
Staffing Policies	—	—	.11	.11	.74
Active Involvement	—	—	.44	.44	.86
Staff Valued	.32	.06	.32	—	.85
School Autonomy	.35	.09	.35	—	.87

Note. JknStd refers to the *Jackknife Standard Error* of the Direct Effects path coefficient.
    d is the residual standard error.

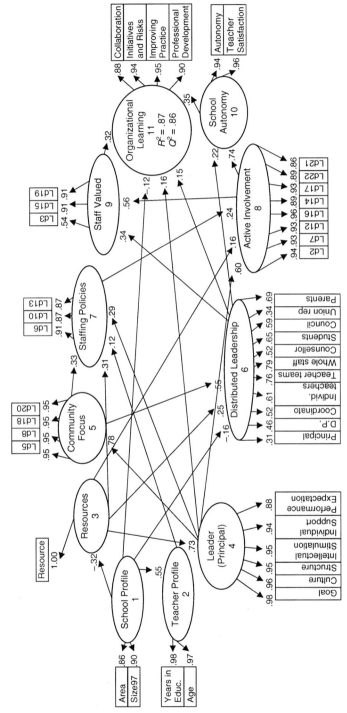

Figure 1. Model of the relationships between variables influencing Organizational Learning.

ANSWERING THE RESEARCH QUESTIONS

What Are the Identifying Characteristics of Secondary Schools Where OL Is Promoted and Facilitated?

Model 1 clearly indicates the four categories of characteristics that identify Australian secondary schools as learning organizations. These are described in Table 2 as characteristics:

- indicative of a collaborative climate; schools where staff collaboration is the norm;
- that facilitate taking initiatives and risks; schools where staff feel free to experiment;
- that support a shared and monitored mission; schools where the staff review programs and performance regularly; and,
- that encourage professional development; schools where staff engage in professional development activities.

An examination of the estimated loadings of these four factors, provided in Table 3, defining the variable OL, indicates that the four observed variables all loaded strongly on this latent construct. These four categories of characteristics were empirically confirmed as being valid and reliable representations of what is understood by the OL construct in Australian secondary schools.

What Conditions Inside and Outside Australian High Schools Account for Variations in OL? That Is, Why Are Some Schools Seen as Learning Organizations and Others Are Not?

Model 1 indicates the nature and strength of the relationships between the variables predicting OL. Size of school was a significant characteristic of the school in this model. The principal's gender was not a factor in promoting OL. The larger metropolitan schools, staffed by experienced and ageing teachers, did not provide the environment most conducive to OL. The smaller metropolitan and country schools were more likely to perceive that sufficient resources were available to promote staff effectiveness. This perception of sufficiency was usually associated with a school principal employing transformational practices. Such practices were instrumental in establishing school characteristics that promoted OL.

The principal in this model was visible, accessible, and interested in student progress. This active involvement in the core work of the school helped to generate teacher satisfaction with leadership and a sense of school autonomy, which was strongly associated with OL. The principal's interest and involvement in the school also established a school climate in which staff contributions were valued and OL fostered. The principal often established strong links and a productive working relationship with the community. Responsiveness to the community supported a greater distribution of leadership in the school that influenced OL directly as well as indirectly through valuing staff contributions, influencing teacher satisfaction with leadership, and establishing a high degree of school autonomy.

The evidence from this research has demonstrated clearly that the predominant conditions accounting for variations in OL between Australian secondary schools are perceived availability of resources together with a principal skilled in transformational leadership and actively involved in the core work of the school. Effects of these conditions are mediated and supported in schools where teachers are satisfied with the leadership and experience higher levels of school autonomy. A strong condition explaining the variation in OL between schools was the process of distributing leadership in the school so that a wider range of sources of leadership was identified by teachers, such as whole school staff working together, teacher teams, students, parents, and other members of the community.

What Proportion of OL Is Accounted for by School Leadership?

The best estimate of the proportion of OL accounted for by school leadership in Model 1 can be calculated by multiplying the path coefficient of the direct effect of leadership on OL by their correlation. The proportion of OL accounted for by the principal (Leader) is 13% (0.16 x 0.84). The variable Distributed Leadership represents all other sources of leadership in the school. The proportion of OL accounted for by the whole school staff, teacher teams, community members, and students is 12% (0.15 x 0.80). The total proportion of OL accounted for by the total sources of school leadership is 25%. This provides clear evidence for the strong contribution of school leadership to explaining the variation in OL between schools.

What Leadership Practices Promote OL in Schools?

Evidence for the key role of transformational leadership practices in the internal processes of the school has been provided by other studies (Leithwood, Tomlinson & Genge, 1996; Silins, 1994a). This research has supported six factors as promoting OL. These six factors correspond reasonably closely to the transformational leadership concept developed by Leithwood and his collaborators. These are described in Table 2 as: Vision and Goals; Culture; Structure; Intellectual Stimulation; Individual Support; and Performance Expectation. An examination of the estimation loadings provided in Table 3 of the six factors defining the variable, Leader, indicates that the six observed variables all load strongly on this latent construct. All six factors contributed to defining the kind of leadership practices that promote OL.

CONCLUSION

Peters (1987) is right when he says that the core paradox in a world of massive change "is fostering (creating) internal stability in order to encourage the pursuit of constant change" (p. 395). If educational reforms are not to continue to be thwarted by the robust nature of established school practice, then stability for change, moving ahead without losing their roots, becomes the challenge (Mulford, 1998). This challenge may be able to be met in education and elsewhere by focussing on a change strategy where learning comes to be seen as "the single most important resource for organizational renewal in the postmodern age" (Hargreaves, 1995, p. 11). In this strategy, the school is viewed and treated as a learning organization.

The range of factors that contribute to OL, and what it means for an Australian secondary school to provide stability or equilibrium (Leithwood & Louis, 1998) through OL, is now clearer. The results of the LOLSO Project confirm and sharpen the newly evolving research literature on OL in schools and, in particular, the contribution of leadership to OL. We identified four factors that contribute to OL in Australian secondary schools. These four factors are collaborative climate, taking initiatives and risks, shared and monitored mission, and professional development.

First, the collaborative climate factor confirms that the change in paradigm is away from the teacher in his or her own classroom to the development of learning communities which value differences, support critical reflection and encourage members to question, challenge and debate teaching and learning issues (Peters, Dobbins, & Johnson, 1996). Our findings agree with others (e.g., Leithwood & Louis, 1998; Lieberman, 1988; Newmann et al., 1996;) who have concluded that collective responsibility for student learning, in addition to improved technical teaching practices and curriculum, is fundamental to educational reform. In brief, de-privatization of teacher practice is the key. De-privatization is most likely to occur in a transparent, inclusive, collaborative school climate. A climate where there is a spirit of openness, honesty and trust. A climate where staff are valued, committed, and mutually support one another.

Second, we show that OL involves taking initiatives and risks. It means acting rather than always reacting. Support, including reward and organizational structures, is used to promote inquiry, experimentation, and initiative. We believe that this finding counters a major criticism of the nonschool OL literature in its contention (Gheradi, 1999, p. 103) that the field of OL has been "developed and institutionalized as problem-driven, as the production of instrumental knowledge." Our findings show that OL is not just problem-driven but also involves what Turner (1991) coined as "learning in the face of mystery." Learning in the face of mystery is important because it acts to reinforce the importance of the de-privatisation of teacher practice.

Our belief is reinforced by the third of four factors defining OL in secondary schools, Shared and Monitored Mission. Regular and critical monitoring of the environment and examination of current practices, both in the light of achieving school goals and the relevance of those goals ensures the school is continuously learning. It also ensures the school does not feel constrained to look "outside the box"—outside its existing goals, processes and structures (Weick & Westley, 1996).

Fourth, we show that OL means recognizing and acting on the need for staff to be continuously learning. This includes learning how to work, and learn, in teams. Ongoing professional development involving readings and the use of internal and external expertise is of high priority.

A condition of note explaining the variation in OL between secondary schools is the process of distributing leadership in the school so that a wider range of sources of leadership is identified by teachers. These sources of leadership include whole school staff working together, teacher teams, students, parents and other members of the community. We suspect that there are strong implications here for a need in secondary schools to work across the traditional subject department boundaries. Distributed leadership contributed directly to OL and indirectly through its contribution to staff feeling valued and to beliefs that the school had secured a high degree of autonomy.

The direct and indirect contributions of leadership to OL in secondary schools are not only becoming clearer but are shown to be significant. The predominant direct conditions accounting for variations in OL between Australian secondary schools are size of school together with a principal skilled in transformational leadership and actively involved in the core work of the school. Along with Leithwood, Jantzi, and Steinbach (1999), we found that the transformational leadership practices included identifying and articulating a vision, fostering the acceptance of group goals, structuring the school to enhance participation in decisions, providing intellectual stimulation, and conveying high expectations. The principal's leadership embraced the active involvement of others in leadership roles and promoted the commitment of all school leaders to the core work of the school and to being visible and accessible; these elements of leadership proved to be important predictors of OL.

OL offers a way for a school to make sense of paradox, to ride the "see-saws" of change (Handy, 1994), and to establish and maintain a sense of connectedness, direction, and continuity. OL offers the potential of stability for change, an opportunity for schools and the societies they serve to move ahead without losing their roots. In other words, it is a change strategy with the potential to address current change agendas. As such, it is a change strategy that continues to be worthy of support, further development, and analysis[7].

---

[7] At least three areas of analysis identified in this chapter deserve further attention: the sequential and developmental nature of the identifying characteristics of OL; the importance of partnership with bodies external to the school, especially central office; and, the relationship between OL and student outcomes. Early data on the last of these areas, student outcomes, can be found in Silins, Zarins and Mulford (1999).

REFERENCES

Adams, R. J., & Khoo, S. T. (1993). Quest – The interactive test analysis system [computer software]. Hawthorn, Victoria: Australian Council for Educational Research.

Berends, M., Heilbrunn, J., McKelvey, C., & Sullivan, T. (1998). *Monitoring the progress of new American schools: A description of implementing schools in a longitudinal sample* (Draft series paper DRU-1935-NAS for RAND). Santa Monica, CA: RAND.

Bishop, P., & Mulford, B. (1999). When will they ever learn?: Another failure of centrally-imposed change. *School Leadership and Management, 19*(2),179-187.

Blase, J. (1993). The micropolitics of effective school-based leadership: Teachers' perspectives. *Educational Administration Quarterly, 29*(2), 142-163.

Bodilly, S. (1998). Lessons from new American schools' scale-up phase. Santa Monica, CA: RAND.

Brown, M., Boyle, B., & Boyle, T. (1999, April). Commonalities between perception and practice in models of school decision making systems in secondary schools in England and Wales. Paper presented at the annual meeting of the American Educational Research Association, Montreal.

Chapman, J. (1997).Leading the learning community. *Leading and Managing, 3*(3), 151-170.

Deal, T., & Peterson, K. (1994). The leadership paradox: Balancing logic and artistry in schools. San Francisco: Jossey-Bass.

Duke, D., & Leithwood, K. (1994). *Defining effective leadership for Connecticut's schools* (A monograph prepared for the Connecticut Administrator Appraisal Project). Hartford, CT: University of Connecticut.

Geijsel, F., Van Den Berg, R., & Sleegers, P. (1999). The innovative capacity of schools in primary education: A qualitative study. *International Journal of Qualitative Studies in Education, 12*(2), 175-191.

Gheradi, S. (1999). Learning as problem-driven or learning in the face of mystery. *Organization Studies, 20*(1), 101-124.

Glennan, T. (1998). *New American schools after six years.* Santa Monica, CA: RAND.

Handy, C. (1994). *The age of paradox.* Boston, MA: Harvard Business School Press.

Hannay, L., & Ross, J. (1999, April). *Self-renewing secondary schools: The relationship between structural and cultural change.* Paper presented at the annual meeting of the American Educational Research Association, Montreal.

Hargreaves, A. (1995). Paradoxes of change: School renewal in the postmodern age. *Educational Leadership, 52*(7), 14-19.

Jöreskog, K. G., & Sörbom, D. (1993). *New features in LISREL 8.* Chicago, IL: Scientific Software International.

Leithwood, K. (1992). The move toward transformational leadership. *Educational Leadership, 49*(5), 8-12.

Leithwood, K. (1993, October). *Contributions of transformational leadership to school restructuring.* Invited address, annual conference of the University Council for Educational Administration, Houston, TX.

Leithwood, K. (1994). Leadership for school restructuring. *Educational Administration Quarterly, 30*(4), 498-518.

Leithwood, K., & Duke, D. (1999). A century's quest to understand school leadership. In J. Murphy & K. Louis. (Eds.), *Handbook of research on educational administration* (pp. 45-72). Washington, DC: American Educational Research Association.

Leithwood, K., & Louis, K. S. (Eds.). (1998). *Organizational learning in schools.* Lisse, the Netherlands: Swets & Zeitlinger.

Leithwood, K., Jantzi, D., & Steinbach, R. (1998). Leadership and other conditions which foster organizational learning in schools. In K. Leithwood & K. S. Louis (Eds.), *Organizational learning in schools* (pp. 67-90). Lisse, the Netherlands: Swets & Zeitlinger.

Leithwood, K., Jantzi, D., & Steinbach, R. (1999). *Changing leadership for changing times.* Buckingham, UK: Open University Press.

Leithwood, K., Leonard, L., & Sharratt, L. (1998). Conditions fostering organizational learning in schools. *Educational Administration Quarterly, 34*(2), 243-276.

Leithwood, K., Tomlinson, D., & Genge, M. (1998). Transformational school leadership. In K. Leithwood (Ed.), *International handbook on educational leadership* (pp. 785-840). Norwell, MA: Kluwer Academic Press.

Lieberman, A. (1988). *Building a professional culture in schools*. New York: Teachers College Press.

Limerick, B., & Nielsen, H. (Eds.). (1995). *School and community relations*. Sydney: Harcourt Brace.

Louden, W., & Wallace, J. (1994). *Too soon to tell: School restructuring and the National Schools Project* (Monograph No. 17). Melbourne: Australian Council for Educational Administration.

Louis, K. S. (1994). Beyond "managed change": Rethinking how schools improve. *School Effectiveness and School Improvement, 5*(1), 2-24.

Louis, K. S., & Marks, K. (1998). Does professional community affect the classroom? Teachers work and student experiences in restructuring schools. *American Journal of Education, 106* (August), 532-575.

McLaughlin, M. (1998). Listening and learning from the field: Tales of policy implementation and situated practice. In A. Hargreaves, A. Lieberman, M. Fullan, & D. Hopkins (Eds.), *International handbook of educational change* (pp. 70-84). Dordrecht, the Netherlands: Kluwer.

Mulford, B. (1994). *Shaping tomorrow's schools* . (Monograph No. 15). Melbourne: Australian Council for Educational Administration.

Mulford, B. (1998). Learning organisations and change: Educational literature, research, and issues. In A. Hargreaves, A. Lieberman, M. Fullan, & D. Hopkins (Eds), *International handbook of organizational change* (pp. 616-641). Norwell, MA: Kluwer Academic Publishers.

Mulford, W., Hogan, D., & Lamb, S. (1997). *Local school management in Tasmania: The views of principals and teachers*. Launceston: University of Tasmania.

Mulford, W., & Silins, H. (1998, September). *School leadership for organisational learning and student outcomes: The LOLSO Project*. Paper presented at the 25th national conference of the Australian Council for Educational Administration, Gold Coast, Australia.

Newmann, F., & associates. (1996). Authentic achievement: Restructuring schools for intellectual quality. San Francisco: Jossey-Bass.

Peters, J., Dobbins, D., & Johnson, B. (1996). *Restructuring and organisational culture* (Research Paper No. 4). Ryde, New South Wales: National Schools Network.

Peters, T. (1987). *Thriving on chaos*. London: Harper & Row.

Reitzug, U. (1994). A case study of empowering principal behavior. *American Educational Research Journal, 31*(2), 283-307.

Sarason, S. (1998). *Political leadership and educational failure*. San Francisco: Jossey-Bass.

Sellin, N., & Keeves J. P. (1997). Path analysis with latent variables. In J. P. Keeves (Ed.), *Educational research, methodology, and measurement: An international handbook*. (2nd ed., pp. 633-640). Oxford: Pergamon Press.

Sheppard, B., & Brown, J. (1999, April). *Leadership approach, the new work of teachers and successful change*. Paper presented at the annual meeting of the American Educational Research Association, Montreal.

Silins, H. C. (1992). Effective leadership for school reform. *The Alberta Journal of Educational Research, 38*(4), 317-334.

Silins, H. C. (1994a). The relationship between transformational and transactional leadership and school improvement outcomes. *School Effectiveness and School Improvement, 5*(3), 272-298.

Silins, H. C. (1994b). Leadership characteristics and school improvement. *Australian Journal of Education, 38*(3), 266-281.

Silins, H., Zarins, S., & Mulford, W. (1998, November). *What characteristics and processes define a school as a learning organisation? Is this a useful concept for schools?* Paper presented at the national conference of the Australian Association for Research in Education, Adelaide, Australia.

Silins, H., Zarins, S., & Mulford, W. (1999, April). *Leadership for organizational learning and student outcomes—the LOLSO Project*. Paper presented at the annual meeting of the American Educational Research Association, Montreal, Canada.

Smylie, M., Lazarus, V., & Brownlee-Conyers, J. (1996). Instructional outcomes of school-based participative decision making. *Educational Evaluation and Policy Analysis, 18*(3),181-198.

Turner, B. (1991, September). *Rethinking organizations: Organizational learning in the nineties*. Paper presented at the European Foundation for Management Development annual meeting, Isida, Palermo.

Van Den Berg, R., & Sleegers, P. (1996). The innovative capacity of secondary schools: A qualitative study. *International Journal of Qualitative Studies in Education, 9*(2), 201-223.

Watkins, K. E., & Marsick, V. J. (1993). *Sculpting the learning organization*. San Francisco: Jossey-Bass.

Weick, K. E., & Westley, F. (1996). Oganizational learning: Affirming an oxymoron. In S. Clegg, C. Hardy, & W. R. Nord (Eds.), *Handbook of organizational studies* (pp. 440-458). Thousand Oaks, CA: Sage Publications.

APPENDIX 3

THE ALTONA CASE STUDY: SHORT VERSION

SETTING THE SCENE

Altona High School is a Grade 7 to 10 (ages 13 to 16) government school in a state which has a three-tier schooling system, primary (Kindergarten to Grade 6), high (Grades 7 to 10), and college (Grades 11 and 12). Many regard Altona as being "on the wrong side of the tracks." Typically, the statistics for Altona show extremes: the area records amongst the highest on elements of social disadvantage and near to, or the lowest, on social indicators which point to privilege.

Four in every 10 Altona households have no men in them, brought about by limited job opportunities, premature deaths, gaol terms, and partner separations. In one sense the suburb of Altona is a young person's place, with a median age of 24. Altona has the lowest proportion of people with post school educational qualifications: only one in five Altona citizens aged 15 years and over has a qualification. Given the shifts in industry and labour market patterns, it is thus not surprising that Altona residents have been particularly affected by unemployment. More than 30% of those who are eligible to work are unemployed, which is about three times the unemployment rate experienced by residents in more affluent nearby suburbs. Whereas the median individual income of residents in nearby suburbs is $13,451, an Altona resident's median income is $9,547. Despite the relatively cheaper nature of housing in Altona, less than one third of occupied private dwellings are owned or being purchased. Affluent nearby suburbs, by contrast, have home ownership or purchase rates of 67%.

THE LEADERSHIP TEAM: CREATING INTERGENERATIONAL LINKS

In his eighth year as principal at the school, Ian Davidson is synonymous with Altona High. Davidson firmly believes that these days, schools need to be more adventurous in what they do and more conscious of the links they can create for students between business, training, and further education. For example, the contacts and networks which many families used to draw on when a son or a daughter wanted an apprenticeship are now not easily found amongst Altona families, so "we have had to step in and replace a lot of that." He cites examples of grandparents and parents of students who have been unemployed throughout the last decade, and is acutely aware of the harsh labour market that awaits many of the young, especially those from less materially-privileged areas like Altona. His descriptions of the personal and social dislocation which can come from being unemployed are supported by a wealth of statistics and "seeing so much of it."

Known for his straight-talking and straight-dealing, Davidson's impatience with politicians who deflect criticism about society and young Australians on to schools is matched by his contempt for a minority of teachers who are not committed to teaching. According to Davidson, Altona has only a couple of poorly motivated teachers amongst a full-time staff of thirty. Poorly motivated teachers are an impediment to Altona "because we want a good deal for our kids." In a similar vein, any centrally-located departmental bureaucrats who are unhelpful to the school's efforts are deemed as having little to offer. By contrast, edicts and personnel from central or district office who evidence a willingness to talk with, rather than only talk at schools, are appreciated.

"When Ian Davidson gets one of his ideas, he becomes driven," said June Syme, the Grade 9 coordinator of Altona High School. "He can get an idea at four in the morning and, by the time he gets to school, that's all he wants to talk about. He isn't easily put off." Despite Syme's concern with her principal's often single-minded efforts to improve Altona High, which sometimes means a lack of consultation, and despite his questionable organizational skills, she considers the school benefits from being led by Davidson. "While he expects a lot from the staff and is very focussed on advancing the interests of students, Ian can also see the humorous as well as heart-rendering aspects of school life. For staff, that sort of leadership is important because, sometimes here, if you didn't laugh or crack a joke, you'd cry."

In the early years of his principalship at Altona, Davidson was authoritarian, a style which, when employed, frequently failed with both teachers and students. These days, his greater knowledge of teachers' qualities and motives translates into support and encouragement for those teachers who are keen to offer interesting and unique learning experiences to students.

A deeply religious man, Davidson's sense of satisfaction with his colleagues and the school is apparent in conversations about the extent and sources of achievement at Altona, "this is a school that really cares about its kids. It is very much to do with the people I work with." Davidson's pride with the school's progress and his contributions, which form part of a long-term mission that is underpinned by beliefs about humanity, community, and social justice, leave him convinced that Altona can create further successes for their students. At the same time, he believes the community needs to accept responsibility for problems such as literacy. "We do magnificent work in improving their [students'] language skills. Huge commitment to it. The problem is solvable, but not by the education sector. The problem is solvable by a turn-around in community attitude. The community has got to take responsibility for it."

In an era when politicians are increasingly focussing on student outcomes and league ladders of schools' literacy and numeracy achievements, Davidson bristles at the notion of all schools being compared to one another in this way. Such comparisons underplay the nature of many students' lives at Altona. "You have a proportion of students who are so far behind the eightball when they begin school— there has never been a book in their house, parents have not been able to read to their kids. There is not a culture which values that sort of thing." The complexity of many students' out-of-school experiences is frequently reflected in their practices at school.

The priority which Davidson and his staff place on meeting each student's "individual needs" often leaves teachers with insufficient time for adequately attending to everything the school would like to do. One up-shot of such attempts to improve what is offered to students is that teachers rarely feel they have adequate time in which to do work to their satisfaction.

For Davidson, the volume-of-work challenges often are met by putting in further hours. He is constantly hunting for extra monies for Altona in order for some additional school-based initiatives to be funded, conscious that this activity is often at the expense of offering instructional leadership. In the absence of being able to provide detailed instructional leadership to staff, Davidson relies on his assistant principal Sally Green, whose office is based next door.

Green has a productive working association with Davidson. Although staunchly loyal to her principal, she does not refrain from telling Davidson—or anyone else at Altona—how she feels if something important at the school is dysfunctional or unsuitable for implementation. In the main, Green believes her principal's ideas over the past 4 years have been sound and ultimately resulted in favourable improvements for the school. Green is in no doubt that her role is to support her principal and staff on agreed policy and program matters. One of the myriad ways in which she does this is "by providing a link between what happens in the trenches." Like many school administrators, Green has a regular teaching load, which allows her to lead by example.

In the relatively short time that Green has been the assistant principal at Altona, staff have come to appreciate her leadership. She is uniformly regarded by teachers and Davidson as being committed to the school and what it is attempting to achieve in the interests of Altona students. Teacher Sandra Miere explained that "Sally Green cares about the students and teachers and isn't self-serving. She puts in 100%—you know where you are with her."

The complementarity of Altona's two administrators is highly productive. It is a working synergy underpinned by a belief in one another's competencies and intentions. In this sense, it is not surprising that each has invested considerable trust in the other, and both believe the trust has been warranted.

Green, like Davidson, acknowledges that time challenges in schools invariably privilege the immediate and the practical. At Altona, classroom imperatives, individual student crises, and, to a lesser extent, timetable and bureaucratic routines, continue to demand much of administrators' and teachers' time. Because of this, documentation of the school's education policy and, in particular, the curriculum policy, have not kept pace with the changes that have occurred at Altona over the last 4 years, and Green accepts the need for the school to review and update its curriculum. On the other hand, she is sceptical and unconcerned about the absence of working documents which outline the school's mission, believing that the mission is known by staff, but not written down. She does, however, acknowledge the potential value of the state Department of Education's Assisted School Self-Review process. "It will give us a chance to write down our goals and it will be concrete. That will be a good thing because they have been floating around in the air for far too long. So if it can do that, that will be good."

Like Davidson, Green is intolerant of any individual's or group's actions which interfere with the school's efforts to assist students in ways that are legitimate educationally, and in keeping with how things are usually done at Altona. She describes as "slack" those teachers who choose not to fulfil their professional obligations to students. Her disdain for uncommitted teachers lies in marked contrast to her empathy and support for those teachers who, whilst at Altona, have experienced difficulties with student behaviour. Most colleagues and the administration provide those teachers with coping and teaching strategies as well as, when necessary, helping to deal with a difficult student or grade. "In this school, you help each other. ... Here, you work as a team. People pull together."

CONTINUING WITH THE STATUS QUO NO LONGER AN OPTION: A RATTLING OF CAGES

In 1993, Ian Davidson vacated the Altona principalship for a year in order to take up an interstate fellowship, as part of a professional development initiative. He returned to a school in which students' cultures prevailed. To many students, educators had become another problem, in much the same way that some of their parents, and other adults in their lives had. In addition, the principal of Altona had left the school which, despite his return, was not dissimilar—in the eyes of students—to what many parents in Altona households did.

Overlying widespread feelings of disenchantment by students was their inability or unwillingness to find classes meaningful. Rather than school being a means of achieving employment, it had become a place where students had little choice but to attend. Absenteeism was unusually high in 1994, and teachers were drawn into daily school-based manifestations of a disenfranchised student population. Teacher Peta Reece recalled that "we were in chaos. It was a crisis and the school was walking away bit by bit. It was being trashed. Student behaviour was totally unacceptable ... spitting, swearing, slagging off at people and there was a general lack of respect plus a lot of graffiti around." Inside classrooms, "there was no teaching, just survival."

The often hostile learning culture of students contributed to a growing sense of frustration and tiredness amongst Altona teachers. Added to that, various structures which at one stage had worked effectively and complemented teachers' work, no longer suited the school's circumstances. In particular, the four part sub-school system which had been most viable in earlier years when there were as many as 800 students, had become dysfunctional. The absence of a "critical mass" of students in each sub-school, plus their failure to operate as a symbolic, rallying-identity for students, left Altona with an outdated structural system that had given rise to a culture of aggression amongst students in which bullying and physical violence had become daily events during break times. Yard duty had become so difficult for teachers that "staff would pair on duty. They didn't feel safe on duty. Staff hated being at Altona," said teacher Margaret Evans.

In the first few months following his return to the school, Ian Davidson's response to what he found was to adopt a domineering style, particularly in relation to students who misbehaved. It was an approach that he thought was, ultimately, of limited value, because it was a style of interaction that differed little from what they experienced in their homes, to which they had become immune.

Teachers' disenchantment with the school, plus what they then saw as unhelpful leadership responses, characterized many of Altona's collegial conversations during break times. As a result, Joanne Little, who was highly respected by teachers and had been at the school for nearly 7 years, finally spoke with Davidson about changing the restrictive nature of his leadership style and the importance of remaining open and positive to finding solutions. The conversation involved a degree of risk for both Davidson and Little—there was a chance for offence to be taken and a possibility of their professional association suffering. However, Davidson trusted Little's motives for approaching him, as well as her leadership and teaching capacities. Almost immediately, Davidson attempted to temper his style by becoming more collaborative and encouraging of teachers, especially those who were canvassing new ways of improving the school.

Essentially, teacher despair and exhaustion, coupled with Davidson's professional development in 1993, were the catalysts for change. Following discussions with staff, in mid 1994, Davidson suggested that several widely respected and high profile teachers, including Wayne Falls and Joanne Little, should visit various schools within the State which had middle schools in operation, with a view to implementing a similar model at Altona. On their return, they spoke strongly in favour of implementing a middle school system into Altona's organizational structure, and at a staff meeting three quarters of the staff voted in favour of making the structural change.

At the end of 1994, 17 out of a total of 30 teachers transferred to other schools. Included amongst those who left the school that year were many teachers who did not want to be part of the middle school initiative, to be implemented at the start of the 1995 school year.

CHANGES EVERYWHERE: TRUST, PERSISTENCE, AND RISK-TAKING

One key purpose of the new middle school structure was to provide students with a reduced range of teachers, for 22 of their 30 class periods. While few middle school teachers relished the opportunity to teach out of area, they recognized the need to restore productive working relations with students and to build a positive learning culture.

"Relatively little time was found to prepare middle school teachers for the following year's work, so it meant teaching on-the-run," said Joanne Little. However, lack of preparation was offset by several strategies. "Middle school teachers had high energy levels and great commitment to the initiative," said John

Westbrook, who was a member of the team. "So we put in extra time and effort as well as having two timetabled sessions where we could all meet to share ideas and plan," recalled Westbrook. According to Westbrook, the preparedness of middle school teachers to give additional time to the job was made easier because of the ongoing support and encouragement they received from Joanne Little.

In order to build the skills and knowledge of middle school teachers, many planning sessions were held that involved teachers explaining to one another how they would conduct a lesson on a specific topic, so that it could be adapted or followed by colleagues in a subsequent class. In the course of those sessions, teachers shared resources which they had cobbled together or developed themselves. "Over time this meant we built up stacks of resources and became more structured. During the course of 1995, middle school teachers also took part in various professional development activities, which were held at locations outside the school. However, within the year, most middle school teachers stopped attending many, if not all external in-services because of the behavioural difficulties they subsequently encountered in their classes once they returned. In response to students' reaction to teacher absences, the school then occasionally brought professional development consultants into the school and arranged for them to meet with teachers either after school or during non-teaching times.

The difficulties which teachers encountered in the middle school in terms of student rebellion and resistance to learning were accepted by most Grade 7 and 8 teachers as an interim legacy of the changed structure. Importantly, according to Joanne Little, the middle school coordinator, the new structure "shifted the behaviour management focus to the class teacher." Hence there was a greater chance for interaction and on-going engagement between a teacher and a student who misbehaved.

There was mixed reaction to the middle school structure by Grade 9 and 10 teachers, with most eager for the initiative to succeed, and some unconvinced that the new structure could lead to improved student outcomes. Nevertheless, all teachers actively implemented new procedures for dealing with student behavioural problems—especially those which occurred in the school grounds. The heightened attention to discipline was intended to complement the middle school initiative and more generally signal to Altona's student population that "the ways things are done around here have changed." A "Time-Out" room was initiated by several teachers, for students whose classroom behaviour was best responded to by separating them for up to one period from their classmates. "I knew in many ways it wouldn't solve the problem with those kids but it was a symbolic thing for them. The message to students who really misbehaved was 'we don't accept you in the class when you behave like that'," said one of the initiating teachers, Carl Thomas. Over time, and mostly as a result of continually trying to understand the students, trial and error use of strategies, and dialogue with colleagues, teachers learned which ways of handling Time-Out students worked. Students also slowly learned to follow the procedures which came with attending the Time-Out room.

In a routine that was familiar to Altona's staff, Davidson addressed teachers at a staff meeting in mid 1995 with another initiative, Work Plus, a scheme intended to ensure that, once Grade 10 students had successfully completed their final year at the school, they would go on to either a job, further education, or job training. Altona High, with the assistance of business and community networks, was to act as the students' broker, organising each student's "transition contract." Davidson wanted—and knew he needed—staff support to ensure success of the initiative. The proposal was, to many teachers, another impost. It was also an initiative that did not evolve from a widely-felt need for it amongst staff, and, hence from the outset, was not fully "owned" by teachers.

Whilst the "bulldozing" through of Work Plus at the staff meeting was helped by an impassioned speech from Davidson about its anticipated benefits to students, it was also helped by a staff-wide belief that their principal's motives were worthy and student-focussed. In addition, because Davidson trusted most staff to make caring and highly competent decisions in their classes, his empowering faith in them was reciprocated when staff endorsed the Work Plus initiative. Work Plus was subsequently implemented, and at the end of 1995, almost every Grade 10 student left Altona to undertake further study, job training, or employment.

The beginning of the 1996 school year was the second year of middle school operation. With the benefit of the previous year's experience behind them, most middle school teachers and some Grade 9 and 10 teachers responded to the situation by continuing to develop relationships with their students, and continuing to provide curriculum by building on students' interests. Davidson encouraged staff to initiate learning opportunities that would allow them to build stronger relationships with their students, such as Grade 10 class visits to a local primary school, and the Grade 9 graffiti-cleaning day. Again, however, lack of time was an issue, with new teacher Louise Griffin reflecting that "It came back to having the time to think about those whole new approaches or new ideas to be able to actually implement them. If you didn't get that time or that motivation to do it, then the risk was fairly minimal, because you stuck to what you knew."

Ongoing problems with student learning continued to be seen as relating to larger social problems, such as the absence of a male figure in many homes. Because of this, "A lot of the boys in the school had trouble coping with authority," recalled teacher Greg Panetta. "Ian got an At-Risk campus program going that year and it was designed to deal with anger management and help students to cope when parents left home," said Panetta. As with all innovations, the At-Risk campus, which was located about a kilometre away from the school, had shortcomings as well as many advantages attached to it. One of its chief limitations was the lack of communication between those who initially ran the At-Risk campus and mainstream class teachers. The At-Risk campus subsequently improved the effectiveness of its operation, but many staff remain unsure about whether the advantages which flow from its existence outweigh what could be achieved by mainstreaming those students and spreading the funds across the whole school. Coordinator of the At-Risk campus, Gillian Anderson, reflected that "I think without Ian Davidson's fierce protection and support of the At-Risk campus, much of what happens here, couldn't happen. This campus is very much to do with Ian Davidson's philosophy, which is that kids learn in lots of different ways and that we need to respond to that positively."

Conscious of the need to cater also for the educational requirements of Altona students who were highly capable and motivated learners, in 1996 Davidson determined that the school should provide an Accelerated learning curriculum. As had occurred with all of his major initiatives, Davidson sought and obtained staff support for the venture. However, as with the At-Risk and Work Plus initiatives, whilst staff supported the proposal, many saw their endorsement of the Accelerated campus decision as a fait accompli. "Again, the idea was good. But it wasn't seen like the middle school initiative, which most teachers felt they owned. With the middle school concept, it was investigated, debated, and implemented by staff members. Everyone had a say, whereas with the other initiatives, we knew it was a case of Ian really wanting them to go ahead," said teacher Jenny Warner.

At Altona in 1997, teachers overwhelmingly sought to accommodate the demands brought about by student involvement in the At-Risk and Accelerated campuses through their school and class programs. Despite this practical support for the external campuses, many teachers questioned the impact on mainstream school which flowed from having an extensive range of programs. Altona's successful efforts at embracing multiple initiatives also meant that, during 1997, less time and energy was available to evaluate and further develop the school's core curriculum programs. This inability to systematically review mainstream curriculum on a school-wide basis left some teachers wondering whether or not Altona was offering the best possible whole school program.

RE-CREATION, LESSONS, CHALLENGES

By 1998, staff who had witnessed first-hand the improvement in Altona students' attitudes towards their learning, teachers, and school friends were convinced that the school had achieved much since 1994. There was a reduction in student absences, and Altona students' learning culture had most noticeably impacted those students who, in 1995, had started in Grade 7. "We are reaping the benefits of all the effort attached to the middle school initiative. You still get the odd student who is not going to do any work but they are a real minority and, in most cases, they are not the disruption in classes that they were last year or in previous years," said Terry Faine.

However, the difficulties many students continued to encounter would not easily be overcome in the short or medium term. Sustaining developmentally appropriate teaching can be as or more difficult than the beginning efforts required by such an approach. Invariably, most teachers needed substantial, ongoing professional development in order to maximize their theoretical understandings and build a repertoire of classroom strategies. Limited funds plus a perpetuation of the negative classroom reactions of students toward staff who undertook professional development outside of the school figured in many teachers' decisions to continue to not develop themselves in this way. Nevertheless, for most Altona staff, professional development in 1998 comprised their own and colleagues' school-based efforts at sharing expertise and ideas, drawing on the gains from particular individuals' postgraduate studies plus occasionally being addressed at the school by an "outside" speaker. Collegial conversations in the staffroom and other rooms where teachers gathered for a meeting or during break-times still usually focussed, in large part, on school, curriculum, or classroom matters.

At the same time, administrators needed to be aware of teacher and student stress levels, and act in a timely way to alleviate them. Within Altona's administration, both Davidson and Green were conscious of teachers' stress levels. Green maintained a regular personal exercise regime and, in combination with Davidson, endeavoured to operationally support staff across the school so as to partially offset the demands of teaching. In addition, her reputation for thoroughly and quickly following through teacher complaints about excessively unruly behaviour by individual students left most teachers feeling they were given responsive, helpful support when required.

Ever conscious of the need to promote a greater alliance between the school and the parents of Altona students, in order to alleviate student stress and promote a learning culture within the school community, in 1994 Davidson set out to inform and "invite" parents into the school. As well as holding numerous award and information sessions for parents and Altona citizens since then, Davidson ensured that various achievements by students were celebrated formally. Those events contributed to a growing sense of partnership between the school and most parents, and to a belief that "It does not matter what category a youngster fits into—whether they are the brightest of bright or the ones who need fixing up, the ones who need intervention because of problems that they are currently experiencing in their learning. Or those whose parents may need motivating and switching on to their kid's education. We can demonstrate that we do all of that very, very well," he said.

Amidst the many broad-based achievements that have occurred at Altona over the past 5 years, the most compelling one is that many students have given effect to their right to learn, regardless of their individual circumstances. By and large, students are more actively, and productively, learning in classes, and a greater number of Altona teachers continue to adapt what they teach as an outcome of their understandings of the types of students they have in class. In reflecting on the quality of staff contributions to the school during the past 5 years in particular, Davidson claimed that the willingness to remain open to new ways of improving the school as well as holding on to what was educationally important helped the school to make much progress. The practice of teachers viewing critically many of his ideas and any which might, in future, be imposed on schools from federal or state governments was, according to Davidson, a healthy feature of Altona. "Because at the end of the day, teachers will run with agendas that they believe in. They will be dismissive of the agendas that are imposed where they can see that it is not going to make a difference to them and their work and the outcomes for their students."

While Altona's administration and staff have made considerable gains in rebutting negative images of the school and its students, many prejudices remain throughout the surrounding non-Altona community, in particular. These limited, stereotyped views of the suburb, the school, and Altona's youth still imply that the area and its people are on "the wrong side of the tracks." It is likely to take many decades, and numerous celebrations of further achievements, before such stereotypical views will be largely ameliorated.

APPENDIX 4

THE HERONWOOD CASE STUDY: SHORT VERSION

SETTING THE SCENE

In a similar vein to many towns nearby, 90% of Heronwood's population of 10,000 was born in Australia. The once burgeoning population of mostly working class people in Heronwood had not escaped several key changes which affected almost all who lived in the state's regional localities during the 1980s. As a result, by 1991, the town found itself with increasing unemployment, poverty, family breakdowns and alienation. It was annually losing about 30 citizens, as individuals relocated in order to find work or resettled elsewhere due to marital or partner separations. Two in 10 Heronwood households (with children) had no men in them, and 1 in 10 Heronwood citizens between the ages of 25 and 64 years was unemployed. For those aged between 15 and 24 years who were able to work, the unemployment rate was twice as bad. One in four families survived on a total annual income of less than $16,000, markedly lower income levels than nearby more affluent towns.

The dominant industries in Heronwood were wholesale and retail trade, manufacturing and community services. Together, those industries employed nearly two-thirds of the town's employees. The most common post-school level of attainment amongst the town's people was a skilled vocational qualification. Nonetheless, for every adult in Heronwood who held a post-school qualification, there were two who had no qualifications. By the early 1990's, Heronwood was characterized by a population that was qualified for a manufacturing era, despite the onset of an Information Age, which was heavily geared by technology.

By the time Andrew Ingram took up the principalship of Heronwood High, a Grade 7 to 10 (ages 13 to 16) government school in a state which has a three-tier schooling system: primary (Kindergarten to Grade 6), high (Grades 7 to 10), and college (Grades 11 and 12), in February 1991, more than half of the school's 47 full- and part-time teachers knew to expect considerable change. Although Ingram had lived on the outskirts of Heronwood for 15 years, he knew much about "what happened in town and how things ticked." Prior to taking up the principalship Ingram talked with teachers and listened intently to their often lengthy comments about the school. He learned that, under the previous principal, no teacher had been promoted out of the school in 11 years. "That was an incredible statistic. It wasn't that there weren't good teachers, it was just that the principal was keeping them at the school. There was a very, very strong teaching staff—many of whom should have been promoted in order to develop their skills, learn more and grow," said Ingram.

Consequently, the school had not benefited from the diversity of experiences, ideas and standpoints which often accompany the arrival of new staff, and a culture of repetition rather than renewal characterized much of teachers' work. Of particular concern to Ingram, once he started at the school was that, by and large, he "wasn't seeing kids turned on by their learning." By contrast, Ingram's observations of classrooms in his early days at the school resulted in him seeing "a lot of really good, positive interactions between teachers and kids. That was the strength of the school—the quality of the teaching staff and their interactions with the kids."

CHANGING LEADERS, CHANGING TIMES

At one of his first addresses to staff, Ingram expressed his confidence in the capacities of Heronwood teachers. "I trust you to do the job," he told them. As well, Ingram promised to provide an open style of leadership that was characterized by consistency and fairness. "I was always both consistent and fair, which was 90% of the battle, on two fronts. If the people who walked through my door found the same person every day of the week at any time of the day, under any circumstances, I figured that was of real value …". Part of the transparency, on his part, would include "opening up all those lines of communication and an open sharing of information." He signalled to staff a commitment to collaborative planning processes. At the same time, "The other thing I did was really push the notion of professionalism, with things like confidentiality, and made sure that teachers were aware that, with the increased flow of communication, came increased responsibilities as well."

Ingram's stance represented a marked and refreshing difference to his predecessor, under whom there had been a leadership vacuum. The vacuum had been responded to by the assistant principal and key teachers initiating those actions considered necessary for the functioning of the school and classrooms. Because of what Ingram had been told about the school and its leadership, he believed that staff needed considerable additional support. One form of support he promised at a staff meeting, related to trust. "We talked about trust, so that from then on, they could trust me to do the things I was going to do and follow up things I said I was going to follow up."

Ingram's quickly established, daily habit of being in the school and being available to teachers at short notice helped to build connections with staff who sought clarification of issues or required assistance of some sort. By walking around the school at least twice daily observing classrooms along the way, Ingram rapidly built up a dense understanding of the school's culture. In turn, his roving presence was interpreted by many staff as early evidence of the priority Ingram gave to teaching and learning in the school.

At other staff meetings early in his tenure, Ingram raised the matter of teachers' professional development, "because the amount of professional learning that had been occurring here was almost nil, and clarified with teachers what professional development they'd undertaken and would like to undertake. ... It also established a lot of trust, because it meant I had a profile of the staff that I was then able to acknowledge to them." The readiness, and in many instances keenness, of staff to access further learning soon resulted in teachers frequently undertaking professional development activities both within and beyond the school. Teacher Debra Hyams noted that the encouragement and material support Ingram provided to teachers who took up professional development opportunities "helped some of us feel that he was committed to teachers as well as the benefits which would flow to the kids."

Coinciding with schools in the state gaining greater decision-making capacity over their budgets, was a heightened capacity for autonomous planning. To take advantage of greater decision making powers "we established a Planning Group," said Ingram. Within the umbrella group were many smaller committees that focussed on feeding back recommendations about specific issues. While particular members made up specific committees and groups, any staff member could attend any meetings and, with the exception of confidential matters, participate fully in decisionmaking.

THE SECOND YEAR

By the start of the second year of Ingram's tenure, eight new teachers joined Heronwood High's staff. Whilst most were pleased with the transfers, they soon became aware of grumbling from some of the established staff about student discipline. These staff were critical of their principal's level of empathy with "difficult students who misbehaved. Many staff believed that Andrew was too supportive of students, especially in relation to students who played up. They also felt that Andrew needed to be more pro-teacher," said Anthea Andrianopolous.

Ingram, however, sought to affirm students by engaging troubled or troubling students in an honest conversation, identifying mutually acceptable or reasonable behaviour and endorsing their teacher's efforts. In the course of students reporting to Ingram over behavioural difficulties, their principal wanted them to know that they had a right to state their case and have it considered. This "helped his standing in the eyes of many teachers as well as the student population," said teacher Betty Palmer. "His regular presence in the school grounds during break times plus the fact that he taught—and taught extraordinarily well—added to his credibility," she claimed.

Having an open-door policy, however, did not mean Ingram accepted or endorsed everything that was told to him in his office. Indeed, as a result of hearing about the marginalisation of some students by other students one day, Ingram organized a special assembly, which was attended by nearly 700 students and staff. "The kids from Room 45 always got a hard time. They were our Special Ed. Kids.

As you'd expect, there was always a bit of a thing amongst the kids and the Special kids were targeted," said Ingram. At the assembly Ingram "ran it with just those kids and got a few of them to say what it meant to be ridiculed in the way they had been. It was a bit of a tear-jerker really, but it had a significant impact on the way the student population subsequently accepted others into the school."

Resistance and suspicion toward incoming teachers from much of the student population had long been "part of the scene at Heronwood," according to Catriona Lorimer. However, it was particularly difficult for some new staff "because they came into a very student empowered school—and that wasn't typical of many high schools." Lorimer, who was widely regarded on staff as being one of Heronwood High's outstanding teachers, claimed that the empowerment of students had occurred, in large part, because of and during Ingram's leadership at the school. At the same time, she noted that the difficulties new teachers to the school experienced in being accepted by students were ultimately reduced over the time they were there, provided it became clear that, in classes, teachers cared.

One offspring from the heavy investment in teachers' professional development ushered in by Ingram was an increasing effort by teachers like Catriona Lorimer to negotiate with students on curriculum matters. Lorimer believed it was an effective avenue for engaging students and providing them with meaningful learning experiences. Recognising the value of staff like Lorimer in promoting change, Ingram eventually persuaded her to share her skills and knowledge at a series of staff development sessions.

Ingram recognized that a traditional antipathy toward non-school-based personnel and externally-developed policies existed across much of Heronwood staff. At the same time, neither he nor the school were immune to the influences of Central or District edicts. Honouring his commitment to collaborative planning, teacher Louis Stedman explained that with key Departmental demands, "Andrew sat down and made judgements with the staff or Planning Groups about the suitability of many of those initiatives. … [He] learnt early that if something was being pushed that we—the people who were applying it—didn't want, that was to be accepted. He knew that without sufficient support, anything implemented under those circumstances would be only given a half-hearted attempt."

THE THIRD YEAR

By the third year of Ingram's tenure, the frustrations from pressurized home lives showed through more and more in the playground and class behaviours of students at Heronwood. Fights in the school grounds during breaktimes and "rudeness in classrooms" were becoming a more common feature of school life at Heronwood. One of the responses from Ingram and Heronwood teachers was to undertake professional development which expanded staff understandings of student behaviour management. Most teachers considered those professional development sessions provided staff with more explicit and coherent strategies to use, and given the perceived need for them, they were ultimately consistently applied by staff in an effort to improve student behaviour. At the same time, Ingram reminded "teachers to not take things too seriously, when the going gets tough," and continued to use humour and engaged in "good natured stirring" as a means of connecting with teachers and "encouraging them to put things in perspective."

Ingram's own outstanding record as a teacher had convinced the Heronwood principal that the better the interpersonal relationships between students and their teacher, the less problematic were discipline problems in classes. It was a key reason why teachers also continued to receive ongoing encouragement and financial support from Ingram to attend seminars which focussed on improving teaching and learning, and to use their initiative and experiment with new ideas and practices in the classroom.

Some staff, however, were unconvinced about the need to expand their teaching strategies, with a deeply-held view that students needed to behave well, irrespective of who was teaching them or what was being taught. Several teachers also remained unconvinced about the need to change their teaching practices, concerned about shortage of time and the risks to content and coverage from, for example, facilitating more group work in classes. Although sympathetic to their argument, Ingram believed that the changing nature of children's lives plus the poor learning culture amongst much of the Heronwood student population, meant that teachers needed to adapt what they did if students were ultimately going to respond more positively within classes.

Ingram was determined that any dissent at Heronwood on prized school matters should not be crushed. Rather, as well as hearing but only selectively challenging the claims of teachers who saw insufficient reasons to change classroom practice, Ingram sought to better use their talents. "He led with wisdom. To do that, he empowered every bastard in the place he could, just like we tried to do with our students. He picked up and brought every talent of every person with whom he worked," said Catriona Lorimer. The demonstration of Ingram's commitment to workplace diversity—whether or not he agreed with different teachers' viewpoints—reinforced his largely favourable standing in the eyes of many trenchant critics of change.

THE FOURTH YEAR

On her arrival, new teacher Celia Warne was surprised at the dispiriting culture amongst Heronwood students. "They struck me as pretty small-town minded. There wasn't a desire to get out of or beyond Heronwood. There was a lack of inquisitiveness, a lack of motivation to know anything much about what existed apart from in their immediate little world." At the same time, Warne soon experienced an avalanche of questioning about the legitimacy of her instructions to students. The nature of students' comments left Warne feeling that being a new teacher, as well as a female, accounted for what she experienced, and that resistance was related to the hardship in which many students lived and the narrow, ingrained attitudes which characterized some families. Also new to the school in the fourth year of Ingram's tenure, Assistant Principal Bob Muscat was alarmed by what he "suspected" was an all increasing development amongst some Heronwood families.

"When students needed parental support, it just wasn't there for some students. The kids were, in effect, on their own."

The growing difficulties many students were experiencing "at home" were accelerating concerns about negative class and school ground behaviour from new and long-standing Heronwood teachers. While there was an emerging consensus about the difficulties that teachers—and many students—were experiencing due to poor behaviour, there was disagreement amongst staff about what could or should be done about it. One solution, which achieved the support of staff, led to an increase in the number of excursions and "special event" activities that were organized for students. Another response saw additional professional development being provided to teachers who wished to expand their understanding of student discipline strategies. As well, student opinions were actively sought in the course of further refining the school's discipline policy. A further strategy which was initiated from Heronwood's Planning Group resulted in the appointment of counsellors to each grade level. Augmented by a professional guidance officer, teachers on staff met weekly with interested colleagues to talk about "kids and the problems kids were having," said Trevor Warburton, one of the junior grade counsellors.

At the same time, further initiatives were being developed to galvanise the learning opportunities of students. Supported by Ingram and the highly effective leadership team at Heronwood, Muscat started work on reframing the school's curriculum to better equip students to "think critically". The focus away from content, and towards teaching students how to think, would represent a major departure from the traditional curriculum. By talking informally with teachers who had indicated an openness to reviewing curriculum and, after subsequently raising the matter with Ingram and at Planning Group, Muscat and several staff met regularly on the issue. In concert with other teachers, Muscat spent the balance of the year researching and evaluating the content and design of various whole-school curricula. Throughout that period Muscat's group regularly fed back progress summaries to Planning Group meetings and staff gatherings.

THE FIFTH YEAR

From the time Ingram took up the principalship at Heronwood, the school had conducted research as a means of informing "both our planning and direction," so that a survey conducted in the fifth year of his tenure built upon earlier initiatives that were designed to identify whether the school was catering to parent, community, student and teacher expectations. Ingram was pleased that the findings "were overwhelmingly positive about the things the school was offering." Throughout Ingram's first 5 years at Heronwood "two important things repeatedly emerged that the school community valued—apart from being consulted—basic skills and supporting a caring environment for children."

However, amongst staff, there continued to be a lack of unanimity about student learning, effective teaching strategies and curriculum content. Ingram was, in one sense, unconcerned about those differences of opinion amongst staff. He believed that critical thinking from staff would, in the end, produce decisions that could have a much greater chance of being effective than anything that was "top-down, imposed on staff." On the other hand, Ingram continued whenever possible to highlight the work of "exemplary teachers and make them available to staff" in a variety of ways, "in an effort to shift some colleagues' teaching practices."

Paralleling Heronwood's efforts to improve the quality of teaching and learning, were increasingly specific requirements from the state Department of Education concerning the student learning outcomes. In general Ingram embraced initiatives from the Centre which were targeted at improving what students, in particular, experienced at school. Ingram suspected that the genuinely supportive and helpful role adopted by the Centre towards schools reflected the state Department of Education's growing recognition "of school personnel as professionals," and an awareness that if it "wanted stuff implemented, it had to grow from what teachers were doing and what teachers wanted to do," said Ingram.

THE SIXTH YEAR

The 15 new staff appointed in the sixth year were able to familiarize themselves quickly with the workings of Heronwood High because of effective staff induction processes, supportive staff, and Ingram's outstanding leadership. New teacher Warren Wallace recalls "that Andrew was a really strong principal, and there was a vision for where the school was going in the future. In terms of where the school was taking the kids, there was a definite plan, a definite vision. As soon as I walked into the school, I picked that up." Wallace was also impressed by Ingram's instructional leadership, specifically his capacity "to demonstrate good teaching practice and talk generally about teaching as well as offer ideas." He had not before experienced a situation where "the principal interacted with the kids in ways to help them become independent learners. Andrew gave the kids a lot of freedom to move about and get on with their learning. It was an example of the way he wanted the school to operate and the outcome was that students were pretty independent learners."

When teaching and other duties permitted, Bob Muscat continued to spend time reviewing the school's curriculum, in conjunction with a small group of interested teachers. Abner Mirna, who had been at the school for many years, was deeply sceptical about curriculum reviews, although in his own classes, Mirna was teaching in ways that were similar to what Muscat's group promoted—especially in relation to developing students' critical thinking capacities. Because of the importance of what Mirna was achieving with his class, Ingram and Muscat finally persuaded him to take an active role in the school's curriculum review. Mirna had concluded that the review was motivated by colleagues who genuinely had the interests of students at heart. He also realized, from his own teaching experiences, that the anticipated change—if effectively implemented—would provide most Heronwood High students with vastly improved learning opportunities, and therefore became "one of the most credible advocates for change amongst staff," said Warren Wallace.

At the same time as the school was grappling with the prospect of redrafting the curriculum, Heronwood High became involved in the Assisted School Self-Review

(ASSR), which was to be undertaken by willing public schools throughout the state. It was unsurprising to Ingram that the staff had agreed to take part in the first "intake" of the rolling process, readily identifying the likely benefit to the school from gathering a wide range of data and again, canvassing the views of Heronwood's school community, as they had been doing for the past 6 years.

THE SEVENTH YEAR

Again, the start of the new school year at Heronwood High brought with it many new staff, due to the Department of Education's transfer policy, which requires teachers to move after seven years in one position. The culture shock which frequently characterized the experiences of incoming staff in relation to students, added to the arguments which motivated many of the claims by Muscat's curriculum review group. Not only was the need for curriculum change propelled, in Muscat's view, by the need to counter students' limited life experiences through radically different class-based learning opportunities, there was an urgency about the time Heronwood High was taking to make such changes.

Even though Ingram empathized with concerns about the protracted nature of curriculum reform, he was undisturbed by the matter. Those, like District Office, who wanted a quicker pace needed to be patient. Ingram believed that proponents of the reforms needed to recognize what they had already achieved. Compared to when Ingram began at Heronwood, the changes to the school's teaching and learning were dramatic. "What they had done was exciting and quite different," said Ingram. Another reason Ingram comfortably accepted that the "transformation of the school's curriculum required even further time to develop" was because he considered lasting change would only be implemented when teachers genuinely believed it was feasible. It was, he claimed, "no good to say 'right, critical thinking—that is where we're going to go to'." To have expected teachers who were not ready or able to work out where critical thinking fitted "in the big scheme of things would have resulted in it neither being implemented nor effective."

THE EIGHTH YEAR

Although there was still some opposition to curriculum change by Ingram's eighth year, there was increasing support for the initiative from staff, and a firm belief that it would be a lasting change. Recognising that "It will be a big risk for many teachers, requiring them to take a leap of faith in not only the new program, but themselves as teachers," teachers such as Catriona Lorimer also strongly believed that teachers' fears, inadequacies, shortages of time and territorial problems would, in the end, be placed second to the "circumstances and futures of kids … [because] these days that's the only way we can teach."

However, Ingram's primary efforts were elsewhere for much of the year. After nearly a decade of effort by teachers and Ingram in developing a deeply caring ethos toward students, by 1998 Ingram believed the school was "treading water" on the issue and not making adequate progress to curb the hostility and aggression displayed by some students toward others. He was not prepared to accept that bullying and harassment were a normal part of adolescence, and feared the nature and frequency of "bullying and harassment in the school might be above the national average." One dimension of the problem to Ingram was an increasing recognition "that there is an underclass of children in school now who are disenfranchised financially, economically and socially. ... those kids are more and more strident in an institution which seeks to maintain community and family values. They are values those kids have never been exposed to." A further dimension was the comparatively recent arrival in town of "street kids." During school hours, and especially at lunch times, several street kids regularly gathered just outside of the school grounds in an effort to talk with, fight or verbally harass particular Heronwood High students. Given the importance Ingram gave to a school providing "students with an environment in which they can grow strongly as social individuals—to make decent citizens for the future," he subsequently intensified the time and effort he gave to the issue. One of Ingram's responses to the problem involved timetabling either himself or one of the Assistant Principals to yard duty every lunchtime.

CHALLENGES

While the school was considered one of the best in the state and had been effective in ensuring an increasing number of Grade 10 students went on to further education, the town's preference for locals to remain local represented a huge and ongoing challenge for Heronwood High to contend with.

Other challenges related to the poor behaviour and learning culture of some students, and the unrelenting practice of bullying especially in the school grounds and, in some instances, after hours in the streets and houses in which students lived. Whereas under Ingram's leadership the school had been effective in stemming the use of physical violence amongst students, as a means of resolving conflict, Heronwood High was, more frequently, having to contend with psychological bullying by students. Although Ingram and Muscat realized the practice of verbal intimidation had begun to take hold amongst "pockets" of students, the underlying triggers to such actions were, in the main, considered by them to lie outside of the school. The continuing economic and social pressures that the town of Heronwood was experiencing and the resultant family "implosions" were, according to Muscat, expected to continue at least in the medium-term. Given the considerable effort the school continued to expend on promoting the well-being of all children, the interim response of Heronwood High was, Ingram indicated, "to put even more effort into dealing with the issue, because, in the end, schools are about being supportive learning environments for the total well-being of children."

At the same time, the anticipated changes to curriculum—which most expected would eventuate—left many subject-trained teachers concerned about their future capacity to operate effectively in classes, despite the prolific provision and use of professional development at Heronwood High. The ongoing efforts of Ingram and Muscat, in particular, to expand teachers' understandings of the ever-changing labour market requirements of school graduates, had not been fully grasped by many Heronwood High teachers. Hence, the beliefs which underpinned the proposed changes to curriculum in terms of equipping students as critical and adaptive learners, had not convinced those staff.

REFERENCES

Adams, R. J., & Khoo, S. T. (1993). *Quest – The interactive test analysis system* [computer software]. Hawthorn, Victoria: Australian Council for Educational Research.

Albanese, M., & Mitchell, S. (1993). Problem-based learning: A review of literature on its outcomes and implementation issues. *Academic Medicine, 68,* 52-81.

Barnett, K., McCormick, T., & Conners, R. (2001). Transformational leadership in schools. *Journal of Educational Administration, 39,* 24-46.

Begley, P., & Johansson, O. (2003). *The ethical dimensions of school leadership.* Dordrecht, the Netherlands: Kluwer.

Ben-Peretz, M., & Schonmann, S. (1998). Informal learning communities and their effects. In K. Leithwood & K. Louis. (Eds.), *Organisational learning in schools* (pp. 47-66). Lisse, the Netherlands: Swets & Zeitlinger.

Berends, M. (2000). Teacher-reported effects of New American School design: Exploring relationships to teacher background and school context. *Educational Evaluation and Policy Analysis, 22,* 65-82.

Bishop, P., & Mulford, B. (1996). Empowerment in four primary schools: They don't really care. *International Journal of Educational Reform, 5,*193-204.

Bishop, P., & Mulford, B. (1999). When will they ever learn? Another failure of centrally-imposed change. *School Leadership and Management, 19,* 179-187.

Bransford, J., Franks, J., Vye, N., & Sherwood, R. (1989) New approaches to instruction: Because wisdom can't be told. In S. Vosniadou & A. Ortony (Eds.), *Similarity and analogical reasoning* (pp. 470-496). New York: Cambridge University Press.

Bridges, E., & Hallinger. P. (1992). *Problem-based learning for administrators.* Eugene, OR: ERIC Clearinghouse for Educational Management.

Brown, P., & Appel, A. L. (1993). Problem based learning in graduate nursing education: How effective is it? In G. Ryan (Ed.), *Research and development in problem based learning* (pp. 83-98). Campbelltown, NSW: Australian Problem Based Learning Network.

Busher, H., & Harris, A. (2000). *Subject leadership and school improvement.* London: Paul Chapman Publishing.

Cooper, B., & Boyd, W. (1987). The evolution of training. In J. Murphy & P. Hallinger (Eds.), *Approaches to administrative training in education* (pp. 3-27). Albany, NY: State University of New York Press.

Cotton, K. (1997). *School size, school climate, and student performance* [On-line]. Available: www.nwrel.org/scpd/sirs/10/c020.html

Coughlan, S. (2001). *How mentors make a difference* [On-line]. Available: http://news.bbc.co.uk/1/hi/education/1132928.stm

Cousins, B. (1998). Organisational consequences of participatory evaluation: School district case study. In K. Leithwood & K. Louis (Eds.), *Organisational learning in schools* (pp. 93-126). Lisse, the Netherlands: Swets & Zeitlinger.

Cronbach, L. J., Gleser, G. C., Nanda, H., & Rajaratnam, N. (1972). The dependability of behavioral measurements: Theory of generalizability for scores and profiles. New York: Wiley.

Cullingford, C. (2001, July). *Pupil attitudes to schools.* Paper presented at The Learning Conference, Spetses, Greece.

Department for Education and Science [DfES]. (2001). *Schools - achieving success* [On-line]. Available: http://www.dfes.gov.uk/achievingsuccess/

Department for Education and Training [DfEE]. (1999). *All our futures: Creativity, culture and education.* Sunbury, UK: Department for Education and Employment.

Elliott, D., & Voss, H. (1974). *Delinquency and dropout.* Lexington, MA: Lexington Books.

Evidence for Policy and Practice Information [EPPI] and Co-ordinating Centre. (2001). *Core keywording strategy: Data Collection for a Register of Educational Research* (Version 0.9.4). London: Author.

Feinstein, L. (2000). *The relative economic importance of academic, psychological and behavioural attributes developed in childhood.* London: London School of Economics and Political Science, Centre for Economic Performance.

Fielding, M. (1999). Target setting, policy pathology and student perspectives: Learning to labour in new times. *Cambridge Journal of Education, 29,* 277-287.

Galton, M. (2000). Big change questions: Should pedagogical change be mandated? Dumbing down on classroom standards: The perils of a technician's approach to pedagogy. *Journal of Educational Change, 1,* 199-204.

Goddard, R., Hoy, W., & Hoy, A. (2000). Collective teacher efficacy: Its meaning, measure, and impact on student achievement. *American Educational Research Journal, 37,* 479-507.

Grady, N., Mulford, B., & Macpherson, R. (1995). Problem-based learning in educational administration through block delivery modes. *International Studies in Educational Administration, 23,* 58-64.

Gronn, P. (2002). Leader formation. . In K. Leithwood & P. Hallinger (Eds.), *Second international handbook of educational leadership and administration* (pp. 1010-1049). Norwell, MA: Kluwer.

Hallinger, P., & Bridges, E. (1995). *Implementing problem-based learning in leadership development.* Eugene, OR: ERIC Clearinghouse for Educational Management.

Hallinger, P., & Wimpleberg, R. (1992). *Developing expert leaders for future schools.* Bristol: Falmer Press.

Hannaway, J. (1978). Administrative structures why do they grow? *Teachers College Record, 79,* 416-417.

Harris, A., & Chapman, C. (2001, September). *Leadership in schools in challenging contexts.* Paper presented at British Educational Research Association conference, Lancaster.

Hay-McBer. (n.d.). *Models of excellence for school leaders* [On-line].
Available: http://www.ncsl.org.uk/index.cfm?pageid=hayhome2

Heck, R. (2000). Examining the impact of school quality on school outcomes and improvement: A value-added approach. *Educational Administration Quarterly, 36,* 513-552.

Hersey, P., & Blanchard, K. (1988). *Management of organizational behavior: Utilizing human resources.* Englewood Cliffs, NJ: Prentice-Hall.

Hodges, A. (2000, April). *Web of support for personalised, academic foundation.* Paper presented at the annual meeting of the American Educational Research Association, New Orleans, LA.

Hurst, D. (1995). *Crisis and renewal.* Boston, MA: Harvard Business School Press.

Johnston, D., & Johnston, F. (1975). *Joining together: Group theory and group skills.* Englewood Cliffs, NJ: Prentice-Hall.

Jöreskog, K. G., & Sörbom, D. (1993). *New features in LISREL 8.* Chicago, IL: Scientific Software International.

Kaplan, A. (1964). *The conduct of inquiry.* San Francisco, CA: Chandler.

Kaplan, A. (1997). Scientific methods in educational research. In J. P. Keeves (Ed.), *Educational research, methodology, and measurement: An international handbook* (2nd ed., pp. 112-119). Oxford: Pergamon Press.

Keeves, J. P. (1986). Aspiration, motivation and achievement: Different methods of analysis and different results. *International Journal of Educational Research, 10,* 115-243.

Kilpatrick, S., Johns, S., Mulford, B., Falk, I., & Prescott, L. (2002). *More than education: Leadership for rural school-community partnerships* [On-line].
Available: http://www.rirdc.gov.au/reports/HCC/02-055.pdf

Lao-tzu. (1986). *The way of life according to Lao-tzu* (W. Bynner, Trans.). New York: Capricorn Books.

Leadership. Everyone talks about it, everyone wants it. But who are the people who will lead us into the new millennium? (1998, July 4). *Herald Sun Weekend* [lift-out supplement].

Lee, V., & Loeb, S. (2000). School size in Chicago elementary schools: Effects on teachers' attitudes and student achievement. *American Educational Research Journal, 37,* 3-31.

Lee, V., & Smith, J. (2001). Restructuring high schools for equity and excellence: What works? NY: Teachers College Press.

Leithwood, K. (Ed.). (2000). *Understanding schools as intelligent systems.* Stamford, CT: JAI Press.

Leithwood, K., & Duke, D. (1999). A century's quest to understand school leadership. In J. Murphy & K. S. Louis (Eds.), *Handbook of research on educational administration* (2nd ed., pp. 45-72). Washington, DC: American Educational Research Association.

Leithwood, K., & Louis, K. (Eds.). (1998). *Organisational learning in schools.* Lisse, the Netherlands: Swets & Zeitlinger.

Leithwood, K., Hallinger, P., Furman, G., Gronn, P., MacBeath, J., Mulford, B., & Riley, K. (Eds.). (2002). *Second international handbook of educational leadership and administration.* Norwell, MA: Kluwer.

Leithwood, K., Jantzi, D., & Steinbach, R. (1998). Leadership and other conditions which foster organisational learning in schools. In K. Leithwood & K. Louis (Eds.), *Organisational learning in schools* (pp. 67-90). Lisse, the Netherlands: Swets & Zeitlinger.

Louden, W., & Wallace, J. (1994). *Too soon to tell: School restructuring and the National Schools Project* (Monograph No. 17). Melbourne: Australian Council for Educational Administration.

Louis, K., & Kruse, S. (1998). Creating community in reform: Images of organisational learning in inner-city schools. In K. Leithwood & K. Louis (Eds.), *Organisational learning in schools* (pp. 17-46). Lisse, the Netherlands: Swets & Zeitlinger.

Maden, M. (Ed.). (2001). Success against the odds – five years on: Revisiting effective schools in disadvantaged areas. London: Routledge Falmer.

Marks, H., Louis, K., & Printy, S. (2000). The capacity for organisational learning: Implications for pedagogical quality and student achievement. In K. Leithwood (Ed.), *Understanding schools as intelligent systems* (pp. 239-265). Stamford, CT: JAI Press.

McCall, J., Smith, I., Stoll, L., Thomas, S., Sammons, P., Smees, R., MacBeath, J., Boyd, B., & MacGilchrist, B. (2001). Views of pupils, parents and teachers: Vital indicators of effectiveness and for improvement. In J. MacBeath & P. Mortimore (Eds.), *Improving school effectiveness* (pp. 74-101). Buckingham, UK: Open University Press.

McGaw, B., Piper, K., Banks, D., & Evans, B. (1992). *Making schools more effective* (Report of the Australian Effective Schools Project). Hawthorn, Victoria: Australian Council for Educational Research.

McLaughlin, M. (1998). Listening and learning from the field: Tales of policy implementation and situated practice. In A. Hargreaves, A. Lieberman, M. Fullan, & D. Hopkins (Eds.), *International handbook of educational change* (pp. 70-84). Dordrecht, the Netherlands: Kluwer.

Mitchell, C., & Sackney, L. (1998). Learning about organisational learning. In K. Leithwood & K. Louis (Eds.), *Organisational learning in schools* (pp. 177-199). Lisse, the Netherlands: Swets & Zeitlinger.

Mulford, B. (1998). Organisational learning and educational change. In A. Hargreaves, A. Lieberman, M. Fullan, & D. Hopkins (Eds.), *International handbook of educational change* (pp. 616-641). Norwell, MA: Kluwer.

Mulford, B. (2002a). Leadership in education: Losing sight of our interests? In N. Bennett, M. Crawford, & M. Cartwright (Eds), *Effective educational leadership* (pp. 3-13). London: Open University Press and Paul Chapman Publishing.

Mulford, B. (2002b). The global challenge: A matter of balance. *Educational Management & Administration, 30,* 123-138. Also available on-line: http://www.cdesign.com.au/acea2000/pages/con03.htm

Mulford, B., Kendall, L., Kendall, D., Bishop, P., & Hogan, D. (2000). Decision making in primary schools. *International Studies in Educational Administration, 28,* 5-22.

Mulford, B., Kendall, L., Kendall, D., Lamb, S., & Hogan, D. (2001). Decision making in Australian high schools. *International Studies in Educational Administration, 29,* 49-73.

Mulford, B., Watson, H., & Vallee, J. (1981). *Structured experiences and group development.* Canberra: Dominion Press for the Curriculum Development Centre.

Mulford, W. (1994). *Shaping tomorrow's schools* (Monograph No. 15). Melbourne, Victoria: Australian Council for Educational Administration.

Murphy, J. (1990). The reform of school administration: Pressures and calls for change. In J. Murphy (Ed.), *The reform of American public education in the 1980s: Themes and cases* (pp. 3-55). Berkeley, CA: McCutchan.

National College for School Leadership [NCSL]. (2001). *Leading by a head* [On-line]. Available: www.ncsl.org.uk

National College for School Leadership [NCSL]. (n.d.). *First Corporate Plan: Launch Year 2001-2.* Nottingham: Author.

Organization for Economic Cooperation and Development [OECD]. (2001a). *Knowledge and skills for life: First results from PISA 2000.* Paris: Author.

Organization for Economic Cooperation and Development [OECD]. (2001b). *New school management approaches*. Paris: Author.

Osterman, K. (2000). Students' need for belonging in the school community. *Review of Educational Research, 70*, 323-367.

Peters, J., Dobbins, D., & Johnson, B. (1996). *Restructuring and organisational culture* (Research Paper No. 4). Ryde, New South Wales: National Schools Network.

Pfeiffer, W. (Ed.). *The 1991 annual developing human resources*. San Diego: University Associates.

Prestine, N. (1998, April). *Disposable reform? Assessing the durability of secondary school reform.* Paper presented at the annual meeting of the American Educational Research Association, San Diego, CA.

Radice, S. (Tuesday July 31, 2001). Our adult friend. *Guardian Education* [On-line]. Available: http://www.dfee.goe.uk/thelearninggateway/mentoring/index.htm;

Reynolds, D. (n.d.). *Effective school leadership: The contribution of school effectiveness research* [On-line]. Available: http://www.ncsl.org.uk/index.cfm?pageid=ev.auth_reynolds

Riley, K., & Louis, K. S. (Eds.). (2000). *Leadership for change and school reform: International perspectives*. London: Routledge Falmer.

Rudduck, J., & Flutter, J. (2000). Pupil participation and pupil perspective: Carving a new order of experience. *Cambridge Journal of Education, 30*, 75-89.

Sammons, P., Thomas, S., Mortimore, P., Owen, C., & Pennell, H. (1994). *Assessing school effectiveness: Developing measures to put school performance in* context. London: Office for Standards in Education (OFSTED).

Sarason, S. (1998). *Political leadership and educational failure*. San Francisco: Jossey-Bass.

Schmuck, R., & Runkel, P. (1994). *The handbook of organization development in schools and colleges*. Prospect Heights, IL: Waveland Press.

Schmuck, R., & Schmuck, P. (1988). *Group processes in the classroom*. Dubuque, IA: Wm. C. Brown.

Sellin, N. (1990). PLSPATH (Version 3.01 User's Manual). Hamburg.

Sellin, N., & Keeves, J. P. (1997). Path analysis with latent variables. In J. P. Keeves (Ed.), *Educational research, methodology, and measurement: An international handbook* (2nd ed., pp. 633-640). Oxford: Pergamon Press.

Senge, P., Kleiner, A., Roberts, C., Ross, R., Roth, G., & Smith, B. (1999). *The dance of change: The challenges to sustaining momentum in learning organisations*. New York: Currency Doubleday.

Sergiovanni, T. (2000). *The lifeworld of leadership*. San Francisco: Jossey-Bass.

Silberman, M. (Ed.). (1999). *The 1999 team and organization development handbook*. New York: McGraw-Hill.

Silins, H. & Murray-Harvey, R. (2000). Students as the central concern. *Journal of Educational Administration, 28*, 230-246.

Silins, H., & Mulford, B. (2001). Leadership for organisational learning and improved student outcomes – what do we know? *NSIN Research Matters, 15*, 1-8.

Silins, H., & Mulford, B. (2002a). Leadership and school results. In K. Leithwood & P. Hallinger (Eds.), *Second international handbook of educational leadership and administration* (pp. 561-612). Dordrecht, the Netherlands: Kluwer.

Silins, H., & Mulford, B. (2002b). Reframing schools: The case for system, teacher and student learning. In B. Cope & M. Kalantzis (Eds.), *Learning for the future* (pp. 3-31). Melbourne: Common Ground Publishing.

Silins, H., & Mulford, B. (2002c). Schools as learning organisations: The case for system, teacher and student learning. *The Journal of Educational Administration, 40*, 425-446.

Silins, H., & Mulford, B. (2003). Leadership for organisational learning and improved student outcomes – what do we know? *Cambridge Journal of Education, 33*, 175-195.

Silins, H., & Mulford, B., & Zarins, S. (2002). Organisational learning and school change. *Educational Administration Quarterly, 38*, 613-642.

Silins, H., Mulford, B., Zarins, S., & Bishop, P. (2000). Leadership for organisational learning in Australian secondary schools. In K. Leithwood (Ed.), *Understanding schools as intelligent systems* (pp. 267-291). Stamford, CT: JAI Press.

Silins, H., Zarins, S., & Mulford, B. (2002). What characteristics and processes define a school as a learning organisation? Is this a useful concept to apply to schools? *International Education Journal, 3*, 24-32.

Sizer, T. (1984). *Horace's compromise*. Boston: Houghton-Mifflin.

Slavin, R. (1996). *Education for all*. Lisse, the Netherlands: Swets & Zeitlinger.

Smylie, M., Lazarus, V., & Brownlee-Conyers, J. (1996). Instructional outcomes of school-based participative decision making. *Educational Evaluation and Policy Analysis, 18*, 181-198.

Stoll, L., MacBeath, J., Smith, I., & Robertson, P. (2001). The change equation: Capacity for improvement. In J. MacBeath & P. Mortimore (Eds.), *Improving school effectiveness* (pp. 169-191). Buckingham, UK: Open University Press.

Stringfield, S. (1998). Organisational learning and current reform efforts: From exploitation to exploration. In K. Leithwood & K. Louis (Eds.), *Organisational learning in schools* (pp. 261-274). Lisse, the Netherlands: Swets & Zeitlinger.

OTHER READINGS

Ackerman, R., Donaldson, G., & van der Bogert, R. (1996). *Making sense as a school leader: Persisting questions, creative opportunities*. San Francisco: Jossey-Bass.

Ackerman, R., & Maslin-Ostrowski. (2002). *The wounded leader*. San Francisco: Jossey-Bass.

Askew, S. (Ed.). (2000). *Feedback for learning*. New York: Routledge Falmer.

Barber, M. (1997). The learning game: Arguments for a learning revolution. London: Indigo.

Begley, P. (Ed.). (1999). *Values and educational* leadership. Albany, NY: State University of New York Press.

Cousins, B. (1996). Understanding organisational learning for educational leadership and school reform. In K. Leithwood (Ed.), *International handbook of leadership and administration*. (pp. 589-652). Dordrecht, the Netherlands: Kluwer.

Day, C., Harris, A., Hadfiield, M., Tolley, H., & Beresford, J. (2000). *Leading schools in times of change*. Buckingham, UK: Open University Press.

Fink, D. (2000). Good school/real school: Why school reform doesn't last. New York: Teachers College Press.

Gronn, P. (1999). *The making of educational leaders*. London: Cassell.

Hajnal, V., Walker, K., & Sackney, L. (1998). Leadership, organisational learning and selected factors related to the institutionalisation of school improvement initiatives. *The Alberta Journal of Educational Research, 44*, 70-89.

Hallinger, P. (1999). Schools as learning organisations: Framework and assumptions. *The Practicing Administrator, 21*, 6-8, 41-43.

Harris, A., & Bennett, N. (Ed.). (2001). School effectiveness and school improvement: Alternative perspectives. London: Continuum.

Heck, R. (1993). School context, principal leadership, and achievement: The case of secondary schools in Singapore. *The Urban Review, 25*, 151-166.

Leithwood, K., Leonard, L., & Sharratt, L. (1998). Conditions fostering organisational learning in schools. *Educational Administration Quarterly, 34*, 243-276.

Marks, H., & Seashore-Louis, K. (1999). Teacher empowerment and capacity for organisational learning. *Educational Administration Quarterly, 35*(supplemental), 707-750.

Newmann, F., & Wehlage, G. (1995). *Successful school restructuring*. Madison, WI: Wisconsin Centre for Education Research, University of Wisconsin.

Organization for Economic Cooperation and Development [OECD]. (2001). *What schools for the future?* Paris: Author.

Stoll, L., & Myers, K. (Eds.). (1998). *No quick fixes: Perspectives on schools in difficulty*. London: Falmer.

Teddlie, C., & Reynolds, D. (2000). International handbook of school effectiveness research. London: Falmer.

Watkins, K. E., & Marsick, V. J. (1993). *Sculpting the learning organization*. San Francisco: Jossey-Bass.

STUDIES IN EDUCATIONAL LEADERSHIP

KLUWER ACADEMIC PUBLISHERS – DORDRECHT / BOSTON / LONDON